BORO TALES

Middlesbrough Football Club's extraordinary highs and lows through the eyes of Teesside legends

ROB STEWART
FOREWORD BY GRAEME SOUNESS

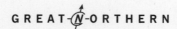

GREAT N-ORTHERN

Rob Stewart is a football writer who chronicled the highs and lows of Middlesbrough Football Club from 2002 to 2011 for the *Daily Telegraph*, but his claim to journalistic fame is breaking the story about Fabrizio Ravanelli's sensational Boro move in 1996. Boro Tales is his second book with Great Northern Books, following a successful debut with *Huddersfield Town: The 101 Club*. He lives in Bristol with his family.

Great Northern Books Limited
PO Box 1380, Bradford, BD5 5FB
www.greatnorthernbooks.co.uk

Every effort has been made to acknowledge correctly and contact the copyright holders of material in this book. Great Northern Books Limited apologises for any unintentional errors or omissions, which should be notified to the publisher.

ISBN: 978-1-912101-75-7

Design and layout: David Burrill

CIP Data
A catalogue for this book is available from the British Library

FOREWORD

By Graeme Souness

There will always be a special place in my heart for Boro because of Middlesbrough people and Teesside as a whole.

I owe the area so much - I grew up as a person when I lived in Middlesbrough and finally found my feet as a footballer, so I've got loads of great memories.

I came up from London, a bit too big for my boots, and lived in digs at 53 Chipchase Road, just off Linthorpe Road. The landlady was Phoebe Haigh and I can hardly begin to tell you how good she was to me.

There was always a lovely cooked meal for me at the end of the day, a glass of milk waiting for me at bedtime and even a nice little sandwich and piece of cake after a night out with the boys.

She treated me so well – in fact she spoilt me rotten in a way that even my own mother never did.

Phoebe had two daughters, Beryl and June, and I was the son that she'd never had. I was one lucky boy.

But it was the whole package for me – I enjoyed my football, I had great pals at Middlesbrough and my lifestyle changed for the better.

I learnt a wee bit about getting a better balance in my life when I arrived from Tottenham and I kicked on.

I still enjoyed myself socially, but when it came to training and match days I was always at it and I had five great years on Teesside.

For the first time in my life I had a few bob in my pocket and I sort of enjoyed being recognised in the street.

I was, if you like, a big fish in a smaller pond. The supporters took to me and I count myself very lucky in that respect.

I was that happy that when I got the call from the club to go to the Queen's Hotel in Leeds because someone was interested in me I was all set for staying put.

It was all hush-hush. The club wouldn't tell me who it was that I was meeting and they weren't keen to sell. I knew Man City and Leeds United wanted me and I knew, because of my good pal Phil Boersma, Liverpool wanted me.

Driving down the A1, I had made my mind up that if it was Leeds or Man City, I was going nowhere – I'd only leave if it was Liverpool.

When I got there, Bob Paisley, the Liverpool manager, was waiting for me, with John Smith, the chairman, and Peter Robinson, the chief executive.

They were sitting around a table in the middle of a grand ballroom. I was swept off my feet, but I couldn't show it.

But in my heart of hearts, I knew that no one in their right mind would have been able to say 'no' to them.

And yet still, I remember heading straight over the Pennines along the M62 to have a medical and sign on the dotted line at Anfield with Peter Robinson in my

BMW, thinking, 'Do I really flipping want this?' That was because my life was so good at Middlesbrough.

So I left Middlesbrough with a heavy heart - even though I was joining the champions of Europe.

If there was any consolation it was that Boro had played their hand well because they got £352,000 for me - a record fee between English clubs, so everyone was happy.

It really was a wrench to go but, to this day, part of me is sad that I never got the opportunity to go back and manage Middlesbrough Football Club. I knew Boro and me would have been a good fit.

There were times while I was in management when Boro were on the lookout for managers and I thought this could be the time. They never came knocking, but hey ho, I'll have to live with that.

The owner, Steve Gibson, clearly never really fancied me, which is disappointing because I'd have loved the chance to go back.

Steve is rightly regarded as one of the best football club owners in British football – if not the very best - and I have enormous respect for what he has done for Middlesbrough, bringing the League Cup back to Teesside and giving the fans a proper taste of European football.

The seven years I had at Liverpool superseded my time with Boro when it came to football. But for different reasons the five years on Teesside were the happiest time of my life.

That is why I love meeting up with my old Boro teammates for reunions. It's also why I'm looking forward to Boro getting back where they belong - in the Premier League.

Graeme Souness.

Author's Note

Looking back, it seems quite fitting that my professional relationship with Middlesbrough Football Club got off to the most incredible start.

It was in the summer of 1996 and I'd made my way to Teesside from the *Hull Daily Mail* newsroom for an *Evening Gazette* birthday bash and got the biggest scoop of my life.

Boro, I was told as tongues loosened, were all set to sign Fabrizio Ravanelli for the princely sum of £7 million just weeks after he'd helped Juventus win the Champions League.

This was according to someone's neighbour, who was a club bigwig. Still, surely not. As Ravanelli says in *Boro Tales*, it's like Karim Benzema joining Watford from Real Madrid this summer.

But one thing led to another, it got checked out, and the Ravanelli transfer story was broken by *The Sun* on its back page one Saturday morning.

It was the most sensational football story of the summer. It also set the tone for the most extraordinary phase of the club's history once Ravanelli settled into his Hutton Rudby home.

The Ravanelli transfer was one of those 'you couldn't make it up' stories, but ones of a similar ilk followed and thankfully, I had the privilege of reporting on them as I covered Boro for the *Daily Telegraph* for almost a decade from 2002.

What still stands out is the honour of being in the Press box when Gareth Southgate lifted the Carling Cup in Cardiff and 128 years of hurt were ended as Boro won a major honour for the first time.

While the UEFA Cup run two years later did not have a happy ending it was still a monumental achievement for 'Just a Small Town in Europe' to see Boro do the region proud by contesting a major European final.

It was a joy to be on that road with Boro. Along the way, I began interviewing former Boro players, staff and managers after being invited to contribute to the match-day programme, *Red Square*, by the club's former head of media, Dave Allan.

There were so many great tales, told from the heart, and this is my collection of favourite interviews with heroes ranging from Rolando Ugolini to Mark Schwarzer and Lindy Delapenha to Stewart Downing, from a variety of media outlets, and there are brand new stories too, especially for the book.

The structure of *Boro Tales* is based on players' positions, but there are also special segments on club mavericks, managers, backroom staff, the academy, the 'season from hell', fans' tales and then, to end on a high, the road to glory in Cardiff.

It's been a labour of love speaking to so many people who served Boro with such distinction. I do hope you enjoy the book as much as I've enjoyed producing it.

UTB.

Rob Stewart

THE LAST LINE OF DEFENCE
– *Goalkeepers*

Ugolini's Matthews Shame

Rolando Ugolini had plenty to be proud of thanks to his days keeping goal for Boro.

But he also admitted to having reason to be embarrassed till his dying days by an occasion when he pitted his wits against football legend Sir Stanley Matthews.

Having played 334 times for Boro after making his debut in a 1-0 defeat by Chelsea, he had many memories but one really stood out – thanks to his own uncharacteristic misjudgment.

"The best and worst memory has to be playing against Sir Stanley Matthews when he was at Blackpool," Ugolini recalled.

"We were winning 1-0 and there were a few minutes left when the ball went out for a corner.

"We both went for the ball, but I got there before him to waste time and I grabbed the ball and went back to the goal and then I threw it to him.

"He came over to me and said, 'Look, sonny boy, if that is the kind of sport you are, I won't even take the corner kick.'

"I felt terrible. Afterwards I knocked on their dressing room door and apologised. We talked about it every time we met afterwards. He was a tremendous player and tremendous person."

The so-called 'Wizard of the Dribble' was not, though, the best player on the scene as far as Ugolini was concerned and instead that personal accolade went to Welsh legend John Charles.

"John was the best all-round player I ever came up against and a real gentleman as well.

"He was a nice man and when he'd come to Middlesbrough with Cardiff he stayed at the big hotel in Saltburn where we met up.

"We'd go there afterwards and he used to sing and he was as good a singer as he was a footballer, so it was great fun. Those were the days."

Ugolini shunned the bright lights of London for down-to-earth Teesside and insists it was the best move of his life.

The Italian-born, Glasgow-raised goalkeeper chose Boro over Chelsea when he left Scottish giants Celtic.

And he went on to cement his place in Boro folklore, playing more than 300 games for the club after becoming a first-team regular in 1948.

"I loved it in Middlesbrough - everything was right about the club for me as a goalkeeper and as a person.

"It was the best decision I have ever made in football to go to Ayresome Park."

Ugolini was just a toddler when his parents left Tuscany in 1925 to run a fish-and-chip business in Glasgow.

He lent a helping hand, peeling potatoes and cleaning up, but shone between the sticks with local junior club Armadale Thistle and that won him a trial with Hearts.

He spent a season at Tynecastle and four at Celtic where he was restricted to a handful of appearances by Scottish international Willie Miller before moving to Boro in a £7,000-deal.

"When I was at Celtic I only got a game when Willie was injured or playing for Scotland.

"I tried for two years to get away from Celtic and they just wouldn't let me go.

"But Chelsea and Middlesbrough came in for me and they relented because, at last, there was money on the table.

"They made me a good offer, but the fact it was nearer to home was one reason I ended up on the Tees.

"But the main thing was that I'd heard they were a good team then as well and I was proved right."

Ugolini – or Roland, Lando, Ugo or 'The Cat', as his Boro colleagues knew him - used to live on Hutton Road.

He rubbed shoulders with Boro legends Wilf Mannion and George Hardwick as well as the up-and-coming striker Brian Clough as he established himself.

"It was a great club to be at and we had the most wonderful manager in David Jack who was a gentleman and a scholar.

"There were lots of tremendous footballers and characters, such as Lindy Delapenha and Cloughie who was a reserve, but came through to get into the first team.

"I enjoyed being with them all - they were really nice people and very, very good footballers.

"We had such a fine team and we could and should have won the FA Cup, but we were unlucky and ended up losing against sides we should have beaten, so sadly it was not to be."

Ugolini, an Inter Milan fan due to his Italian roots, put into perspective just how football has changed over the years from a goalkeeper's perspective.

"It was tough being a goalkeeper compared to the modern game.

"You can't charge goalies now, but if I had the ball in my arms they'd barge into you, knock man and ball into the back of the net and it would be a goal.

"But it was more like rugby. That all seems comical looking back, but I can tell you it was far from funny. I got bumped about all the time."

There were also grounds for concern for Ugolini due to the state of the pitches.

"The football fields then were shocking, especially in the goalmouth, as the season wore on. I had to keep my wits about me.

"Being a fitness fanatic, I was agile, but I was only 5ft 9in which was small, but the goalmouth was about six inches deep and there was no grass so it made life difficult for little old me.

"Now the grounds are beautiful and balls are brilliant, but that makes life tough for goalies.

"When there is even a slight wind it's harder because players can bend that ball and make it do tricks. You couldn't do that in our day.

"The game is now much quicker because the ball is much quicker; it flies about, so I enjoy it more than ever."

Ugolini would lose his place to Clough's future managerial partner Peter Taylor in 1956 after dislocating his shoulder at the end of the 1955-56 season.

He moved to Wrexham before finishing his career with Dundee United and then running a bookies' shop in Edinburgh before retirement.

Every now and again Ugolini took a walk down Memory Lane when he headed down the A1 from his Edinburgh home to Middlesbrough with the club's Former Players' Association.

"I love going back because Middlesbrough people are so warm and friendly and Riverside is a fantastic stadium.

"And it makes me feel privileged to have played for the Boro. I just wish that we'd played at a ground like that in our day."

Rolando Ugolini died at the age of 89 in April 2014.

Appleby's Tricks of the Trade

Bob Appleby always had a trick or two up his sleeve.

As well as being a solid last line of defence thanks to his goalkeeping agility, he could also revert to deceiving Boro friends and foes alike.

"I could do a whistle like you'd get from the shrill of a referee's whistle and I wasn't afraid to use it," Appleby said in an interview at his Newcastle home.

"When I was at Middlesbrough I perfected it - I can still do it to this day, mind - so if a player was racing in on goal at me I'd whistle.

"Then he'd stop in his tracks and I'd pick the ball up. I'd carry on as if nothing had happened. You wouldn't get away with it nowadays.

"My teammates loved it, but Cloughie (Brian Clough) used to hate it when I did it in training. He'd go mad.

"I used to be able to make the ball spin like nobody's business when I threw it out. I had the lads bamboozled.

"They didn't know whether they were coming or going. But I loved doing it because it made them run.

"The lads always seemed to fall for it and I never got tired of doing it and it was good for team spirit because it made everyone laugh."

Appleby used to clean Brian Clough's boots but knew he would always owe him a huge debt of gratitude.

The teenager was struggling to make a living as a rookie goalkeeper on Teesside until Boro legend Clough intervened.

"I was on less than half what the other players were being paid until Cloughie heard about it and got things put right, so I owed him."

"I'd just broken into the first team and Cloughie asked me how much I got paid. I told him I was on £12 a week and he saw red, he wasn't having it.

"He led me straight into the office, told them to put me on the £25-a-week the rest of the lads were on straight away, so I doubled my wages thanks to him."

Appleby, who displaced Clough's future right-hand man Peter Taylor as Boro's goalkeeper, relished playing alongside the man who went on to lead Nottingham Forest to European Cup glory.

"He wasn't everyone's cup of tea because he had a high opinion of himself and always spoke his mind.

"People said he was self-centred and greedy as a player, but that business with my wage showed that he always thought of others as well.

"Some of the senior players didn't like him, but Cloughie was a team player through-and-through who wanted the best for us all.

"Plus he was a fabulous goalscorer for us and sadly for Sunderland because – like a lot of our best players – he ended up leaving Boro for pastures new, which was a shame."

Appleby was brought up in the Northumberland coastal town of Warkworth and was a striker until persuaded to change positions by a PE teacher whose own team needed a goalkeeper.

"I ended up playing in goal for his team, Amble Welfare, on Saturday afternoons, but that worked out well because I was spotted by a scout and told to go to Middlesbrough for a trial.

"Three of us went to Middlesbrough, me from Warkworth and two from Amble who were sent back.

"I felt like a right country bumpkin because I'd never even seen a double-decker bus until I went there, but it went well and I joined the ground staff as a lad.

"I cleaned Cloughie's boots as well as the terraces, showers and toilets, but I didn't mind that graft. It served me well. I went through the juniors, the reserves and then made it into the first team.

"Bob Dennison was the manager who gave me my big chance. He called me into his office and asked me if I was ready. It was like a test of my confidence, a test of character.

"I told him I should've been in a fortnight ago. I was 19. I didn't let him down. My debut was in a 1-0 win against Stoke at Ayresome and I was man of the match in the newspapers."

The young goalkeeper was also making news after he was married to Pauline at Warkworth Parish Church.

"We received a load of telegrams when we got back to the reception, but one of them really stood out.

"It was one that ended my honeymoon before it began, as it came from the club telling me to come back sharpish because they needed my services.

"That came right out of the blue. I'd been injured, but I had to go back because of other injuries."

As well as being a solid last line of defence, the 5ft 10in Appleby was also key to club spirit thanks to an array of tricks.

Appleby worked in a butcher's shop to supplement his wages – a role that helped him when he was forced to retire at the age of 29.

That was when he was on Hereford's books due to a back injury sustained in a cup-tie between Boro and Manchester United at Old Trafford.

"I ended up as a water bailiff near Cockermouth in the Lake District, basically looking out for people that were illegally fishing for salmon.

"And then I landed a job as a gamekeeper on the Holkham Estate on the North Norfolk coast which was great.

"I had a cracking shot which was possibly down to my dad having been a poacher to put food on the table for his family.

"I was such a good shot that I finished second in a clay pigeon shooting competition that had a field of 300, and I also worked in the Yorkshire Dales before we moved to Tyneside."

The 73-year-old occasionally visited the Riverside as a guest of the Middlesbrough Former Players' Association but he's now more likely to be seen at his local playing fields, watching his grandson.

"He plays three times a weekend and I watch him when I can. He's a fast little fella and he loves his football. The only bad thing is that he's a Newcastle fan. But hopefully I'll convert him to Boro."

Platt's Homesick Blues

Jim Platt yearned for the green, green grass of his Emerald Isle home after swapping Northern Ireland for Teesside.

The young goalkeeper's future in English football was in serious doubt because he couldn't wait to get back home after joining Boro.

But he overcame a severe bout of homesickness, knuckled down and ended up establishing himself as one of the club's all-time greats.

"My first six weeks of learning the ropes with Middlesbrough were great because being a professional footballer was my dream," Platt said.

"But still I didn't settle and all I wanted to do was go home as soon as I possibly could every weekend.

"I used to make a five-hour drive up to Stranraer to get the last boat back to Belfast on Friday nights and returned on the last boat back on a Sunday.

"I was seriously homesick and if I hadn't have signed a two-year contract I would have stayed back home for good.

"It was my first time away from my family, which is a fairly big deal, and I wasn't playing as well as I could have so things looked bleak."

Thankfully, he sought counsel from Bertie Peacock, who played for Northern Ireland and Celtic and was Coleraine's manager.

"I knew his son and I bumped into Bertie and told him things were not going too good with Middlesbrough.

"He said just the right thing. 'Well, get yourself back there and give it your best shot, because if you don't you will regret it for the rest of your life.'

"I heeded his advice, I got stuck in and the rest is history."

And once he found his feet, Platt went on to become one of the club's most distinguished servants.

Platt is fifth in the list of all-time Boro appearances as he went on to play 481 times for Boro following that pep talk.

And he fulfilled the potential seen in him by Boro talent-spotter Bobby McAuley after he made his debut in the Irish League at the age of 16 with Ballymenna.

He spent a fortnight on trial with Liverpool but the Anfield club had already signed future England goalkeeper Ray Clemence, whose presence blocked that particular pathway.

So, when he became available, Boro grabbed him with both hands following a scouting mission by then coach Harold Shepherdson who watched him in action in an Irish Cup semi-final.

A £10,000 transfer deal saw him cross the Irish Sea and he worked his way through the ranks at Boro.

Finally making his debut in 1971 after Willie Whigham was dropped following a 4-1 defeat at Sunderland, Platt marked his first game with a clean sheet as Blackpool were beaten 1-0.

"Everyone remembers their debut, but one game I remember really clearly was at Liverpool.

"Someone shot, I went to catch the ball and thought I'd missed it, but it hit the top of my hand and flew over the crossbar.

"The next thing is the papers were saying it was a fantastic save. And then I said to myself okay it was. It was just the stroke of luck I needed."

His fondest memories are those of the Jack Charlton era.

"We only had a 13-man squad, but we won the old Division Two title by a country mile.

"That was because of the camaraderie that developed, the quality of players like

Bobby Murdoch, Graeme Souness, John Hickton, John Craggs, Stuart Boam and David Armstrong and Jack's astute managerial acumen.

"It was funny the way things started. Pre-season went brilliantly, we had a rather lucky win down at Portsmouth, then we went and lost the next game at home 2-0 to two late goals.

"That meant we incurred Jack's wrath for the first time. He was ranting and raving, effing and blinding, telling us that we had to realise this league can be so tight that points here and then could make all the difference.

"Stuart Boam spoke and Jack really lost his temper. He held a meeting to apologise and he lost his temper again, but we then went on a long unbeaten run, so it didn't do us any harm."

Platt twice won the Boro player of the season accolade in 1972 and 1981 when he was also named North East player of the year.

As well as serving Boro with such distinction, Platt also represented Northern Ireland on 23 occasions and would have played plenty more had it not been for the legendary Pat Jennings' presence.

"I had 13 great years at Boro, but I have to admit my biggest achievement was playing for my country.

"I went to two World Cups - 1986 to Mexico and also to Spain in 1982 when we surprised everyone by beating Spain to reach the quarter-finals, which was the equivalent of winning it for us.

"We had a really good team and a really good manager in Billy Bingham and we won the old Home Championship in 1980, which was quite an achievement."

After he quit playing, Platt went into management with Coleraine and helped launch the careers of future Northern Ireland manager Michael O'Neill and former Manchester City midfielder Steve Lomas.

He had a spell in charge of Darlington and took the club to the League Two play-offs.

Nowadays, Platt remains closely linked with the Riverside as a matchday host and as secretary of the Middlesbrough Former Players' Association.

He launched the organisation with Alan Peacock and Gordon Jones and they were joined on their committee by BBC Tees' late Boro commentator Ali Brownlee and former club communications manager Dave Allan.

"We've helped a lot of old boys without telling anyone, but unfortunately the older players are too proud to come to us and say they need assistance.

"It is only through third parties that we find out they need a bit of support because they are unwell or broke.

"We still need younger members. Once we give up, the worry is that it will be finished because the modern players will never require the help that the older ones needed."

Pears' Penalty Prize

It was a case of saving the best till last for Stephen Pears in his days as Boro's goalkeeper.

Pears carved his place into Boro folklore thanks to his shot-stopping expertise in front of the adoring Holgate End.

But he also has a very different niche in the club history books because he has gone down as the last Boro player to score at Ayresome Park.

It was just a week after Boro had won the Division One title that a testimonial game took place in County Durham-born Pears' honour.

The feel-good factor was tangible as the Football League trophy was paraded around the ground - and Pears ensured the feeling of well-being continued by slotting home the winner in his Boro swansong.

"I'd been on a subs' bench most of the season behind Alan Miller, but I still went out on a high in front of a crowd of about 20,000 in my testimonial," Pears said.

"We were awarded a last-minute pen because the game was refereed by a good mate – an old school teacher of mine, John Sinclair, who sadly passed away a few years ago.

"I'd promised to have John as our man in the middle if I ever had a testimonial and I knew he wouldn't let me down because he was a top bloke.

"It wasn't the best of penalties, but it was still immensely satisfying because it rounded off a great evening and a great season.

"It was a really good laugh and we had Boro players, old and new, on each side, apart from Peter Beardsley, who was our special guest."

Beardsley and Pears went back a long way – to their days on Manchester United's books as apprentices.

It was when Pears was representing Durham Boys that his potential was spotted. He was asked by Leeds boss Jimmy Adamson to go for trials at Elland Road but was persuaded to join United instead.

"That just felt that it was the club for me and I had seven fantastic years in Manchester.

"I had a great upbringing and superb goalkeeping coach, thanks to legendary Harry Gregg, who was one of the only coaches around at that time."

Beardsley headed off for pastures new but Pears stuck around and played alongside people like Alan Davies, future best man Gary Worrall (who played for Peterborough and Carlisle), Mark Hughes, Norman Whiteside and Mick Duxbury.

"At times in United's reserves there were 10 internationals and me and the bonus was that we always played at Old Trafford when the first team was away.

"But what stands out is reaching the FA Youth Cup semi-final where we took on Man City and we were watched by 35,000 fans over two legs.

"They had some really good players, like goalie Alex Williams, Tommy Catton, and Nicky Reid, and they beat us, so they had the local bragging rights."

An understudy to Gary Bailey, Pears featured just five times for the Red Devils first team and was on the substitutes' bench for the 1985 FA Cup final with

Everton.

"That wasn't as good as it sounds because there was just one sub in those days, so I didn't even get an FA Cup winner's medal.

"But I did get a great view of Norman's amazing curling winner after Kevin Moran had been sent off by Peter Willis, a referee who came from up the road from me in Meadowfield."

Pears would leave United at the age of 21 in search of regular first-team football.

He was brought in on loan at Boro by Malcolm Allison where he played 20 games and was unbeaten in nine home games before being signed by Willie Maddren.

"I'd had enough of being at United because I needed first-team football and I could have gone elsewhere, but wanted to come back to the North East.

"QPR and Leeds were keen, but sometimes you just have to feel comfortable and at home and that's how I felt at Boro."

Yet there would be no full-time goalkeeping coach for Pears to develop his skills.

"In those days you had to look after yourself, but I'd had a great upbringing with Harry, so I knew the game.

"Joe Corrigan, who played for England and City, was a freelance football coach, and he popped over a few times, but it was Harry who taught me how to play."

Gregg clearly did a sterling job and Pears prospered under Bruce Rioch as relegated Boro flirted with extinction, boasting an unprecedented 32 clean sheets as the club won promotion from the Third Division.

"Willie left Bruce a lot of good players, but didn't get enough praise for work he did.

"Willie was a fantastic man and I loved him to bits. He was a nice chap and he loved football and was himself a great player. If it weren't for his knees, he'd have played for England.

"He knew a player as well – he brought through people like Colin Cooper, Gary Pallister and Stuart Ripley, who all played for England and Gary Parkinson and Tony Mowbray.

"It was a tough time financially because we were on the brink, but I stayed because I wanted to achieve things and that's what we did with back-to-back promotions into the old First Division."

Pears has countless memories but there is one game that means more than any other.

It was his first appearance following a lengthy lay-off after his father died while his son, despite being injured, had travelled down to Barnsley with the first team.

"He died of a heart attack when he was just 61 and I was 27. Then I got really ill with colitis, which came through the shock of losing my dad.

"There was definitely a link. I lost three months of the season and three-and-a-half stone in weight. It was awful. I was really poorly. It was tough to get over.

"I got turned round by time, and the way the club looked after me. They were really good; they gave me time, which is all I needed. Colin Todd was my manager and he was great."

It was one Friday night when Todd asked him if he was ready to return to first-team action against Leicester.

"We were up against Kevin Campbell, who was very impressive, but that was my best game ever.

"We beat them 4-1, but it seemed like one-way traffic in their favour.

"In those days there were marks out of 10 in the Sunday People and I was awarded a ten."

There is plenty more for Pears to be proud of. He set a club record with seven straight clean sheets in the 1987-88 season and was named North East Player of the Year in 1992.

He was also called into the England squad to face Czechoslovakia but his international dreams faded when he suffered a broken cheekbone in a collision with Cambridge United striker Dion Dublin.

After being released by Boro boss Bryan Robson, Pears joined Liverpool (on the recommendation of Reds goalkeeping coach Corrigan), as understudy to David James and back-up keeper Tony Warner.

"Unfortunately, I broke a finger on my first day and then at Christmas time fractured my jaw in a reserves game. My Liverpool debut was destined not to happen, but it was still great to work alongside greats like John Barnes."

He returned to the North East with Hartlepool where he finished his career before joining Boro's academy as a goalkeeping coach, where he saw the likes of Ross Turnbull, Brad Jones, David Knight and Jason Steele flourish.

"I taught them the way I was taught which meant I was very demanding - Harry Gregg was hard on me at United and I was hard on my goalies.

"You teach them how to play, read the game, all the technical side and how to be a good person. You just pass on your knowledge.

"I always said I just wanted to make you make a living out of football and that was the right way forward.

"It helped that I had a reputation and I'd been around the block a few times, because it meant they'd stand upright with me because they wanted to learn."

Pears spent 16 years as a coach and had stints with Hartlepool and Gateshead before calling it quits.

He went on to make a living in the building trade, making the most of talents that had seen him help former Boro team-mates Mark Proctor and James Pollock build new homes.

"You get sick of being sacked because football's not a stable career and when you're in your 50s you don't want to be moving around.

"So I decided I would pack it in and do something else and I moved into the building game.

"It's harder as you get older, but still enjoyable, but I'll always miss the day-to-day life that football gives you as a player and coach."

Poole's Height of Achievement

They say size isn't everything and that old adage certainly rings true when it comes to golden oldie Kevin Poole.

He was told that he was not big enough to make it between the sticks during his time at Villa Park by Graham Taylor but was still going strong at the age of 48.

A quarter-of-a-century after being told that, at 5ft 10in, he did not have the required stature, Poole has defied his doubters and the ageing process.

As he approached his 50s, he was still registered to play for Burton Albion where he was the back-up goalkeeper as well as goalkeeping coach.

"Everyone is entitled to their own opinion, but to this day I still disagree with what happened when Graham Taylor released me at Villa because he figured I was too small for a goalkeeper," Poole said

"You don't have to be massive to make it as a goalkeeper, and let's face it, Fabien Barthez won the World Cup for France and played for Manchester United and he was the same size as me, so that helps prove my point."

Poole certainly proved Taylor wrong as he went on to thrive as a goalkeeper at Boro and then six other clubs in a long and distinguished career.

"I must say it felt like a wrench to leave Villa. I spent seven years there after starting off as an apprentice.

"The club was in my blood because I used to watch them with my dad on the Holte End, but I was determined to kick on and luckily Bruce Rioch came calling when he was Boro manager."

Poole was on Boro's books from 1987–1991 but played just 34 times.

"I knew Bruce from time at Villa Park when he was a player, and also Brian Little who was my youth team manager there, and was reserve team manager at Boro, and so together they got me to move to Teesside.

"I had some good times up at Boro. I really enjoyed playing at Ayresome because it was a nice and compact ground, which meant that there was always a good atmosphere there, so I had a few enjoyable years up there.

"Plus, it was great playing behind people like Tony Mowbray, a great skipper, Gary Pallister, Colin Cooper and Gary Parkinson, because they were great characters and great defenders. They were a formidable unit.

"But then Bruce left the club and Colin Todd took over. I played under him for a little bit, but we had a little fall-out.

"I went to Hartlepool on loan for a few months which was excellent. I don't think we lost when I was there and we got promoted from the Fourth Division.

"So all in all, I have lots of fond memories of the area. It was great living in the North East. Our place in Yarm was excellent and the people in the area were great which meant a lot."

A Privileged Position for Walsh

Gary Walsh says he feels "privileged" to have been part of Bryan Robson's stunning Riverside Revolution.

Like former England skipper Robson, Walsh left Manchester United for Middlesbrough in a £600,000 deal in August 1995.

"Bryan had a massive impact and he took the club to a new level," Walsh said.

"Robbo was amazing to play with and he was the main reason I headed to Boro.

"He was incredible on the field and incredible off it as well. He had some pull as a manager and attracted some amazing players to Boro.

"It was Robbo's reputation, but also Steve Gibson's powers of persuasion that got us top players. They were a great double act. The players respected them both so much.

Walsh helped Boro take the Premier League by storm following promotion.

"I enjoyed every minute of my time at Boro - the buzz was massive.

"When I was with Boro, the stadium seemed full every match. There was a really great feel-good factor about the whole place.

"The first year really was great and in the run-up to Christmas we felt like we could be world-beaters. Everyone had a spring in their step.

"If we'd beaten Everton on Boxing Day we'd have gone second, but we lost and then slid down the table."

Wigan-born Walsh had played rugby league as a schoolboy but his whole life changed when he went to watch a friend play football for his town's representative side.

"The goalie didn't turn up, so I volunteered and in the game after Man U were watching and I must have played well - they rang up that night and offered me a contract. It was meant to be."

He came through the ranks at United as Sir Alex Ferguson worked his magic.

"I was part of something special at a truly great club. Sir Alex gave me my debut at Villa Park at the age of 18, which was a big thing for me.

"But it got frustrating at Old Trafford because there was a certain gentleman called Peter Schmeichel between the posts.

"I had a few years being behind Peter in the pecking order and could've stayed for the rest of my career, but I came to the age of 27 and wanted to play games."

He headed to Teesside as Alan Miller's deputy but "knew I had a better chance of getting into the first team."

It worked out as he established himself as Robson's last line of defence until Ben Roberts came through the ranks and Mark Schwarzer arrived from Bradford.

Walsh - who lived in Sedgefield with his wife and their two children – slipped down the pecking order but does not reckon Boro fans saw the best of him.

It was, he admits, only after his Riverside days – where he was tutored by England legend Peter Shilton – that he peaked.

"I was fortunate enough to be coached by Peter Shilton at Boro and Neville

Southall, although my best coach – and first goalie coach at the age of 19 - was Man U's Alan Hopkinson.

"If you can't learn from them you'll never learn, but I didn't show my best at Boro.

"I went from not playing regularly at Man United to playing week-in week-out and, to tell you the truth, I found that quite difficult.

"But the experience I gained at Boro was invaluable and that stood me in good stead for Bradford. That was where I reached my peak. I was battle-hardened."

Walsh, who left Boro for Bradford in a £500,000-deal in October 1997, would move to Wigan to fulfill a long-term ambition to turn out for his local side.

He had a stint as a player-coach at hometown club Wigan before heading to Derby with Paul Jewell and then had a spell at Hartlepool before moving to Hull.

"It was good to go back to the Boro with Hull (as a coach) in the Championship.

"It reminded me how privileged I was to play for Boro and how passionate the fans are and how great the Riverside is, especially when they're really behind the team.

Walsh is now goalkeeping coach at Aston Villa, working for another former United legend in Steve Bruce.

"I'm certainly enjoying what I'm doing and I'll have to pack it in because I've got no right leg.

"I've had lots of ups and downs, but I count myself very lucky. I've always got a smile on my face. I played as much as I could and was ready to become a coach, which is something I always wanted to be."

Roberts' Wembley Woe

Ben Roberts had an unwanted place in football history.

The former Boro goalkeeper's dubious claim to fame was down to conceding the fastest goal in FA Cup final history.

He ended up picking the ball out of the net when he was beaten after just 42 seconds by Chelsea's Roberto Di Matteo at Wembley Stadium in 1997.

It looked like Roberts' place in trivia quizzes might last at least a lifetime until he was replaced in the record books by Chelsea's Petr Cech in 2009.

Everton's Louis Saha shaved 17 seconds off Di Matteo's record before Chelsea recovered to win 2-1 – but you won't find Roberts thanking the striker.

"I was on holiday with my mate, the Boro physio Adam Reed, and we were messing about in the water with his son and my phone started going mad by the side of the pool," Roberts said.

"We weren't even watching the game and I went and looked and there were about 15 text messages.

"So straight away you think something is wrong at home and thankfully it was everyone texting to say the record had been beaten.

"It always gets mentioned and I get stick about it, but I was a bit gutted to be honest to lose the record. I'd learned to live with it."

It was, though, "demoralising at the time" for Roberts.

"As that goal went in, all I was thinking about was what my mum was feeling sat in the stands right behind me.

"It wasn't nice. I don't think she cried, but I don't think she was too happy – like the rest of the Boro fans.

"I still believe that if that had happened after half-an-hour I would have got it. But I paid the price for being in a false position.

"Early in the game you're always on the front foot trying to get a positive touch. So I was looking for a through-ball and little did I know that he was just going to belt one.

"From where I was stood it was unstoppable, but later in the game I would have got that."

While that shot may have been stoppable, a back injury would prove virtually inescapable.

"I had a great time at Boro apart from that last season when I seemed to be continually injured.

"The thing is, I couldn't get over it, which became soul-destroying because you want to play and train every day and when your body doesn't let you it's hard.

"In the end, I was there from the age of 13 to 25. I met some really good people, played with some great players. It's just a shame we didn't win something."

Nowadays Roberts, who was born in Bishop Auckland, is goalkeeping coach at Brighton.

He was forced to retire from the game by injury but the intervening period was an eventful one for this globetrotter.

"I retired because of that long-standing back injury that started at Boro when I was 20 and just kept coming back.

"I'd had my second operation on it and so I had to make a decision on it and I retired, which was heart-wrenching.

"I moved to Brazil for nine months because my girlfriend was finishing university there, just to take a break from football and see what my next step was going to be."

During his time in Brazil, Roberts lived in the city of Belo Horizonte where he joined a gym in a bid to regain his fitness.

And then he hit the road again as a backpacker, bringing a whole new meaning to the 'journeyman footballer' cliché.

"It was a great experience living in Brazil. I rehabbed every day. Six weeks after my op, when I could walk properly, I joined a nice gym where I worked out twice a day.

"Once I was in good shape again, I went travelling around South America and then Asia – Singapore to India overland for four months. It was a great year.

"I went backpacking because I tried to do it properly. I didn't want to do it by staying in nice hotels. I vowed never to pay more than $20 a night for accommodation.

"I did it proper, proper rough, but it was enjoyable. I spent a month with my girlfriend, a month with a mate and for the rest of the time I was a free spirit."

Roberts saw England play cricket in "highly-charged Tests" in the Indian cities of Mumbai and Delhi and as well as playing plenty of beach football he witnessed an "awe-inspiring" Buenos Aires derby between Argentine giants Boca Juniors and River Plate.

Then, with horizons broadened, Roberts returned to professional football

"I got back from Brazil and started doing coaching badges and then began playing again. I went to train with Brighton for six months and nearly ended up signing again.

"Things didn't work out, so I went to university at Roehampton on a PFA-sponsored sports science degree alongside my coaching at Yeovil where one of my best friends, Nathan Jones, was assistant manager.

"It gave me a second career in football. I was so pleased to be back in football again with Yeovil - even though the lads never missed a chance to rib me about that FA Cup final goal."

Crossley: Playing Second Fiddle

Mark Crossley was just about to board a plane for Scotland at East Midlands Airport when he was suddenly diverted towards Teesside.

The experienced goalkeeper was poised to swap Nottingham Forest for Scottish Premier League side Hibernian when Boro boss Bryan Robson called.

"My Forest career came to an end because our manager, David Platt, wanted to bring in youngsters instead of players who'd been there a long time," Crossley said.

"I never really wanted to leave, but I got a call from Hibernian and I was relishing the chance to head to Edinburgh for a fresh challenge.

"But then, out of the blue, I got a call from Bryan Robson when I was on my way to the airport.

"He asked what my movements were and I told him I'd agreed to sign a contract for Hibs.

"He said, 'Tell them your flight has been delayed and get over here because I want to have a chat with you.'

And, Crossley said, he "didn't have to give it a second thought."

"I knew Colin Cooper from our days at Forest, so I knew what it was all about and that Boro had a magnificent training facility, brilliant fans and the North East was a great part of the world to play your football.

"I fancied a move to Yorkshire and everything fell into place. I went for a medical, signed the same day and had to ring Alex McLeish and tell him I wasn't joining his club. That was the only problem."

Crossley joined as Mark Schwarzer's understudy but has mixed feelings when he looks back on his three years on the Riverside books.

"I knew I was coming as a No2, but I was confident I could offer Mark serious competition for his place.

"So, in the end, I was really disappointed because I got in the team and did really well, but as soon as Mark was back I got left out.

"I knew that every time Mark was available I would be out of the team. That was fair enough because I had made that commitment anyway.

"I had no arguments about that, but I still felt a bit miffed that I was not given a longer period in the first team.

"If I was in charge, I would have kept the person in that was doing well. It wasn't as though the results were bad - I kept nine clean sheets in 22 games.

"I'd stick with the player in form and wait until that changes before you take him out of the team, because that will destroy confidence. It did with me a bit.

"Once I went home and I was upset. Paul Barron (goalkeeping coach) came round to explain, but really he had no need to. I knew the score.

"I loved working with Paul. I was the fittest I had ever been when I was at Boro, so I was ready for a starting slot, but still…"

Crossley learned the goalkeeping ropes at Forest under Middlesbrough-born manager Brian Clough who made no secret of his goal-scoring prowess at Boro.

"It was a privilege to have worked under Cloughie for six years - on many an occasion he told me what a brilliant striker he was.

"Goalie coaches were not around then, there was never specialist practice. When we trained, goalies were made to be in the thick of it and play out-field.

"He used to tell me if you can take care of the ball you've got a chance. There was no one better to learn from than him. He inspired me.

"He was a little bit too old to stick me in goals and show me exactly how good he was in his Boro days because his knees had gone, which was a shame."

Career Sea-change For Turnbull

It was a visit to the seaside when everything changed for Ross Turnbull.

That trip to Blackpool still stands out as a crucial turning point in his football journey.

It was at a junior football tournament on the Lancashire coast that Turnbull's childhood dreams of becoming the next Alan Shearer ended.

But it was also where Turnbull took the first steps towards becoming a professional goalkeeper with Boro.

"It's funny looking back, but I never really wanted to be a goalkeeper when I was a kid," Turnbull said.

"I was always outfield, but then we went to that youth tournament in Blackpool and it all changed.

"We were messing about and I went in goal and then it turned out I was pretty good at it, so I ended up in nets for the weekend and stayed there all season.

"It all happened very quickly. One thing led to another and then you can't really change your position.

"But I'm definitely glad it happened that way because there's no way on earth I would have made it as an outfield player."

Turnbull was representing his local team, Newton Aycliffe Football Club, at Under-12 level when he had his change of fortune in the seaside town.

It is as if fate had intervened because as luck would have it, closer to home, future Boro academy manager Dave Parnaby was in charge of Turnbull's Bishop Auckland district side.

And before he knew it, the once reluctant goalkeeper grabbed his chances with both hands and ended up at Rockliffe Park.

It also meant that Turnbull started to aspire to be like new heroes Peter Schmeichel and David James.

"I had been on trial at Sunderland and come back to Newton Aycliffe and then gone on trial at Darlington for nine or ten weeks.

"They were really happy with me, but no one came and said, 'Do you want to sign forms?' And then out of the blue Dave rang my parents and asked if I wanted to come down for trial at Boro.

"All he wanted was another goalkeeper for the age group, which was, from what I can remember, under-13. I spent six weeks there and then signed up until I was 16."

Like most of his fellow academy graduates, Turnbull feels he owes a massive debt to former mentor Parnaby.

"I've got so much admiration for Dave – he's an absolutely fantastic coach and fantastic person.

"I know him from his son, Stuart, and his older son, so I speak to him quite a bit as a friend and everyone that has been at the academy feels the same as me - they think he's the bee's knees.

"He's done a great job, as you can tell by the amount of players that have come through the academy.

"Virtually each and every one of us has been brought in the right way in terms of football and life in general, which is just as important."

However, the former Byerley Park Primary School and Woodham Community Technology College pupil feels that it is goalkeeping coach, Stephen Pears, to whom he remains the most indebted.

"It is fair to say that if it weren't for Stephen Pears and the way he coached and guided me, I wouldn't have made it.

"He was a brilliant coach and it was superb working with him. I learned so much it was untrue from Stephen, in terms of things like preparation, shot-stopping, organising, reading of the game, decision-making and focus."

Turnbull thrived under Parnaby and Pears' expert tutelage and was a member of the team beaten in the FA Youth Cup final by Manchester United in 2003 – the year before Tony McMahon captained the Under-18s to victory over Aston Villa in the showpiece event.

"When we reached the final, there was Andrew Davies, me and Chris Brunt, but the rest of the side was younger.

"Afterwards they were saying, 'Don't worry, we will win it next year,' and they did, so fair play to them. The experience they gained from our run suited them perfectly."

Nor did it do Turnbull any harm either, as he came through the ranks and a series of loan spells – including a lengthy one at Barnsley – helped him into Boro's first team.

It also earned him a place in the history books when Steve McClaren fielded a team of locally produced players at Fulham at the end of the 2005-06 season.

"A lot of the time I went out on loan because Mark Schwarzer was there as the No1 and he was playing fantastically well.

"But from my point of view, I was still young and I wanted to play football and get the experience which I did on loan.

"That day down at Fulham was a special day for everyone. It was just my second game, as I'd played before against Bolton, and because we were all together and putting on such a performance it was brilliant.

"Okay, we lost 1-0 to a penalty, but we were the better team and deserved to win. The whole club could have been proud of us."

In the end, Turnbull got what he described as "the offer of a lifetime" when Chelsea came calling on his services as back-up to Petr Cech at Stamford Bridge.

"When a club like Chelsea shows an interest, it is one of those situations that every player would want.

"I say that because it was the chance to play with one of the clubs at the pinnacle of English football.

"It was an amazing opportunity for me, and Gareth Southgate couldn't guarantee me I'd play after relegation, so I was thinking it was the right career move.

"I knew I wasn't going to get first-team football the majority of times, but when I got the opportunity I had the chance to show what I could do at the highest level.

"You don't want to turn down that type of opportunity because how many other players get the chance to move to what is one of the best clubs in the world."

Turnbull might have found first-team openings at Chelsea hard to come by thanks to Cech's enduring excellence but that did not stop him being as professional as possible.

"Maybe I've not played as much as I would like, but I always take the positives out of it - the main one is working with one of the best goalkeepers in the world in Petr.

"That always helps and I really progressed by practising with him. Goalkeepers are like that. They always try to help each other, unlike outfield players, who can feel threatened by younger players.

"We're like a team within a team. You don't wish injury or suspension on anyone, but I still give it everything I have got just in case.

"You've got to apply yourself at all times. That's something Dave Parnaby and Stephen Pears always drilled into us all."

BACK IN TIME
– Right, Left and Wing Backs

The Right Chemistry for McNeil

There has always been a certain chemistry between Mick McNeil and Boro.

It was a passion for Boro that started burning brightly when he marveled at the likes of Wilf Mannion from the Ayresome Park terraces.

By his own admission, Middlesbrough-born McNeil, who attended St Francis Junior School and Middlesbrough Tech, had an "unconventional route" into football.

He was studying to be an analytical chemist on Teesside and playing for Cargo Fleet while his fellow aspiring Boro stars were following the beaten track at Ayresome Park.

It was only when it dawned on him a mishap in the chemical laboratory could stop the Middlesbrough Boys prospect realising a childhood dream that he decided to concentrate on building a career in football.

It proved to be a wise choice as the full-back established himself as a first-team fixture and won England international honours.

"Funnily enough, I was never an apprentice like the rest of the lads, because I wanted to get behind me something to fall back on, so I went to Pattinson and Stead after my GCEs and trained to be an analytical chemist," McNeil said.

"The trouble was, though, the work involved a very volatile process that could sometimes explode and one day it did and damaged the edge of a man's eye.

"That made me realise how dangerous the job could be. It showed you could lose an eye and my career would have been over before it had started.

"Thankfully, the powers-that-be at Boro, the coach Jimmy Gordon I think it was, asked me to turn professional when I was 17.

"I figured I was better off doing so and enjoying football before it was taken from me. An accident was 90 per cent unlikely, but there was just that odd chance.

"I was lucky enough to get straight into the first team, because Derek Stonehouse was injured. I was thrown in at the deep end. I'd not even played for the reserves."

It was an auspicious debut, as Boro won 6-4 at Brighton and McNeil went on to become an ever-present for the following four years.

"I went from going to watch Boro with my father and brother, standing and cheering on the likes of Wilf Mannion and my other heroes, so to follow in their footsteps was fantastic.

"I was invited to West Brom for trials, but wasn't interested in playing for anyone but Boro. Every game was something special. Nothing beats playing for your own club.

"My father was on professional forms with Rotherham, but his dad died so he came home to work in the steelworks, so he was thrilled to bits when I picked up the baton.

"I loved playing for Middlesbrough and got on really well with my teammates because the camaraderie was fantastic and everyone pulled in the same direction for each other."

His family lived in Green Lane and then Hemlington, "because my father wanted a garden."

McNeil, who remains close friends with former Boro goalkeeper Bob Appleby with whom he enjoyed going fishing, impressed so much that England came calling.

"It was so exciting because playing for Boro was my boyhood dream and playing for England was the icing on the cake.

"I was playing well, I got into England Under-23s at a time when the full side was not settled, and I was next in line to come up when an injury hit Roger Byrne, who was a great full-back, and I got my chance.

"I played in nine consecutive games over the course of two years and was never on a losing side, but then I got a knee injury against Liverpool and had to pull out of the 1962 World Cup squad.

"That was a regret, as I never really got back to my very best because, unfortunately, they didn't know as much about the intricacies of the knee as they do today.

"It was difficult to regain the speed I had with one injury to the knee. It slowed me right down."

McNeil, who was 21 when he earned his last cap, played alongside legendary figures such as Bobby Robson, Ron Flowers, Bobby Charlton, Johnny Haynes, Jimmy Greaves, Brian Douglas and Jimmy Armfield.

However, his failure to hit it off with another legendary figure in the shape of manager Raich Carter led to McNeil's departure from Boro.

"I couldn't get on with Raich Carter - we didn't see eye-to-eye.

"It was a clash of personalities and attitudes to football. He wanted long ball stuff; I liked to play football.

"All he wanted from his full-backs was for them to cross the ball from one side of the pitch to the other.

"I didn't think it was the way forward. I just felt I wanted to get away. I didn't want to leave the town or club so I went with a heavy heart."

Ipswich manager Bill McGarry welcomed him with open arms at Portman Road and he liked Suffolk so much he stayed there and made Bury St Edmonds his home.

McNeil, who describes Ron Greenwood, under whom he played at England Under-23 level, as the best manager he ever served, toyed with the idea of becoming a manager when he hung up his boots.

"I always thought I'd go into management, but after talking to people in the game I changed my mind and went into business.

"That's because I found out how much time away from home you spend as a manager and, having a young family, I didn't want to be leaving them.

"I ended up owning seven sports shops in Suffolk, so I guess I didn't do too badly.

"I'm retired now and I might live a long way from Middlesbrough, but there will always be a huge place in my heart for Boro.

"The club gave me a chance to fulfill a boyhood ambition and make football a career. For that I'll always be grateful."

Future Written In The Stars For Jones

Like scores of teenagers across Teesside, Gordon Jones' eyes lit up as he read his local newspaper, the *Evening Gazette*.

The Stockton boys' football team captain had come across an open invitation for budding players to show they had what it took to join Boro.

He would go along to back up words with deeds in a trial match but Jones, who would make 532 appearances for Boro, has admitted he initially feared he would not make the grade at his local club at all.

"It was one day when I was about 15 years old that I saw an advert in the *Gazette* saying if you fancied a trial for Middlesbrough write in," Jones recalled.

"So I put pen to paper and got a letter back saying come in one evening and I turned up and there were two teams ready for a trial match.

"The Boro manager, Bob Dennison, was there with the coach, Jimmy Gordon, so it was my big chance to impress.

"The game got started, it was frantic, but then after just 15 minutes Bob shouted, 'Come off number three.'

"So I went off, head down, deeply disappointed, thinking, 'That's it for me, I'm not good enough,' so I'll have a quick shower and hop on the bus back home to Sedgefield.

"But then Bob and Jimmy walked into the dressing room and said, 'Where do you live? Come on son, we want to go and see your dad – you're signing for Middlesbrough.'

"I had to pinch myself. To go from thinking I'd fluffed my big chance to seeing them give me the thumbs-up really took me aback.

"Thank God for the *Evening Gazette*. From what I can gather, there were practice matches like that going on every night of the week for five or six weeks.

"Of all of the people that took part, there was just myself and a lad called Arthur Proctor who got signed up. But he never made it, so technically I was the only one who did."

Only Tim Williamson, a goalkeeper from North Ormesby, has played more times than Jones for Boro, raking up 602 games early in the 20th century.

Jones had played as a forward at school before fate intervened when the Stockton boys' team left-back failed to turn up and everything fell into place.

"You need a bit of luck and that came my way again because there was a flu epidemic at Boro.

"I was only 15 and a half and I got a game in the reserves team because so many people were ill.

"George Hardwick, who was a columnist with the Gazette, wrote after that game that I was the best prospect he'd ever seen and it went from there.

"It was a great bit of positive publicity and then Micky Fenton, a former England centre forward who was our coach, pushed me for the first team, which helped."

Jones made his first-team debut in a League Cup tie against Cardiff in October 1960 but then got his big break in a League game four months later.

"I was taken along with the first team just so I got a taste of life with the senior side.

"I was 16 or maybe 17, and we went to Southampton. I thought I'd just enjoy the experience but on the way down Derek Stonehouse went down with flu.

"I was the only one there the next day and so they had no choice – they had to play me – and after that they never got me out of the side, either at left-back or right-back.

"My main challenge was that the left-back was Mick McNeil who was the current England full-back. I had to play consistently well week in week out."

Jones made the left-back berth his very own and after winning nine England Under-23 caps was even in the running for the Three Lions squad that won the World Cup in 1966.

"One of the favourite memories was in 1967, when Stan Anderson had made me skipper, and we got promotion against Oxford.

"It was the last game of the season and they say there was a 40,000-crowd there.

"The gates were locked and they were sat round the running track. That night was extra special."

Thanks to John O'Rourke's hat-trick and a goal from John Hickton, Boro beat Oxford 4-1 in front of 39,683 fans to pip Watford to promotion.

Despite his longevity, Jones was booked just twice in his Boro career and he puts that down to a pep-talk from a senior colleague.

"It was when I was a kid of 15, there was a lad called Dicky Robinson who was an England B international. He was a really good player. He said: 'You're not the quickest, so if you get too tight to someone they'll skin you for speed, so you need to position yourself properly. You've got the positional sense to do that, so stand off them and show them where you want them to go.'

"That's the best bit of advice I got - I didn't have to go into 50-50 tackles with people. Very few wingers got past me, so I can only thank Dicky for his words of wisdom."

Jones twice won the club's coveted Player of the Year award and captained Boro for six seasons before moving to Darlington in 1973.

He watched on as Jack Charlton succeeded Stan Anderson as manager and guided Boro to promotion

"In my opinion, Jack's was the best all-round team I've seen at Middlesbrough.

"I'm not talking about individual players here – I'm talking about a team and the way they played.

"I was more or less captain of the side when a load of great players came to the club under Stan Anderson.

"In fact, all Jack's side had been signed by Stan, except for Bobby Murdoch, and I saw it all come together.

"There have been better individuals, but that was even better than the one that won the Carling Cup in terms of consistency. When you look, they are great lads and good players at that."

It was while he was still playing that Jones went into business - and got more than he bargained for.

"We opened up our first shop, but we didn't have anyone to deliver the papers one weekend.

"We played against Manchester United in the FA Cup at Old Trafford and got a draw, which was a very creditable result.

"I was the captain, but the next day I ended up having to deliver about half-a-dozen rounds of Sunday papers which weighed a tonne."

That business acumen still comes in handy, as nowadays, Jones, who lives in Stockton, is treasurer of Boro's Former Players' Association.

• *Gordon Jones is enjoying retirement – two decades after a huge health scare.*

"Believe it or not I've got leukaemia," he says, "and I've had it now for well over 20 years.

"When I was first told I'd got it, I thought that's it – I'll be a goner before I know it.

"But there are about 10 different types and I've got one that is treatable, providing my body would cope with what was going on.

"I've had two rounds of chemotherapy and I go to hospital once a month to have my immune system topped up because I've got none whatsoever.

"I've been told it will come back again probably for a third time, but they can't say where or when.

"But it's now nearly five years since anything happened, so I'm keeping my fingers crossed. The chemo didn't stop me in my tracks and leukaemia hasn't deterred me from leading a normal life."

Craggs: Boro's Geordie Hero

John Craggs was deemed surplus to requirements by Newcastle, but he proved crucial to Boro's top-flight ambitions.

He swapped Tyneside for Teesside and helped Boro surge to promotion to the old First Division.

"I joined Newcastle straight from school as a member of the ground staff when you used to sweep the terraces, clean the players' boots and clear the dressing rooms," Craggs said.

"I played 80 games for the first team and I was in the team that won the Fairs Cup in 1969, but I wasn't a regular because David Craig, an Irish international, was keeping me out of the team.

"I only really got a game when he was injured and it didn't matter whether I played well or not – as soon as he was fit he was back in the team again.

"The manager told me he would let me know if anyone was interested in me and thankfully (then Boro manager) Stan Anderson came in for me.

"He had to sell Hughie McIlmoyle to Preston to finance the deal for me to go to Ayresome for £60,000 - and that was in the days when £60,000 was a fair bit of money."

The right-back was identified as the player who would help Anderson bring top-flight football to Teesside – and his manager was proved right.

"I didn't want to venture too far away from my roots and it just seemed like the perfect move.

"Boro had been knocking on the door of the First Division, but just missed out and Stan wanted me for their big push.

"We just missed out and then Jack came in and we got promoted straight away."

Craggs thrived under Charlton who, according to Dave Allan's book *The Who's Who of Middlesbrough*, rated him as the best attacking full-back in England.

"Jack was only there for four years because he always said he'd only stay at a club for four years, irrespective of whether it was going well or poorly.

"But what a great four years it was, mind, getting promoted and then finishing in the upper reaches of the top division in our first season.

"Everyone said we were a defensive team under Jack because he came from Leeds and was defensive-minded.

"That was fair enough because when he arrived he told us if you don't give any goals away you're halfway there.

"That's what we did, but we scored the most goals that season and conceded the least and won the league with a record number of points.

"We couldn't stop winning and it was great to get back into the top flight and take on the bigger teams. We ended up as a good consistent top-flight team."

It proved too good to last, though, as Boro's success attracted the attention of leading clubs.

"We had a lot of good players, who eventually left for better things, because there wasn't much money in the game. We had to sell to keep the club going.

"That's the way football was, but we had some good players who were coming through when John Neal was the manager and we had a decent few years with John as well."

Craggs, who lives in Yarm, would spend ten years with Boro before Newcastle finally lured him back up the A19.

"I went back to Newcastle and they signed Kevin Keegan a month after I re-joined and the memories of his first game at St James' Park are still vivid.

"It was chock-a-block because everyone wanted to see Kev and he didn't let anyone down – he made it a memorable occasion by scoring the winning goal."

Despite rubbing shoulders with the Geordie icon, Craggs identifies two of his Boro teammates as his most impressive colleagues.

"Bobby Murdoch, when he came down from Celtic, would have to be one of the best I ever played with, second only to Graeme Souness.

"Bobby was coming to the end of his career, but he was still a great player. He could see moves even before he got the ball.

"The number of times he would release the ball first time and get us going quickly was tremendous, but Graeme was probably the best all-round player.

"But when Graeme came to us from Tottenham he didn't get into the first team straight away.

"He was in and out of the side, a bit of a boy, until Jack got hold of him and told him he had to stop burning the candle at both ends.

"He said, 'You have to want it if you're going to get anywhere.' Graeme clearly listened because look at where he went – right to the top of English and European football as the captain of Liverpool."

As farewells go, the send-off John Craggs received from Boro fans could not have been much worse - his testimonial against Newcastle in 1982 attracted just 3,572 fans.

But nothing could spoil Craggs' memories of an eventful decade at Ayresome Park or detract from the sterling service he gave Boro.

"I got a testimonial when they were coming to an end and it came at the end of a season when we were relegated, so it was a bit of a washout.

"I suppose ultimately I was in the wrong place at the wrong time, judging by the paltry attendance, but overall I can say without a shadow of doubt that I had a great time at Boro. I wouldn't change it for the world."

• *John Craggs worked for Boro legend Willie Maddren after his retirement - before being hired by future Newcastle owner Mike Ashley.*

"After I stopped playing I had a couple of jobs like selling cars when Willie asked me to work for him, because he was opening a shop on the retail park when there were only three units there.

"He ended up with three stores but it came to a sticky end. One day I turned up for work and all the doors were locked, but everyone was inside and it turned out we had been taken over by what was then Sport & Ski."

That is what brought him into contact with sports retail magnate Ashley and he worked at his Sports Direct store in Middlesbrough for nearly 20 years.

"Mike's a decent down-to-earth guy. A lot of people don't like him, but he has a fabulous business in Sports Direct and what he's done for Newcastle is unbelievable.

"He got off to a bad start when he was new to the game, but he learned from his mistakes and turned the club around like nobody's business.

"For me, Mike is a smashing bloke. He does what he wants to do because I think he knows he is doing the right thing. People have a go at him in the media, but you never see him coming back at them. He just gets on with things."

Spraggon: Courting Trouble

Frank Spraggon had to prove himself on and off the field in his playing days.

For Spraggon not only had to win over the Boro coaching staff to win a first-team place at Ayresome Park.

But, away from the club, the young defender also had to impress Boro coach Harold Shepherdson because he was courting his daughter, Linda, as well.

And judging by the fact Spraggon served Boro for 13 years, and enjoyed five happy decades of marriage, he was clearly a match for anyone on the pitch and perfect match off it.

"Harold wasn't too chuffed when Linda told her dad she was going out with a footballer," Spraggon said from his Marton home.

"He turned round and said, 'Listen, you're not going out with a footballer, a lot of them are drunkards, a lot of them are womanisers and a lot of them like a bet.'

"Fair play to Harold because he was right about a few people in football, but the thing is I never drank till I left football, I never smoked, I've never gambled and I've been married almost 50 years."

Despite those paternal instincts, Shepherdson, who is best known for being Sir Alf Ramsey's right-hand man when England won the World Cup in 1966, had a positive impact on Spraggon's career.

"It was quite hard because after a match he would sit me down and have a chat about this, that and the other.

"But on the other hand, he was very good because to be given advice by someone of his stature was excellent.

"I'm not just saying this because Harold was my father-in-law, but everyone you spoke to had nothing but good things to say about him.

"When any club came to Middlesbrough, someone would ask about him. His knack was that he never forgot anyone's names, even though he'd done four World Cups.

"He was a down-to-earth Middlesbrough person who was as happy talking to people from St Hilda's, where he was brought up, as he was with top international footballers."

Tyneside-born Spraggon hails from the Gateshead borough of Whickham. He was spotted by Shepherdson, playing in a schoolboys' representative match in Middlesbrough against a side featuring future Boro midfielder Don Masson.

Ignoring Newcastle's overtures, Spraggon left home at 15 to come to Middlesbrough ("it was virtually the first time I'd been out of Tyneside") and before he knew it, he was in the first team under then manager Raich Carter.

"I made my full senior debut in a League Cup game at home against Bradford Park Avenue and that was before I'd even played in the reserves.

"A few days later it was my League debut away at Huddersfield Town's Leeds Road ground and I was amazed. The game just passed me by. But then again I was only 17 years old."

It wasn't the best of starts, but Spraggon went from strength to strength on Teesside.

He looks back with particular fondness to the Jack Charlton era when Boro stormed into the old First Division and Spraggon went from being a centre-half to left-back.

"It was more or less Stan Anderson's team, but when Jack came in from Leeds as manager the place just took off.

"I'd never known anyone like Big Jack - it was a privilege to work under him.

"He brought in a couple of players, sorted out the defence, and we hardly put a foot wrong.

"He got us working on little things, especially in defence, and we ran away with the old Second Division, winning promotion by Easter, and then more than holding our own after we went up."

It was during that era in which Spraggon struck up an unlikely friendship with rising star Graeme Souness.

"Graeme lived in digs nearby to us and he used to come to our house for his tea on a Friday night before a game and we'd give him fillet steak.

"It's funny looking back, because he's a millionaire nowadays. But he was a lovely bloke and a very good footballer who went on to become a great player."

Spraggon's sterling service earned him a testimonial match at Ayresome Park, which gave Boro supporters the chance to pay homage to an unsung hero.

"We couldn't get Celtic because they wanted too much money and we couldn't get Liverpool because we'd just played them, so we went for Continental opposition in the shape of Dynamo Zagreb.

"Some 10,000 fans turned up, which I thought was pretty good going. I wasn't that popular and it was a rainy, foggy night, so I was very pleased. They made me captain, so it was a cracking night."

After Boro, Spraggon headed over to America and played with the Minnesota Kicks with former club colleagues Alan Willey and Peter Brine.

"I was lucky enough to play against Pele in his New York Cosmos days and overall things were fantastic for us, but we were beaten in their final by Eusebio's Toronto team.

"But what stands out still, because it was funny, was the way that you were introduced to the crowd before the match, because it was all about entertainment.

"When it came round to my turn, it was 'At tonight's match, we have at No3, all the way from Middlesbrough, England, Frank Spraggon.'

"You had to go out and wave to the crowd, which obviously I wasn't used to, but when we played the Cosmos, Pele did a lap of honour when it was his turn and everyone lapped it up."

He had a spell coaching in Sweden before returning to Middlesbrough.

"I ended up back at Boro getting the Football Community Centre project in Eston off the ground, doing lots of coaching, working in schools.

"It was something I loved doing and it's great to see the way the scheme has kicked on to become the Football in the Community work, because it's a real force for good.

"I still like to go and watch the Boro and it's nice that they look after people like me so well."

Cooper's Call Of Nature

It was hardly the most conventional approach, but when Terry Cooper answered the call of nature he found it difficult to turn down Jack Charlton's request to join Middlesbrough.

The former Leeds teammates had helped take the Elland Road club to the summit of English football under Middlesbrough-born Don Revie.

And when Charlton was getting stuck into the task of turning Boro into a top-flight force as manager he quickly enlisted Cooper's services.

"I remember going to a dinner in Leeds, getting up to go to the toilet and Jack followed me and tapped me up in the toilet," Cooper said.

"Jack was always straight as a dye, and he just said, 'I think it's time you moved, so why not come and join us?'

"Leeds was changing. It was in a transitional period, so I thought a change might do me good, but I spoke to Don before committing myself.

"After he'd left Leeds for the England job, if you needed any advice, he was always there. He would always give you the best advice possible.

"I remember ringing him and telling him that big Jack had had a word with me and wanted me to go to Ayresome Park.

"He said things were in transition at Leeds, so as long as the deal is fair get yourself off."

Cooper, whose son Mark managed Darlington, now lives in Tenerife, and looks back at his spell with Boro with mixed emotions.

"I had four years, the first two were enjoyable, but then I got an Achilles injury and couldn't get properly fit, which was a great shame.

"Jack had built a really good team, but they were good lads as well, so he had a good spirit there.

"Jack was a good manager, he knew what he wanted and proved that at Boro, Newcastle, Ireland and Sheffield Wednesday.

"He knew how to get the best out of his players and wouldn't stand for any messing about.

"Football is a simple game complicated by bad coaches and players that want to over-complicate it, but Jack was always straight and to the point.

"When I was there, we had a good top-flight side. We had Willie Maddren – God bless him – and Stuart Boam at centre-back, Graeme Souness and Bobby Murdoch in midfield.

"So there was a good mixture of youth and experience, plus there was David Mills and David Armstrong, so we had a good, well-balanced team.

"And Jack knew how he wanted to play. He wanted things kept simple. He wanted us to get forward as quickly as possible and defend well."

Cooper played at left-back alongside centre-half Charlton, but has a special place in Leeds' history because he scored the goal that earned the club its first major honour in the 1968 League Cup final against Arsenal.

"Big Jack went up, the ball fell to me, I closed my eyes, whacked it and it flew into the top corner."

Cooper helped Leeds win the League Championship and broke into the England side, but then professional disaster struck.

"I broke my leg when I was 27 and it took me a long time – about two-and-a-half, three years to get back - because I had complications."

He believes that it is thanks to Charlton that Boro punched above their weight.

"I didn't get my eyes opened until I moved to Middlesbrough with Big Jack. I didn't realise how good or big a club Leeds was until I left.

"Jack didn't have the financial clout to do what Revie did at Leeds. Compared to Leeds, Boro didn't have the facilities or the resources.

"At Leeds we stayed in hotels ahead of home games and away games. If we spent two days a week at home we were lucky. It must have been expensive, but winning helps balance the books.

"The Boro training facilities were okay, but nothing special and the stadium was quite old and it's nice to see they have got a new ground and practice ground.

"It just shows how much progress the club has made over the years."

The rivalry between Middlesbrough-born Leeds managers Revie and Brian Clough was brought to the fore by David Peace's book and the film *The Damned United*, but Cooper was not a fan.

"My son bought it me for Christmas, but after ten minutes I had to turn it off and I can't watch it now because for me it's just not factual at all.

"It's a fairy story. I just felt this wasn't the way it was under Brian Clough, so I couldn't be bothered with it. But I know there was no love lost between them."

Cooper, who managed four clubs including Bristol City and Birmingham, does, though, have fond memories of Revie.

"Middlesbrough as a whole should be proud of Don – he was different class as a man and manager.

"Don was way ahead of his time in terms of training methods, preparation, and diets, whatever.

"At every Christmas party we all had young families and there would be about 40-odd kids and he knew all the kids' names and the wives.

"Don used to be Father Christmas. He was clever that way. If wives are happy, you will be happy.

"He made you want to play for them. He was really good at fostering team spirit.

"He was on the ball and because I'd grown up there I didn't know any different. It's only when you move that you realise not all clubs are the same."

As for Cooper's career as a whole, he says, "It was a dream come true. I came from a small village near Pontefract and all I always wanted to do was play professional football, so even getting £100 a game was great.

"It was a great honour to play for England. I earned 20 caps and every one was special, but I would have had 80 if I hadn't broken my leg.

"It was a privilege to play alongside players such as Bobby Moore, Alan Ball and Bobby Charlton and Jack for England.

"And I count myself really fortunate to have played alongside great players at Leeds and Middlesbrough."

Laying Down The Laws

It was a dream move that turned into a "nightmare" but Brian Laws would still not have it any other way.

The young Geordie defender had relished the prospect of moving back to his native North East with Boro from Huddersfield in the mid-1980s.

Things quickly turned sour as Boro flirted with extinction and even though it was, by his own admission, a "frightening experience" Laws insists he still relishes his Teesside memories.

"When I first signed for Boro I thought it was a fantastic move, because it felt as though I was coming home," Laws said.

"I was convinced it would be one of the most important moves of my career.

"But it turned into a nightmare when administration arose and then liquidation followed.

"To be part of that set-up was the most frightening phase of my career, because things were so uncertain. We didn't even get paid."

Laws, an attacking right-back, was brought to Teesside in 1985 by Boro boss Willie Maddren.

But even though he did well enough on a personal level to briefly become skipper he was unable to prevent his club being relegated to the old Third Division.

The rest is history, of course, and Boro flirted with extinction and bailiffs padlocked the gates to Ayresome Park and the club was wound up.

Laws was in his mid-20s at the time, so it was no wonder he feared for his future as both players and the club struggled to make ends meet.

"It was almost like going back to Sunday league football when the administrators moved in.

"We trained where we could and Bruce Rioch did well to keep 14 players together to form a team.

"Then, when we actually realised that Steve Gibson was paying our wages and supporting the club financially, we got the first game of the season under way, albeit at Hartlepool's ground, instead of Ayresome.

"From that moment on, the togetherness between the players and the supporters was phenomenal. I don't think I will experience anything closer in terms of contact and appreciation of each other than when I was at Boro."

Rioch has described his squad as a 'Band of Brothers' and that analogy with the American World War II television series seems apt judging by Laws' reflections.

"Willie Maddren was one of the nicest guys I have ever come across and I'm grateful he took a chance on me.

"He had a real aura about him with the players, but that was abused by some as well, because he was too nice and maybe that was his downfall.

"He needed someone in there with him with a bit of sternness, because that was not in his make-up.

"When Bruce came along he was a different kettle of fish. He was a sergeant major who was strong with the players and that formed an even stronger bond amongst us.

"It was hard at times to appreciate what he was doing, but in time we all agreed it was the right thing for us.

"He made sure we were clean-cut and well presented with a view to making sure we worked as hard as any other team in the division."

Rioch's methods were certainly effective as Boro bounced back from relegation in style.

"To succeed in that first season, by going up from the old Third Division and following it up by getting back into the top flight, was bred by the dressing room all sticking together.

"It wasn't about money or anything else other than a bond that was very, very strong and a mentality that we wanted to do well for the club and the supporters, who were extraordinary.

"The fans had seen the club almost fall apart to the degree that liquidation meant we didn't technically have a football club, but then a spark ignited the club and I have to say that was provided by Steve Gibson."

Laws remains adamant the Boro chairman was the catalyst to the upturn in fortunes.

"Without Steve Gibson I don't think the club would be where it is today, challenging for a place in the richest league in the world.

"And without Steve Gibson, Boro would have not won the Carling Cup, reached a European final and been a force to be reckoned with in the Premier League.

"I don't think it would have survived - without his input we would have gone under.

"So Steve Gibson has to be at the forefront of all our thoughts and appreciation. "What he's done for the club and the town has been truly incredible and it was an honour for me to play a part in the club's upturn in fortunes."

Laws was eventually lured away by Nottingham Forest manager Brian Clough.

"I had a period in my life where I had lost my mother and I was going through a traumatic time.

"I had just come back from injury, but then I got a call from Brian Clough asking me to come down to have a chat with him and it turned my whole life around.

"Even though it caused me real heartache to leave Boro, I ended up having six amazing years at Forest in terms of success. Wembley was almost our second home. I could not have asked for a better period."

First Impressions Count For Wood

Darren Wood reckons he is the biggest waste of money in Sheffield Wednesday's history.

But the former defender – now a successful Yorkshire-based businessman - still looks pretty much invaluable as far as Boro were concerned.

After being spotted by scout Ray Grant at the age of 13 while playing in his hometown of Scarborough, Wood became a huge asset for Boro in the 1980s.

He was invited for a trial, was, in his words, "lucky enough to be asked back," and never looked back.

"It was a lovely, friendly, homely club, so it could not have been a better start for me," Wood said.

"I stayed at the Medhurst Hotel, Linthorpe Road, with triallists and apprentices from afar.

"It was like an extension of school. We had a great time, but didn't appreciate how lucky we were. We were young and we'd just come out of school.

"When you're young doing something you love, in what was an extension of school, you don't know you're born. We were getting paid for doing something we'd do anyway. It was amazing."

But Wood had a strong work ethic as well, which enabled him to make a career out of football.

"I had to work really hard. Some people are naturally gifted and don't have to work hard, but don't make it.

"I knew that with my limited ability I had to train hard to keep fit, listen to the coaches and do my best."

He puts Boro's legendary World Cup-winning coach Harold Shepherdson and his father, Terry, down as the most influential figures in his career.

"Harold taught me you can't take anything for granted and so the club helped me a lot in terms of character and technique.

"My dad was always full of sound advice, which is what you need when you're young.

"He'd played professional and not made it. He didn't want me to make the same mistakes by not totally dedicating my life to it.

"He roomed with Billy Bremner at Leeds and went to Bolton, but had a knee operation and went to Scarborough where he settled down and had all his children."

The Wood family must have been overwhelmed by his Boro debut exploits.

"We were struggling as a club, which is why I got my breakthrough relatively quickly.

"Bobby Murdoch was in charge and threw me in against Notts County at Ayresome Park. Luckily enough, I intercepted a ball 35 yards out, took a swing and it flew into the top corner.

"More often than not, the ball would have flown 20 yards over, but I got lucky and it got me into the swing of things. Plus, playing in front of a crowd at Ayresome was great."

His dad's former Leeds colleague, Jack Charlton, returned on a temporary basis after Murdoch was sacked, but Wood maintained upward mobility.

"Big Jack steadied the ship and then Malcolm Allison came in and lots was expected from one of the game's most flamboyant characters.

"The history books tell you that it was a poor time, but I was lucky in that I was given a chance that I took with both hands.

"But looking back, it would've been better to have been in and out like it is nowadays. Because of the financial situation, we had to play every week and as a youngster you're very inconsistent. It probably didn't help us or the team."

Wood prospered, but the club was finding it hard going on the financial front and so the need arose to cash in on one of their best assets – although it did not go smoothly.

"It was a shame I had to leave because I was very settled. I had no inclination to move, but unfortunately things were beyond my control.

"I was at home in Scarborough and the chairman, Mike McCulloch, asked me to go and sign for Sheffield Wednesday.

"I didn't sign because Malcolm was away in London and I didn't think it would have been very honourable to move without speaking to him.

"He found out, which didn't go down well, because he'd taken the job on the proviso we didn't sell top players. He had big ideas and was talking about bringing in financial backers, so it looked rosy, but then he got sacked."

Six months later Wood would move to newly-promoted top-flight side Chelsea where he would spend five seasons.

"Initially, it was probably not a good move for me. When you're a youngster, to move that far away from home is hard, and London took a lot of adjusting to.

"It was totally different. Boro was a family club and everyone lived near the ground, 20 miles max, so you could get together anytime.

"At Chelsea, no one lived near the club. They were 50 or 80 miles away. So you lost all your mates, you're on your own 250 miles from home.

"It was not ideal, but sometimes you've just got to do it. You've got no choice. It was all right in the end, though.

"I enjoyed it once I'd settled in. The highlight was playing at Wembley against Man City in the Full Members' Cup final.

"We finished fourth in the league and were up there with the best of them. Having a chance of beating Man United or Arsenal away from home said it all.

"We had a chance of winning the league but just needed one or two more players."

Wood eventually moved to Wednesday, but is certain the club would have regretted renewing their interest in him.

"Looking back, I should have waited and got a medal, because we were on the brink of winning Division Two at Chelsea, but I wanted to move back North," the father-of-three said.

"Wednesday is a great club, but I was a bad buy – probably the worst buy they've ever had, because my back went.

"I only played a few games and I had to retire at 27. It was all very quick.

"It was a ruptured disk that did for me. I had a back operation and couldn't play anymore. I played five-a-side 15 years ago and couldn't walk afterwards.

"I'm just glad I made the most of my time when I was playing."

It was when he was at Hillsborough that he took the first steps into the business world where he has thrived.

"I bought a shop in Halifax market that my father-in-law was selling," said Wood who lives in Thorner, near Harrogate, and whose business - Dale Farm Foods - was based in Morley.

"My dad was in business and, because I knew football was not a long career, by the time I'd finished playing we'd got five shops.

"I've simply applied the same ethics to business as I did with football and worked hard. Believe it or not, I get up at 2.30am and get home at about 5pm.

"The fitness I built up as a footballer has helped in terms of stamina. I haven't put a load of weight on. I'm slightly heavier than when I played, which has been helpful. But when you're working those sorts of hours it's like pre-season every week."

Home Where Hart Is For Parky

Gary Parkinson has a special claim to fame thanks to his time with Boro.

He secured his own niche in Boro history because of the role he played in reviving the club's fortunes during the 1980s amid financial meltdown.

"I'm possibly one of the few players who has actually made a home debut away from home," Parkinson said.

"It was when we played Port Vale at Hartlepool's ground because we'd been locked out of Ayresome Park.

"Many people have said that could be the basis of a good quiz question, but not many people will know the answer.

"But what I do know is that, in football, in the face of adversity, people can achieve great things, because that's what we did."

Parkinson, who was brought up in Thornaby, relishes the memories of that special day which ended in a 2-2 draw.

"It was a surreal experience, but we were just glad to be getting the chance to play a proper match with everything that was going on.

"Little did we know that it would be the start of a bit of a fairytale, with back-to-back promotions against all the odds.

"We nearly went out of business and into extinction. We didn't even have a training ground or a stadium.

"We rose from nothing. And so, for me, being a home-grown boy and coming through the system, it was unbelievable.

"To work under Bruce Rioch and Colin Todd and to play with great players like Tony Mowbray, Gary Pallister, Stuart Ripley and Bernie Slaven was a real treat."

Parkinson had almost slipped through the Boro net after being released by the club as a schoolboy, having come to the club's attention while representing Cleveland and Stockton schools.

"At the age of 14, I was at Boro's centre of excellence, but I was told I'd never be good enough, so I joined Everton as an associate schoolboy and signed the old apprenticeship forms.

"But then I got homesick, I couldn't settle, and after six months I came back home and a great friend of mine called Barry Geldart, who was chief scout, spoke to me.

"That was when I was on the verge of signing for Cyril Knowles at Darlington and Barry got me to sign for Boro on the old YTS forms with no guarantees.

"I got lucky and I'm very grateful to Barry, because I went in there when Willie Maddren was manager and he looked after me and believed in me.

"Then Bruce came in and it was a situation where us young lads were the only ones left, because he'd had to cut costs.

"We were down to bare bones. The team picked itself, so I got my opportunity and that was the stroke of luck I needed. It was surreal."

For Parkinson, an attacking right-back who helped Boro reserves win promotion before repeating the act at first-team level, Rioch's role was crucial in the club's renaissance.

"We had a fantastic manager in Bruce and we all had tremendous faith in him.

"He's a fantastic man, who is a great manager, and that should never be forgotten.

"He got 16 local boys – all home-grown – to achieve massively and that was a catalyst for where the club has been in recent years.

"But he ruled with an iron fist and frightened us all to death. If he said, 'Jump!' we'd ask, 'How high?' He had maximum respect and no one stepped out of line.

"His father was in the army, and while he wasn't regimental, he liked to keep a grip on us. That was how we got our team spirit and team ethic."

Parkinson's days were numbered after Rioch left Teesside and he lost his place to Colin Cooper when Colin Todd became manager before leaving on a free transfer when Lennie Lawrence took the helm.

"I was disappointed to leave, but Lennie came in, and because I'd been there nine years he thought I'd been there too long and needed to be moved on.

"Then it was a case of better the devil you know and I followed Bruce to Bolton."

Parkinson left with "lots of incredible memories."

"The best thing was Chelsea at Stamford Bridge when we beat them on aggregate in the play-off final.

"There was loads of trouble and we had to hit the deck in the coach as we left because it was being bombarded with missiles. It was very intimidating.

"The worst thing was playing Sheffield Wednesday when we were relegated from the old First Division.

"We'd had an unbelievable two years of back-to-back promotions and to get relegated after our first season back was a major disappointment.

"That was the turning point, for things starting to go wrong under Bruce."

Parkinson played 265 times and scored eight goals in a distinguished spell with Boro.

There was an unremarkable spell under Rioch at Bolton, but there was an upturn in fortunes when he joined Burnley.

That was where he scored the winning goal in a Wembley play-off final to cement his place in Clarets folklore.

Then he moved to Preston where he served under David Moyes for three years before, at the age of 34, being transferred to Blackpool where he became head of youth after a spell on Civvy Street.

"I was out of the game for two years. I went into normal working life, which was hard – a real culture shock. I was working for a sport leisure company for Burnley chairman, Barry Kilby.

"But I also had a job delivering parcels, which meant early mornings and was the first time I'd ever had to clock in and out of work. That was an eye-opener and gives you a real grip on what life is like outside football.

"Thankfully, I got a route back in thanks to a friend of mine, Steve Johnson, the first-team coach at Blackpool.

"I jumped at the opportunity and I was guided, in a way, by my time at Boro, but then again I suppose I've always been influenced by my Boro days.

"If I took anything from Bruce it is to be honest and up-front with people, because honesty and hard work can take you a long way in life."

• Gary Parkinson was struck down by locked-in syndrome - a condition that left him unable to speak - in September 2010, while coaching at Blackpool. For details on the Gary Parkinson Trust, visit the website: www.garyparky.co.uk

Double Blow For Morris

Everyone connected with Boro will have painful memories of the way the 1996-97 campaign turned out - but few will have felt worse than Chris Morris.

As if it was not tough enough for the full-back to see his club lose two cup finals and be relegated, Morris had special cause to feel aggrieved.

That is because he was forced to quit football due to injury.

Morris was warned by knee specialists that he would be putting his long-term health at risk if he continued to play football.

"I had a number of knee problems and ended up going to see my surgeon, who said, 'I'd think very carefully about how long you play because this could have a huge impact on you in later life'," Morris said from his Newquay home.

"At the time I was trying to recover from injury, and then I thought it was time to retire, so I went to see the gaffer (Bryan Robson) and (then chief executive) Keith Lamb and decided it wasn't probably worth trying to carry on and I called it quits.

"I could have probably tried to continue a few years, but weighing things up, it was the right thing to do. I have had a fair spell out of football, but I've come back with renewed enthusiasm and on a real quest to learn."

Having sold the family business - Morris Cornish Pasties - the former Republic of Ireland international became immersed again in football, as an FA regional coach.

And he also renewed old Boro acquaintances with Craig Hignett and Stephen Pears as the trio worked towards their coveted UEFA A Licence.

"I rattled through every course there was to be done - I have a real hunger to learn and get better."

Morris can put plenty of his own experience to good use having begun his career at Sheffield Wednesday under Jack Charlton before heading to Scottish giants Celtic.

It was at Parkhead that he had the distinction of being the only player to figure in all 55 games of the club's centenary season and played alongside Boro legend Tony Mowbray.

He headed to Teesside with Derek Whyte in a deal that saw Andy Payton head to Glasgow as Boro manager Lennie Lawrence prepared for the inaugural Premier League season.

"I was two weeks into a new two-year contract at Celtic and got a message from the manager, Liam Brady, to come see him and he told me Middlesbrough wanted me.

"Once you get to the stage where a manager is prepared to let you go, then you have to seriously consider your future, but then again it was great to be part of the brand new world of the Premier League with Boro. It was a really exciting challenge."

But Morris admits to having mixed memories of his time at Boro following a frustrating start to life at his new club.

"The first year was disappointing in that we had high hopes at the start of the Premier League and some of the things we hoped we might achieve, but we didn't because the resources were not there.

"When I signed we were hoping to have a much bigger squad, but those signings never materialised and we suffered when we had injuries, illnesses and suspensions, because our squad was too small and we ended up going down."

After being "stuck in no man's land" in the second tier following relegation, Morris then saw Boro revived when chairman Steve Gibson lured Bryan Robson to the manager's office.

"When Robbo arrived, there was a whole buzz about Ayresome Park and everything took off.

"It was great getting promoted and moving to the Riverside and we had two or three really exciting years, including my last one that included Ravanelli, Juninho and Emerson."

That Morris identifies winning the Championship in Robson's first year in charge as one of the highlights of his career really is saying something, because he also thrived at international level with Ireland.

"I still have fantastic memories of working under Jack Charlton and playing alongside cracking players, such as Ronnie Whelan, Liam Brady, Mark Lawrenson, Andy Townsend, John Aldridge, Paul McGrath and Mick McCarthy.

"Everywhere you looked there were top-quality players in our squad. The highlights were the major tournaments – the 1988 European Championships, when we beat England 1-0 in Stuttgart, which was awesome, and then the 1990 World Cup finals in Italy."

Charlton's team reached the quarter-finals before losing to Italy in the Olympic Stadium in Rome when Toto Schillaci scored the winner.

Geography and work commitments prevent Morris from getting back to Teesside, but he is keeping a close eye on Boro's promotion campaign.

"With a bit of luck, they will go up this time, but whatever happens they are heading in the right direction."

Fleming - Cut Above The Rest

Curtis Fleming swapped the fashion industry for a career in professional football, thanks to Boro.

Fleming was earning a living working in a trendy men's clothes shop in Dublin city centre while playing part-time football.

But his life was transformed when he was spotted playing in a match by Boro's head of recruitment Ron Bone on a scouting mission focused on other players.

"It definitely sounds like a rags-to-riches tale, but it wasn't at the time," Fleming said.

"In fact, in those days, it was all rags and no riches. I had the clothes, but no money in my pocket. But it was an incredible change in fortune for me.

"A lot of lads I knew from football would come in, including on one occasion, Andy Townsend, and a few years later I'd be playing with him, which was surreal."

Fleming had played for Belvedere Boys' Club, but his potential was identified by Bone while he was playing for St Patrick's Athletic and he never looked back.

"From the age of 17 to 21, I'd gone on lots of trials across England and it hadn't worked out for one reason or another. I wondered if I was ever going to make it.

"But then Ron came over to see a game in Dublin between us and Bohemians to look at a couple of their players.

"I ended up getting man of the match and when he came back he said he didn't rate those two, but fancied the right-back, which was lucky for me.

"Then they rang the club and asked if I could come over for a week's trial.

"But I was working in a clothes shop called Neon at the time, and they were a bit miffed at me taking off.

"I'd been away with the Ireland Under-21s and I'd taken my holidays, so I had to beg them for two more days off.

"Thankfully my boss took pity on me and I played in a game for Boro and then they said they would sign me, which was great."

There were still a few bumps in the road for Fleming to navigate.

"When I flew over, Colin Todd was the manager - with John Pickering as his assistant - and Colin said he'd sign me, but not until the start of the new season.

"But I remember being in the shop when I heard on the radio that he'd ended up losing his job, and I thought, 'Jesus! That's my chances scuppered.'

"John and Ron stayed on and Ron rang me to reassure me that whoever came in they would recommend me, so hold on.

"Lennie Lawrence came in and took a chance on me and he would go on say that at £50,000 I was one of his better signings, so I was happy with that."

That Fleming, who was born in Manchester but moved to Dublin as a baby, would make 317 Boro appearances over a ten-year period shows it was a shrewd bit of business.

"I wouldn't say it was a Cinderella-style story, but it was a fantastic break for me. I signed and the first season was unbelievable.

"I was on the bench for the first 15 games, but everyone had been saying I would be in the reserves to start with for so many games, but I was lucky enough that they saw me as first-team material so soon.

"In that first season, we had a Rumbelows Cup semi-final at Old Trafford and then promotion, so I was thinking this is a great life. It wasn't all like that, but it was a fantastic opening season."

For Fleming, the highlights were winning the Championship in 1995, the two 1997 Cup finals and promotion in 1998.

He confesses to being nagged by self-doubt, but he certainly proved himself worthy of being a first-team regular – as a right-back or left-back.

"I know it's a bit of a cliché to say it was a rollercoaster ride, but it was for me.

"When I look back on it, I had a ball. It couldn't have been much better in terms of highs and lows. And I'm really proud of what we achieved.

"But I must admit, I was always doubting myself and I thought I could be going when Bryan Robson brought in Neil Cox.

"But Robbo told me I was his left-back and that was that and having a world-class player like that give you backing was just what the doctor ordered."

The season Boro bounced back from relegation still stirs Fleming.

"Looking back, 1998 was massive because the whole town got behind us with us having been unjustly treated - relegated by having three points docked because we were a Northern club and unfashionable.

"The way we bounced back was incredible. The whole season was brilliant because we were thinking, 'We'll show them!'

"It was like Dogs of War, plus Robbo brought in some good players, most notably Paul Merson, so we were solid and had quality."

After his playing days, Fleming continued living on Teesside with wife Lucie and their three daughters.

He coached the Boro Under-16 side with Paul Jenkins at the club academy with a view to looking to develop his coaching career – which he did under Tony Pulis at the Riverside as first-team coach.

"I did all my badges and, after six years' graft, I received my UEFA Pro Licence, which I gained through the Irish FA and it was presented to me before the Ireland-Uruguay game.

"I was part-time at the academy, which was a great start, because when football is in your blood like it is mine, you just want to do it every day."

Ziege: My Boro Regret

Christian Ziege played for some of the football world's most illustrious clubs - but still regards his time with Boro as the happiest of his career.

AC Milan, Bayern Munich, Liverpool and Spurs are on the former German international's CV, but memories of the year he spent at the Riverside remain particularly fond ones.

"What I remember most is that as a footballer I had the best time of my career at Middlesbrough," Ziege said.

"The supporters were fantastic to me and the way they treated me was the only time – apart from maybe a bit of the time at Tottenham – where the fans were truly great to me.

"It was my first taste of the Premier League and I loved it there, and so did my family. I loved playing for the club, but we loved the people and countryside around Middlesbrough as well."

Ziege remains indebted to former Boro boss Bryan Robson for revitalising his career, which was drifting after his two-year spell in Italy.

"There are so many things I liked at Middlesbrough, but Bryan was particularly good.

"Bryan is a fantastic man and he was a good coach at Middlesbrough. I loved playing under him and I learned a lot from him.

"He was always there for me and because it was my first time in England he helped me a lot, as did the coaches and the players as well.

"I played with great players such as Gazza, Paul Ince and Gary Pallister and Andy Townsend, who were very helpful."

Such esteemed company invigorated Ziege after a morale-sapping spell in Serie A and Liverpool persuaded him to leave Teesside.

"On the one hand, it was a good decision to leave Middlesbrough for Liverpool because we won the UEFA Cup, FA Cup and League Cup.

"But also, when I retired from playing, I felt that I should have stayed with the club longer.

"I regret leaving when I did. You can't change history, but I will always be grateful to everyone at Middlesbrough.

"They helped me get my career back on track - they gave me confidence that I could do very good things.

"The fans were so important in that respect because of the way they got behind the team and the way they backed me.

"Hopefully, the fans can forgive me for leaving and I would like to think they will not hold things against me."

An exciting left-sided player, Ziege endeared himself to the Boro faithful but the relationship ended in acrimony when he left for Liverpool in controversial circumstances.

It was a deal that landed the Reds in trouble with the football authorities and resulted in a heavy fine for the Anfield club.

It caused fury among Boro fans and undermined Robson's preparations for the new season that saw the club flirt with relegation.

"I only have good thoughts about Boro, but the fans' thoughts changed towards me when I went to Liverpool, which I can understand.

"From my point of view, I would never say a bad word about the club or Boro fans, because they played a big part in my career and are still in my thoughts."

Ziege, who most recently had a brief spell in Thailand coaching Somchai Maiwilai's Dragons, also managed Borussia Monchengladbach and coached the German Under-18 team.

"It's really good working with kids because, on the one hand, they are still listening as they are young and they will work hard.

"But on the other hand, we only get together for a few days and that is difficult.

"I have to be honest and say that I did not have the coaches or the facilities that the kids these days have, but I still enjoyed playing from first thing in the morning until the evenings, if I could.

"Playing for the national side as a youngster was always fantastic, but I was always a little bit nervous.

"You are playing with top players and you are representing your country against other nationalities, which was a great honour and a privilege."

Ziege's son, Alessandro, followed in his father's footsteps in professional football and has an advantage over his peers thanks to his dad's cosmopolitan past.

"I learned a lot from my time in England and that helped me as a coach.

"I enjoyed my time in England, and my family did as well, and it has always been in my mind that we would one day go back and live there at some stage, because the people were so friendly and the country was fantastic.

"Life was great in England for us as a family and I enjoyed playing in England under the different coaches. You always take something with you, either from the coaches or the teams you play in or the facilities.

"I have been in Italy, England and Germany and I learned so much from my time with Middlesbrough, Liverpool and Tottenham. If I got the chance to go back I would go back straight away."

Young's Bargain Buy For Southgate

It is fair to say Luke Young got more than he bargained for when he went shopping while on holiday to Portugal.

Young nipped out to an Algarve supermarket to spend a few euros on food and drink for his family, but ended up bringing about a £2.5-million move to Boro – thanks to a chance meeting with Gareth Southgate.

"I'd just been relegated with Charlton, which was devastating, and there was quite a bit of interest in me from various Premier League clubs," Young said.

"Other clubs tried to play little games, probably using me when they had other irons in the fire.

"But then I bumped into Gareth on holiday in Portugal in a supermarket, of all places. He spoke to me as if he really wanted me to come to Boro and they made the most effort to show they really wanted me.

"The fact I met Gareth, him assuring me Boro wanted me and the club moving quickly to get something together, made me think the Riverside was the best place for me and that proved to be the case."

Harlow-born Young settled quickly once a £2.5-million transfer was agreed in July 2007.

"I'd spent all my life in and around London, but I loved living in the North.

"I ended up in Harrogate on the recommendation of Jimmy Floyd Hasselbaink, who'd lived there and said it was a lovely place to stay if I ended up at Boro.

"I spoke to Chris Riggott who said the same. It was great living there and we really missed it when we left, but you often don't know how lucky you are until you move on.

"The only bad thing was that the club did not remain in the Premier League, which was disappointing because I really thought we'd started to get something going up there.

"There were signs we were going to be a really good side. Sadly it didn't work out that way.

"Unfortunately, we started to lose one or two players. There was always speculation about Stewart Downing going, but we lost Jonathan Woodgate and Robert Huth as well, which was too much."

The England international, who played seven times for his country, was a model of consistency at Boro and a hit with fans.

He was also responsible for one of the best individual strikes the Riverside has seen - a long-range thunderbolt against former club Tottenham in a 1-1 draw.

"Even though I say it myself, it was a great goal – one of the best of my life.

"But the most important thing is that it came right in the middle of a poor run of form, when we weren't picking up points, so that draw spurred us on a bit.

"We ended up getting a few results after that, so it was doubly pleasing, as it was against my boyhood team and the place where I learned my trade."

That Young was voted the best right-back to have pulled on a Middlesbrough shirt in a fans' survey says it all about his year on Teesside, which ended when he moved to Aston Villa in a £6-million deal.

"I had a great rapport with the fans - it's just such a shame I couldn't have stayed for longer, because had it not been such a fee the club would have wanted to keep me.

"I loved playing there. The atmosphere was electric at the Riverside in some of the games when we played the bigger teams in the Premier League.

"I remember playing Man United when it was 2-2, and we also beat Arsenal, and the fans played a massive role from the start. If the fans lifted the players and shook up their opponents, then the players could go on and beat anyone."

Young, who joined Boro on a four-year deal, has just one regret about his time at the club. He is just a little sorry he did not stay on Teesside longer.

"I thoroughly enjoyed my time at Middlesbrough, but just feel a bit disappointed I was only there for the one season.

"Once I was up there, I had such a great time. It was certainly good while it lasted, but in the end, me moving on probably suited everyone.

"I was 29 years of age and they were offered what was, in my opinion, very good money at the time for me, and I don't blame Steve Gibson for taking up that option.

"Ultimately, it was close to £6-million with add-ons, so he made the right decision. Anyway, Steve's such a successful businessman who am I to argue with his logic. It made sense.

"I didn't really force through the move, but I sat down with the manager and he said if you want to then go for it, because it's probably best for both parties.

"But I felt sad to be leaving. It wasn't a case of me thinking, 'Great, I'm leaving Boro for Aston Villa,' because I really liked the lads, the staff, the fans and the whole ethos of the club.

"I was caught in two minds, but the whole package was a good deal all round."

Young spent a year at Villa Park before joining Queens Park Rangers in a three-year deal which ran till 2014 when he was forced to quit football.

He had a miserable time at Loftus Road as the club slid into the Championship and he struggled with a hip injury.

"I came back for pre-season, and then something happened on the first day back in training, and in the end I had to have an operation which was very frustrating.

"Our manager, Harry Redknapp, is a great man to work for. It's brilliant with Harry. I didn't have a great time with Mark Hughes, and so as soon as Harry came in he just said get yourself fit, we'll look after you.

"The old regime was trying to ease a few of us out by not being particularly nice to us, so as soon as the new manager came in that all stopped, and Harry treated everyone as professional footballers, which is the way it should be."

Grounds for Optimism

They say that when you get a second chance you're supposed to grab it with both hands.

And that is exactly what former Boro defender Jonathan Grounds did when he was a youngster.

The Teessider recovered from the potentially crushing disappointment at being released by his beloved club and made the most of a fresh opportunity to fulfill a childhood dream and play for Boro's first team.

Grounds was spotted by Boro chief scout Ron Bone at the age of seven and won a place at the club's School of Excellence and held his own as the Academy opened, but then at the age of 12 he received a bombshell.

"I was released because they said I needed to toughen up. It was a bit of a shock to the system, but I was determined to bounce back," Grounds said.

"Thankfully, family and friends rallied round, got me playing for local sides and then I earned a place back at the academy, so it all worked out well in the end.

"But initially it was hard to overcome, because it was everything I knew. I wasn't too interested in school because playing football was what I did, day-in, day-out."

Grounds played with Redcar Town for 18 months before proving himself worthy of a re-call from the Boro Academy.

"I managed to get straight back into football because I'd stayed in touch with my Sunday league coach at Redcar Town, who told me to come and play for his team as soon as I was ready.

"Ron also kept an eye on me, spoke to Academy manager Dave Parnaby a few times, and got me back in to the fold at Boro, and it went from there.

"I was on trial and we played in a Nike tournament in Sunderland, which we won, we went off to America where we played in the world finals, and then I signed back on as a scholar."

Grounds, who hails from Thornaby and attended the town's St Patrick's School, was a season-ticket holder at the Riverside and hero-worshipped Juninho "because he had this ability to light things up for us."

A left-winger, he also had a soft spot for Manchester United winger Ryan Giggs, until he found a niche for himself at left-back where the competition at the Riverside was intense.

"It was injuries to other players that helped me get my opportunity, because we had two established left-backs in Andy Taylor and Emanuel Pogatetz, but they were both crocked when I was on loan at Norwich.

"The manager at the time, Gareth Southgate, rang and told me that he needed to call me back. That was my big break and it came against Liverpool at the Riverside, which was a dream come true."

He would have been forgiven for getting the butterflies, but the policy of loaning players out paid dividends.

"Being that little bit older and having been on loan helped. A lot of players make their debut at 16 or 17, but I was 19, so I'd trained with a first team a lot, but there were still nerves.

"But we had a lot of experienced players in the dressing room, such as George Boateng and Jonathan Woodgate, which helped because they were so encouraging.

"I marked Yossi Benayoun and Ryan Babel, and it was disappointing not to beat Liverpool that day, because the old Fernando Torres produced a bit of magic to get them a draw after George Boateng had put us ahead.

"I wanted to get Torres' and Steven Gerrard's shirts, but by the time I reached them some of the other lads had already got them."

Grounds found first-team opportunities limited before he upped sticks and headed across the Pennines to play for League One outfit Oldham.

"Footballers have to grow up quickly. That's something I learned from my loan moves at Boro, as it was a steep learning curve leaving home for the first time.

"There have been big changes to say the least with moving away from home permanently and becoming a dad, but it's definitely been enjoyable.

"Going out on loan from Boro worked wonders for me. It makes you grow up having to look after yourself and play regular first-team football.

"For me it was vital to get that bit of experience and overall I had good memories of Boro. It was good to learn from different managers."

Grounds has thrived at Birmingham City, but Boro still occupy an important place in his heart. "It's still my club. I'll always be a Boro fan."

CENTRE OF ATTENTION – *Central Defenders*

Boam And Bust

Stuart Boam feared his days were numbered when Jack Charlton arrived on Teesside.

The centre-half thought he was about to become surplus to requirements when Charlton took over as Boro manager.

But those fears could not have been further from the truth and he went on to establish himself as a club legend.

He led Boro to promotion to the old First Division and a place in the upper echelons of the English game during an eight-year stint at Ayresome Park.

"Jack actually signed for Boro as a player-manager from Leeds, so I thought I'd be on my way even though I'd just arrived on Teesside," Boam said.

"I vividly remember when he conducted his first team meeting at chairman Charles Amer's country club.

"Jack went through all the players individually and said what he thought of them and what they could do.

"He left me till last and told everyone I couldn't play. I knew in my own mind I was doing my job okay, but he broke my heart.

"I thought the statement showed he wanted a game or two and I'd suffer, but then not only did I play in practically every game, he made me captain.

"I've since found out that a similar thing happened to him when Don

Revie took over at Leeds. It was man-management, deliberately done to

wake me up a little and make me into a better player.

"So, as it turned out, after many arguments and set-tos between me and Jack, and one thing and another, things worked out well for both of us and, most importantly, the club."

Under Charlton's guidance, Boam helped Boro win promotion to top-flight football by a mammoth 15 points before a seventh-placed finish the next season.

It represented a meteoric rise for Boam who was rejected as a youngster by Nottingham Forest before launching his career at Mansfield where sterling service earned him a £50,000-move to Boro in 1973 during Stan Anderson's rein as manager.

"I remember my wife Janice and I saved up our pennies for 12 months, because

I wasn't getting much money, to buy a house.

"We finally moved into the place on the Friday and then put it up for sale on the Saturday because of my move.

"I was over the moon moving to Middlesbrough, even though I didn't know where it was, but it just about broke her heart because we'd been looking forward to creating a new home for ourselves."

Boam would play 322 times for Boro before a £170,000 transfer to Newcastle in 1979 and was a defensive mainstay.

"Boro had a reputation of scoring a lot, but conceding as many, and so Stan bought myself and Nobby Stiles - who I roomed with for three months - and Johnny Vincent.

"Unfortunately, it didn't click and Stan was sacked mid-way through the season and we had to wait till summer for Jack to take over, because at the time he was playing for Leeds.

"Harold Shepherdson ran the show as caretaker manager for eight games and I was introduced to Willie Maddren, who was a very good player, and from the word 'go' we hit it off.

"I don't think we lost a game under Harold and conceded very few. Out of the blue we'd solved our defensive frailties – by hook or by crook - and that provided the platform for Jack. He was on to a good thing."

Boam was given the seal of approval by World Cup-winning centre-back Charlton by being appointed skipper.

"It was a case of 'what Jack wanted, Jack got' and my job was to ensure the way we played was the way the manager wanted.

"We never altered our style or tactics to suit the opposition. If they were better than us then so be it. We always played a 4-4-2 system.

"It made my job a lot easier because there was no rotation system, unlike the top clubs these days, who change according to their opponents.

"We didn't have enough players to do that – we got by with 13 - and Jack felt we always played to our strengths, rather than worry about weaknesses.

"My job was not only to get us to stick to what we'd been working on, but also to get the best out of each individual player through encouragement or getting on to them.

"Jack let me make changes on the pitch as long as I could justify them either defensively, because we were hanging on for draws, or attacking-wise, if going to win the game.

"You'd get the feel for a game and if we were a goal down you'd know if we had a chance or no chance.

"If we were losing 1-0 I'd let my pal Willie stay up front or I'd stay up front, knock a few people about and hope we'd get a lucky break.

"Sometimes it worked, sometimes it didn't. If my ploy didn't work I'd get a rollicking the day after by Jack."

Boam's team scored 77 goals and conceded just 30 in 42 games during their promotion campaign but were still criticised as unexciting.

"We were labeled as a defensive side, but we weren't really. From front to back, when we had defence on our mind, everybody had a job to do.

"Although all the credit went to the back four, Jack would make sure that John Hickton and David Mills, who mainly played up front, would be part of the defensive set-up when attackers were running at us.

"That promotion year was fantastic. Hardly anything went wrong. We didn't get a lot of goals, but we didn't give many away.

"People used to call us boring. It wasn't that. We just didn't score many because we didn't have the players to knock in our chances.

"Jack made sure we didn't give goals away so we'd always get something out of a game. That served us well."

"We had moments, me and Jack, but we got over everything and we've been good friends ever since. In fact, he's even said some very nice things about me."

So Near But So Far For Nattrass

When Irving Nattrass reflects on his time at Middlesbrough he definitely feels it's a case of what might have been.

Nattrass became Boro's record signing when Newcastle were paid £475,000 for his services in 1979 and his future seemed bright, but it proved to be a false dawn.

"I feel sadness when I look back on my time at Boro," Nattrass said. "It should have been a really successful period, but for one reason and another it didn't work out that way.

"We had some good players, such as Mark Proctor, John Craggs and Bosco Jankovic, but we let our best ones leave when Craig Johnston and David Hodgson headed off to Anfield and David Armstrong went to Southampton.

"We had the makings of a good side, which is why I chose to join Boro, but didn't really replace the players we allowed to leave.

"Then it turned out to be a battle for survival. I rated John Neal really highly and he did well despite having his hands tied behind his back for financial reasons, but he was sacked over the sale of Johnston.

"Thankfully, things have changed drastically since then, and by common consent, Boro have the best chairman in England in Steve Gibson."

His assessment that there was "a missed opportunity" also applies to his time at Newcastle where he carved out a reputation as one of the best defenders in the business at right-back or centre-half.

"Again we had the makings of being a really successful club. We'd reached the League Cup final and finished fifth in the First Division.

"Gordon Lee replaced Joe Harvey, but then it all seemed to fall apart. We sold Malcolm Macdonald who was one of the greatest goalscorers I'd ever seen.

"That in itself was understandable, as long as there were plans to replace him, but shortly afterwards Gordon Lee resigned to join Everton.

"It felt as though he'd done the dirty on us all. I lost all respect for him and we went on a downward spiral just like we would do at Boro."

On a brighter note, Nattrass, appointed skipper by Malcolm Allison, witnessed the emergence of two Boro legends – Gary Pallister and Tony Mowbray.

"Both were up-and-coming players and it was obvious that Gary had great potential, but just needed a kick up the backside because he was so lethargic," said Nattrass, who was born in the County Durham village of Fishburn.

"In that respect, I suppose he couldn't have gone to a better place than Manchester United and Alex Ferguson.

"Tony might not have been the classiest defender, but he played with the biggest heart you could ever imagine, and you could always see him going into management because he was such an influential leader.

"On the other hand, I always thought David Hodgson and Mark Proctor would go on to great things and play for England because they were such fine prospects, but they never really fulfilled their early potential."

Nattrass is another who failed to live up to his early billing after being tipped for great things.

He was denied a place in the 1974 FA Cup final between Newcastle and Liverpool by knee damage and after joining Boro instead of Tottenham and Manchester City his injury jinx struck again.

An anticipated England cap during his Tyneside days failed to materialise for the defender when injury forced him out of the national side's 1977 tour of South America.

"I suppose I picked up injuries that came at precisely the wrong time, both at Newcastle and Boro, and prevented me getting a foothold in the England side," said Nattrass, capped once for England Under-23s in 1976.

"I picked up a few nasty injuries after joining Boro and as I got older niggly things stopped me getting a good run in the team."

Despite the setbacks, Nattrass made 313 appearances for Newcastle and played 220 times for Boro before being forced to retire at the age of 33 and became a successful businessman on Tyneside.

"I could have probably gone on for another season and I thought it might have been a bit early to stop playing, but looking back I'm glad I called it a day when I did.

"Football's a great career, but people don't understand the tremendous toll it takes on your body physically when you're playing and training day-in, day-out.

"Thankfully, I can still play a couple of rounds of golf in one day with just a few aches and pains. But if I'd carried on playing it could have been a dire situation."

Best Of Times For Mogga

It was the best of times and the worst of times for young Tony Mowbray.

He can vividly recall the chilling day as a schoolboy when his blood turned cold – before enjoying one of the happiest days of his childhood.

"I was in the middle of a normal school day when my dad turned up, completely out of the blue, and I just jumped to the conclusion that something was badly wrong," Mowbray said.

"I was only about 10 years old at the time. I was mortified, and I thought, 'Oh no, something dreadful has happened at home,' and things like that.

"I was braced for the worst, but thankfully I could not have been more wrong.

"In actual fact, my dad had come to school to pick me up because he was taking me to my first ever football game – to see the great George Best that afternoon."

Best was in town with Manchester United who were going to play Boro at Ayresome Park.

"It was very unusual because it was a midweek match taking place in the afternoon.

"That was because it was the middle of the miners' strike in the 1970s and the power cuts that were all over the place meant there would be no floodlights for an evening kick-off.

"It is still my first memory of the Boro and although I don't remember too much about the game itself, I'll never forget how bowled over I was when I climbed the steps in the ground and saw this stunningly beautiful green pitch in a great arena laid out in front of me.

"It was awesome. For a kid who'd picked up the football bug watching Pele, Jairzinho, Rivelino and Gerson in front of the telly during the 1970 World Cup, it didn't get much better than this.

"It was also the day when I decided I wanted to become a professional footballer. I was inspired to do everything humanly possible to play for the Boro."

A year later, the Redcar youngster had a successful trial with Boro at the age of 11 and the first steps were taken towards a career that would begin in earnest in the most intimidating of circumstances.

"I went to watch regularly from the Holgate and my favourite player was John Hickton, partly because of the 25-yard run-ups he used to take before smashing home his penalties.

"He was the player most kids my age wanted to be like, but I loved watching Willie Maddren and Stuart Boam the most, because of the way they dominated in defence."

Before long, Mowbray swapped his place on the terraces for a spot in Boro's defence after being handed his first professional contract by then manager John Neal and then being given his debut by Bobby Murdoch in 1982.

"It was an amazing occasion – up at St James' Park, which even then was a great stadium – and we were taking on a Newcastle side featuring local talisman Kevin Keegan.

"It was extra special to play against a megastar like Keegan, and not only that, but I was ordered to man-mark him. We drew 1-1, so I must have had a pretty decent game."

Mowbray would become Boro's defensive mainstay and, at the age of 22, he was appointed as club captain by manager Bruce Rioch.

Together with Boro owner Steve Gibson, Rioch would spearhead the club's resurgence after the padlocks went on the Ayresome Park gates in 1986.

"In the face of adversity caused by liquidation, Bruce took a team of young lads and moulded them into not only a very good football side, but also into a group of very good characters.

"It's a set of lads who have generally enjoyed really good careers and when we meet up the events of 1986 feel as though they happened just a week ago.

"There is a bond there – it's a genuine affinity caused by sticking together during those troubled times."

Rioch, of course, paid tribute to Mowbray by famously uttering the words *which would inspire acclaimed Boro fanzine Fly Me to the Moon*.

'If you were on a rocket ship going to the moon, the man you would want sitting next to you would be Tony Mowbray,' Rioch said.

The feeling of admiration is mutual.

"Bruce is a great man. He never thought that football was purely about ability - the basis of his success was discipline.

"His attitude was that if you are disciplined off the pitch you will be disciplined on it.

"This even meant that we were fined if we turned up unshaven, so designer stubble was out.

"For Bruce, it all meant he could trust his players to do the jobs they were supposed to do and meet the demands he laid down before us."

Mowbray spent 10 years on Boro's books and played 348 games before playing for Celtic following a £1-million move and then Ipswich where he became first team coach.

He had a spell at Portman Road as interim manager before his managerial career began in earnest in Scotland with Hibernian.

Then he was in charge at West Bromwich Albion, Celtic and had a three-year spell at the helm with Boro before taking the reins at Coventry and most recently Blackburn.

"I learned a lot from Bruce, which I put into practice as a player and manager.

"He was always punctual, smartly turned out, he said and did the right things and was always polite.

"I spent a lot of time with him when I was managing Hibs and we played his team, Odense, in Denmark, in the UEFA Cup.

"It was great to catch up with my old boss. The funny thing is, he hadn't changed a bit. I hope he never will."

Cooper - From Rags To Riches

Football really has been a proverbial rags-to-riches tale for Colin Cooper.

He may have endured a relatively tough upbringing as a young footballer, but insists he would not have had it any other way.

Things were looking decidedly grim when Sedgefield-born Cooper joined Boro when the club was in financial meltdown in the mid-80s.

But he is certain he would not have prospered as a footballer with Boro - not once but twice - and gone on to represent his country had things been comfortable.

"After joining Boro on a YTS (Youth Training Scheme) at 16 from school, in my first few years the club was on a downward spiral financially," Cooper said.

"There was none of the new sparkling kit and the gleaming new facilities that kids enjoy now.

"We had to get down to Ayresome Park early to get the best stuff for the pros we were paid to look after, then get the rags we were left for ourselves for training.

"It seems very old-school, but it grounded me as a person and made me appreciate everything as a footballer.

"We weren't treated as prima donnas. All we got was a pair of boots. We rolled up our sleeves and grafted with the groundsman in a way kids don't anymore.

"It was tough, but that makes you appreciate things when it turns in your favour and you move up to become a successful professional."

Cooper followed future Boro manager Tony Mowbray through the ranks as the club overcame the odds to gain back-to-back promotions under the guidance of Bruce Rioch in the mid-80s.

"The crowds were low and the football wasn't very sparkling, even though Boro players are always taught to play in the right way.

"Willie Maddren was my first manager and I had a lot of respect for him, but the condition of the club dictated that the quality of players under him wasn't good enough and we went down and nearly out.

"When I made my league debut the club was close to relegation, and if anyone thinks crowds dwindling to 13,000 are depressing at the Riverside they should have tried playing in front of 3,000 at Ayresome Park. They were the real diehards."

After starting out as a sweeper in central defence under Maddren, Cooper thrived at left-back under Rioch and won eight England Under-21 caps.

"I thought my career was up following liquidation because it would have been a matter of going out on trial everywhere, so I felt it was in danger of disappearing.

"But things really clicked. I got England Under-21 recognition, but we had three hard seasons on the bounce and that top-flight season caught up with us.

"It started to take a toll on body and mind. I played with a fracture in my foot for seven months without knowing it.

"My body packed in and I felt that for 18 months I was drifting along, although I was a decent player. Things came to a head when Lennie Lawrence took over.

"It felt right to move on. It was the best thing for me because my career had levelled off and, in my opinion, was tapering off quickly, so I needed a fresh start.

"Lennie was very complimentary and said he should never have let me go. But I know for a fact that the player I became in years hence I would not have been if I hadn't left."

So it was on to Millwall in a £300,000 move in 1991 and although things worked out well for Cooper, his new colleagues at The Den didn't take to Rioch as their manager.

"I really thought Bruce would be the right person to put me back on track at Millwall.

"It was a bit daunting at first having to mix it with club stalwarts such as Les Briley and Terry Hurlock, but I won them over.

"The older players didn't take to Bruce, who tried to change things and it never worked.

"He had a really disciplined way of being a manager, he could be relaxed, but all he wanted was high standards.

"Trying to impose them on people who'd been there for a long time meant he found himself banging his head against a brick wall."

A change in the manager's office took Cooper's career in a different direction when Mick McCarthy took the helm.

"Mick had been a teammate and friend and when he became manager he said he'd convert me from full-back to centre-half because it would suit my qualities better.

"I was more than willing to oblige and I'd do anything for him because he was a mate and for the club's own sake.

"So there was good judgment on Mick's part and a bit of luck on mine, but I never looked back.

"We had two years where we just failed to make the play-offs and then in 1993 Mick said the club had been made an offer it couldn't refuse and I moved to Nottingham Forest."

Cooper thrived at Forest after a £2.5-million transfer and won two full England caps before coming home and re-joining Boro.

He partnered Gary Pallister in Bryan Robson's defence, played for Terry Venables and Steve McClaren beyond his 38th birthday and became part of the coaching staff.

But his Millwall days have left an indelible mark on Cooper both on and off the field - with fans from The Den rallying behind him following the tragic death of his young son Finlay.

"I know Millwall always get a lot of flak for the way their supporters are.

"But the one thing I always knew from them, and which stood me in good stead down there, is that they are similar to Boro fans.

"If the players who are representing their club give everything for the cause then they will back you to the absolute hilt. But you have to show you care.

"They were not over-fussed about a skinny Northerner arriving, but by the time I left they realised that when I play for a club I give absolutely everything.

"They appreciated that so much that I still speak to a lot of Millwall fans and they still raise money for the charity we formed in Finlay's memory. They get as much respect from me as they gave me, which is saying something."

• *There was an overwhelming sense of déjà vu for Colin Cooper when he embarked on his managerial career with Hartlepool.*

Despite never playing for Boro's neighbours he had a strong sentimental connection with Pools.

It goes back to the day when Cooper was in the Boro side forced to play its first 'home' game of the season at Victoria Park after bailiffs had locked the Ayresome Park gates.

"You've got to remember that but for Hartlepool, Boro might not have been here today," Cooper said.

"We couldn't have played that first league game but for their generosity and dispensation from the Football League to play a home game at The Vic against Port Vale, so we could get our season under way.

"Boro had major financial problems. We were in dire straits. Had we not been able to play, who knows what might have happened.

"Until that week we didn't know if we would have been able to fulfill our league fixtures. Everything was in the balance."

Pallister's Debt To Willie Maddren

From Stockton Sixth Form College's third team to Premier League summit with Manchester United, Gary Pallister's career was the stuff of comic book heroes.

Pallister, of course, helped restore the glory days to Old Trafford alongside Steve Bruce in the heart of Sir Alex Ferguson's defence when Manchester United won the Premier League title in 1993 to end a 26-year wait for domestic supremacy.

But that was only after he had worked his way up from being a sixth-form no-hoper to Northern League outfit Billingham Town and then from Middlesbrough to Old Trafford.

That was when United boss Alex Ferguson had seen enough of the centre-back, who had already made the first of just 22 England appearances - to get chairman Martin Edwards to pay £2.3 million for his services and make him the most expensive defender in British football in 1989.

"Even when I look back at my career now, I think, 'Christ! Did that really happen?'" Pallister said.

"To go from leaving school with nothing in front of you to end up playing for the biggest club in the world, winning trophies and playing in finals - it's fairy-tale stuff."

But it was only thanks to bloody-mindedness that Pallister overcame a series of setbacks to win the 1992 PFA Player of the Year award as he soared to the top of the English game.

"Even when things weren't great, I thought, 'I don't care what any bugger says, I'm going to make it as a professional,' but no one in their right mind could've known where it would go from there."

Born in Ramsgate, Kent, Pallister moved to his dad's native Teesside and was brought up in Norton, attending Billingham Comprehensive where he was able to indulge his passion for sports of all kinds.

"I loved my football with a passion, but I was an all-round sportsman when I was a kid.

"I was a cricketer, an athlete, a footballer and a basketball player and I got district honours at every sport - apart from football.

"I was a centre-forward and I scored plenty of goals, but always remember wondering why I never even got asked to represent Stockton.

"I felt aggrieved. Our team won the league every year and yet I never got asked to have a trial, despite a good goal-scoring record.

"The thing is, though, there was no one you could really ask about how they were making the decisions at the time, which was frustrating.

"I was making my mark in my other sports, and even playing for the county at basketball, but it rankled because football was always my first love."

Despite that he remains an advocate of the virtues of school sport at a time when club academies dominate.

"You've got to let kids develop in their own time and at their own pace, especially at school, but clubs stop kids playing for their own school teams now.

"I disagree with that. It breeds an idea of elitism; that they're better than their peers. That's so wrong. They've got to be able to grow as individuals and deal with the hardships that you get at school."

Things would take a turn for the better, but only thanks to a teammate's extra-curricular activities on a Sunday morning.

"I was 15 and in my last year at school and we took on Conyers who everyone was thrashing.

"But our centre-half had been at an all-night ice skating marathon at Billingham Forum. He hadn't slept a wink. It was 3-3 and he started nodding off on the pitch.

"Our manager, Malcolm Danby, shouted: 'Get off. Pallister centre-half and I'll put a sub on'. So I went into defence and we won 10-3.

"Next, we played our main rivals and Malcolm, who's done a lot of work for Boro over the years, said, 'Pally, it's a tough game, so I want you to play centre-half.'

"But, being a headstrong so-and-so, I turned round and said, 'I don't want to play centre-half.' Malcolm wasn't having any of it. He said, 'Well that's where I'm playing you,' and so for the rest of the season I played at centre-half.

"And that's when it all started to come together - well sort of, because then I went to Stockton Sixth Form College and ended up playing in their 3rd XI. I got dropped from the A-team, dropped after falling out with the manager of the seconds and ended up in the thirds."

Pallister was, though, asked to play for Stockton Wolves in the Teesside Junior League and made his mark to the extent that he went to Billingham Town for a season where he attracted the attention of Football League clubs.

"I got a knock on the door from a chap called Jimmy Mann who asked me to go to Grimsby for a trial and we picked up Peter Beagrie on the way.

"We played a game which went pear-shaped for me. I gave away a penalty two minutes in and yet they invited me back for more trials. But Billingham had other ideas. The seconds had loads of big games and wouldn't let me go back.

"But I was always determined to make it as a professional footballer and I always told my mates I would one day do it."

Grimsby's loss was Boro's gain. He was promoted to the Billingham first team and his performances in the Northern League Second Division caught Boro's eye and he was invited to trials.

But it was only thanks to Boro legend Willie Maddren that Pallister was given the chance to fulfill his boyhood dreams and make it as a professional.

"There were six triallists out to make an impression and about ten minutes in, Malcolm Allison, who was the manager, came to the touchline to watch.

"But 15 minutes later he walked off, evidently not thinking much of us lot, which was a downer. I didn't play well and I sat down in the dressing room feeling disappointed, thinking I'd blown my big chance.

"Then the legendary Willie Maddren, who was the reserves' manager, sat next to me. 'Listen son,' he said. 'I know how you're feeling, but I've seen enough to want to keep an eye on you, so go back to Billingham and I'll keep tabs on you.'

"About a year later, by which time Willie had taken over as manager, I got a call to go back. I think the Boro scout, Barry Geldart, told Willie I was quicker and physically stronger and worth another look.

"I was on the dole at the time, heading nowhere, so it was music to my ears. I played two trial games and Willie asked me to come back for a month's trial. They'd cover expenses, so I'd see what it'd be like to train full-time and we'd take it from there.

"After six weeks I was called into Willie's office. He asked me if I'd like to sign a professional contract and so, for the princely sum of £50 a week, I became a Middlesbrough player. I was 19. It was one of the greatest days of my life."

Pallister says he will be forever indebted to Maddren, who played almost 300 times for the Teessiders, and died in August 2000 of Motor Neurone Disease at the age of 49.

"I'll always owe Willie a huge debt because if it wasn't for his faith in me things would have been very different.

"He saw something in me at a time when I didn't think anyone would have seen anything in me in that first round of trials with Boro. I thought he was just being nice, but he was a man of his word.

"He'd take me out for extra one-on-one training sessions because I'd missed the apprenticeship everyone else had enjoyed. He taught me how to be a centre half and that was a real privilege because he'd been a great defender himself.

"It was Willie who ushered in what was called the 'class of 86', but he never got a chance to see them come to fruition as a manager.

"He had a massive part to play in that team because he had sourced all those players who served Boro so well."

They remained close right until the very end.

"Willie gave me the benefit of the doubt and we stayed good friends for the rest of his life.

"Even after I went off to Manchester, I used to come back to Teesside and go and see Willie in his shop.

"I'm eternally grateful for the help he gave me and his faith in me. He was such a lovely man and it still upsets me when I think about him not being here now. There was so much tragedy about him with his injuries that curtailed his career.

"I was really upset when the news came through about his Motor Neurone Disease diagnosis. It was devastating to watch Willie go the way he did, because of the way the disease took hold and ravaged him. It was really tough to see Willie suffering."

Bruce Rioch, who succeeded Maddren as manager, is credited with galvanising Boro but Pallister did not hit it off with the Scot who had a reputation as a disciplinarian.

"Me and Bruce never saw eye-to-eye. We rubbed each other up the wrong way from the off and as much as he was a great coach, and you can't argue with what he achieved as a manager, I didn't like his man-management style, continually getting fined and being at loggerheads with him.

"In the end, it became one of the reasons why I left, although it was ultimately a professional reason because we'd just been relegated, but it was a personal decision because I wasn't enjoying my football. The rest, as they say, is history."

Over a nine-year period, Pallister helped United win four Premier League titles, three FA Cups and a League Cup as well as European success.

"There are so many highs, but winning the European Cup-Winners' Cup final in 1991 was a massive highlight.

"And the first title after 26 years was a massive thing for the club, because it lit the touch-paper on the dominance Man United had for the next 20 years."

After 317 league games under Ferguson, he would eventually head back to Middlesbrough and a re-union with former United skipper Bryan Robson.

"I came back because Bryan was the manager and because it was my hometown club.

"I could have stayed another year at Old Trafford, but I didn't want to end my time at United getting cynical about not playing. When we brought in Jaap Stam I spoke to Fergie and he told me I'd have to fight for my place.

"They accepted a bid and told me he was looking elsewhere now, and with Wes Brown coming through, I thought it was time to move on but, that said, I don't think I'd have gone anywhere apart from Middlesbrough.

"In hindsight, if I'd have done it a year later without the fee it would have been easier because they ended up paying £2.5million, as opposed to £2.3 million they sold me for, which didn't sit right with me.

"It was a fee that I wasn't worth after the service I'd given to United. That put more pressure on me to play games, but I didn't play the amount I'd have liked.

I played plenty in the first season, but my back started to struggle and then it went completely and I needed surgery.

"Gazza, Andy Townsend and Brian Deane were there and so we played some good football that year and no one who follows Boro will forget that day we won 3-2 at Old Trafford."

Kernaghan's Food For Thought

Professional footballers experience all sorts of problems, but few face what Alan Kernaghan went through during his Boro days.

Forget about injuries, fall-outs or new deals, Kernaghan was left wondering if his whole career was in jeopardy when – out of the blue - a doctor diagnosed him as a diabetic.

But the centre-half refused to let anything get in his way and five years later he was jetting over to the United States for the 1994 World Cup finals in ex-Boro manager Jack Charlton's Republic of Ireland squad.

In a candid interview, Kernaghan has spoken about how his world was turned upside down by his medical condition.

"We were playing at QPR and I'd been feeling a wee bit ropey for a couple of weeks beforehand – just tired and not my usual self," he said.

"It was a really hot day and I felt absolutely exhausted. My mouth felt as dry as dry could be and I just felt a bit lifeless.

"So I told the doctor at half-time that I had to do something about it and he just said, 'Right, we will see how you get on and come in and see me on Monday.'

"I managed to get through the weekend, the weekend of the Hillsborough disaster, and then went to see him on the Monday morning.

"He just did a urine test and that was that. He told me within ten seconds that I was a Type 1 diabetic.

"I went into hospital for about five days. They did all the bits and bobs they had to do and got my blood-sugar levels down to a reasonable rate.

"The first question I asked was whether my football career was over and the doctor just said let's get your health sorted out and take it from there.

"The people at the hospital were very good and they could see no reason why I shouldn't carry on. And away we went.

"It's funny, but the footballer's lifestyle is ideally suited to a diabetic. The food is pretty much perfect for what a diabetic should eat, as is being fit and looking after yourself.

"They aligned themselves to one another and, to end up in the Irish squad at the World Cup finals, showed diabetes is just a bump in the road if you are disciplined with your health."

Nothing, it seems, has been straightforward for Kernaghan. He was born in Yorkshire but brought up in Bangor, Northern Ireland, and played for their national schoolboys' team before switching allegiances and playing for the Republic.

He does, though, count himself fortunate to have ended up at Boro as a schoolboy.

"I was spotted by scouts at the age of 15 and went over to Middlesbrough for the summer holidays and then after every school holiday.

"A friend of mine's dad was an FA coach who used to coach the coaches and we used to go along to his sessions.

"At the end of the night there used to be a game and that's how I was spotted. It was funny, but that's that little bit of luck you need."

Kernaghan joined Boro as an apprentice in 1985 and went on to play 212 times over the next eight years as the club went from bust to boom.

"It was great for me at Boro. Earlier on, there was the disappointment of relegation and the shock of going into administration.

"But that was easily outweighed by the happy times I had, such as winning promotion and getting to Wembley for the ZDS Trophy final against Chelsea.

"And who could forget that 'home' game at Hartlepool? It had been a relief to just play and get the season up and running.

"It was on and off and then we started the game like a house on fire. I was up front in those days and I didn't score, but I was pleased as punch that Archie Stevens got our goals to give us that 2-2 draw with Port Vale."

Kernaghan, it seems, went backwards to go forwards at Boro having started off as a forward before establishing himself as a central defender.

"I played centre-half and striker on and off, just depending on where I was needed, and at times filling in for Tony Mowbray or Gary Pallister.

"But then Colin Todd told me to play centre-half when I was about 21 and that was that.

"I played in the back four with Tony after Gary left and then it was myself and Nicky Mohan and then Derek Whyte.

"I went down to Charlton on loan when Colin Todd was in charge and it was just about to become permanent when, in a weird coincidence, Lennie Lawrence left The Valley for Boro and said, 'I would love you to stay,' which I was only happy to do.

"Lennie was excellent. He wasn't your typical football manager in that he hadn't played, but he was a very good man-manager.

"He didn't overpower anybody. He treated you like you would like to be treated. It wasn't his way and the highway."

Kernaghan's past experiences have ensured he is an upbeat character.

"If the doctors had said your career's over because of diabetes it would have been very depressing.

"But, if anything, it gave me a kick up the backside to knuckle down and work even harder to make something of myself."

From Fan To First-Teamer For Todd

Andy Todd went around the block a few times after launching his career at Boro, but still regards his time on Teesside as his happiest days in football.

He only played eight times for Boro before seeking his fortune elsewhere, yet still looks back fondly on his journey from terraces to first-team dressing room.

"I started at Boro as a kid and in football terms those days have to be the best of my life," said the son of former Boro boss Colin Todd.

"I was only young and only made a handful of appearances, but I look back really warmly on my time there with lads that went on to have really good careers, like Alan Moore, Michael Brown, Craig Liddle, Graham Kavanagh and Andy Collett.

"We had a great laugh in the dressing room. The banter was brilliant in the bottom end of the away dressing room, and the commuting down from Chester-le-Street where I lived was great too, because there was a crew of us.

"We trained at the prison at Kirklevington, college pitches up the road from Ayresome and Redcar beach. We were all over the shop. Facilities weren't up to much, but in John Pickering we had one of the best coaches I've worked with."

The fact Todd had travelled the length and breadth of the country supporting Boro was also a factor as he realised a schoolboy dream.

"I was a Boro fan because my dad was there for a few years before I joined," said Todd, who would play Premier League football for Charlton and Blackburn.

"I used to go to home games on the Holgate End and away games with my mates and was that passionate I once got up at half-five to travel to Brighton.

"I really enjoyed my time at Ayresome Park because I was a fan and my hero, without a shadow of doubt was Tony Mowbray - aggressive, but always made things look easy."

Pearson In Land Of The Brave

They say that fortune favours the brave. And that is the case for Boro as far as Nigel Pearson is concerned.

Pearson led Boro to promotion not once but twice during his four years on Teesside after being appointed skipper by then manager Bryan Robson.

And he also had to lead by example as the club recovered from three cup final defeats and the trauma of relegation.

But he insists that Boro's Carling Cup victory in 2004 was down to the "bravery" shown by club owner Steve Gibson after the players and fans had their hearts broken.

"My period with Boro was a bit of a rollercoaster ride, but trust me, it was really enjoyable," Pearson said during a visit to the Riverside while managing Hull.

"At times, things were difficult to take, but we bounced back. That's because we had a spirit and vision of where we wanted to be.

"When we didn't quite get there we had a good go at doing it. They were fantastic years and Boro's is one of the results I look for first.

"They were interesting times - to say the least - and I still feel privileged to have been a part of that incredible phase of the club's history.

"That period of the club's history was a very transitional period and whatever mistakes were made then were brave mistakes.

"But the club got there in the end by winning major silverware, thanks to the bravery shown at the top of the club by Steve Gibson."

Pearson was persuaded to leave Sheffield Wednesday for Boro in 1994 by Bryan Robson in a £750,000-deal.

And it is the former Manchester United and England captain's influence that he identifies as a key factor in the club's upturn in fortunes.

"When Bryan came in, his very presence changed the perception of the club and the ability of the club to attract bigger name players.

"And it is important to remember that period was the start of Middlesbrough's, if you like, most recent climb into the upper echelons of the English game.

"The key reason for getting promoted twice was that we had a good squad, but we also believed in what we were doing. It's as simple as that.

"We had goal-scorers and we had a decent side. It's always about players and you need players that can go out and win games and do that over the course of a season.

"The first time we got promotion only one team went up automatically and the league was very competitive.

"It's a tough ask, but we showed what favourites can do, but you just have to deal with the pressure and the expectations."

Pearson was eventually forced into retirement due to injury while at Boro, but that still doesn't ruin his memories.

"We had a great time here and my kids still talk really enthusiastically about the time we had here and we have fond memories.

"I finished my career at a club that was on the up, moving forward and was really going places.

"I'd had some tremendous years with Wednesday and I came to Boro when I was 31. When I retired I was 35, so to be involved in a club that was still going in the right direction for a player of that age is fabulous.

"I would like to think that I had a good affiliation with the fans, so I really enjoyed my time up on Teesside.

"They were four great years, but I could not afford to get carried away with that sort of thing when I came back (with Hull) and be sentimental."

Football No Joke For Davies

Andrew Davies was the joker in the Boro pack - but it would be wrong to think football was a laughing matter for him.

He may have provided the off-field entertainment for his teammates but he insists his love of life never interfered with his commitment to the Boro cause.

"You could say I was a bit wild when I was younger - I was 17 when I made my Premier League debut and I suppose I was living the life," Stockton-born Davies said.

"They were funny times but don't get me wrong - although I had a reputation as a joker, football was always my priority.

"Football has always been my life, but I don't let it rule my life. That is the most important thing. For me, if you take football too seriously, I personally believe it will drag you down."

That was not always the case as the student at Billingham's Northfield School was first and foremost a cricketer until football intervened.

He was spotted playing for the Stockton district side by legendary Boro scout Ron Bone at the age of 14 and his sporting life changed direction.

"I was always into my cricket more when I was a kid with my brother, Mark, who went on to be a professional cricketer.

"It was one of those things where I enjoyed my football, but I loved my cricket and the more I played football the more people said I had a great chance of making it.

"I didn't take it seriously until I was signed for Boro. Then I ditched my cricket because in the end I loved my football even more than I did my cricket, which I always thought was impossible.

"My brother played for England in the Lions squad and I played for the England Under-21s, which was a massive achievement for me. We both drive each other on and that's been a massive factor in our careers."

Davies - Dava to his friends - has plenty of happy memories from his time as a Boro player even though his Premier League debut coincided with a 5-2 battering by Aston Villa at the Riverside in January 2003.

"It was a desperately disappointing night, but still an unbelievable experience at such a tender age.

"It was a great era and when you look back some people might forget how good it actually was.

"There were so many local lads coming through the ranks, such as Lee Cattermole, James Morrison and Tony McMahon, who are all good friends of mine, all working their socks off for each other in the same team.

"We used to go out for meals together and then be playing against Chelsea and all their superstars at home, and giving them a good run for their money, too. It seemed crazy.

"We had a mix of players, with exceptionally good experienced players, like Jimmy Floyd Hasselbaink, Jonathan Woodgate, Gaizka Mendieta, Ugo Ehiogu and Gareth Southgate there as well.

"I learned a lot from them and from Steve Round, who was probably the best coach I've ever worked under, and I'll always be very grateful to Steve McClaren for giving me my chance in the Premier League and UEFA Cup.

"Plus, I will never forget the way that I was shown the way forward by Dave Parnaby, Mark Proctor and Stephen Pears and the academy coaches who were second to none."

The UEFA Cup ties with Stuttgart and Roma stand out for Davies, but there is an element of frustration when Davies reflects on his time at the Riverside which saw him make 53 first-team appearances.

It ended when he joined Southampton in October 2007 and he clearly made up for lost time because he was named player of the year at the end of the season.

"I'm a centre-back by trade, but found myself having to fill in at full-back and I gave it my best shot, but it wasn't my best position.

"Whatever happened, I was constantly just behind someone else throughout my time at Boro, whether it be Gareth Southgate, Chris Riggott or Danny Mills.

"Then they signed Robert Huth and a couple of other defenders, so I found myself down the pecking order, having not even played a game, and it was an uphill battle.

"When it got to the stage where I'd played a full season and found myself just behind Luke Young, I thought it was time I got my career going with a move."

Riggott: Agony And Ecstasy

Former Boro star Chris Riggott has opened up his heart about the injury problems that spoiled his time on Teesside.

Riggott played a key role in the most successful period of Boro's history as he helped the club win the Carling Cup and then reach the UEFA Cup final.

But he still feels as though he short-changed fans despite his vital contribution to an amazing era where the last three of his seven years on Boro's books were blighted by injury.

"The fans rightly get frustrated when they see players on long contracts and they're not playing, but no one could have been more frustrated than me when I was at Boro," Riggott said.

"I felt as though I let people down, especially Gareth Southgate when he became manager, because I was never fit for him. But if I look in the mirror, I know in my heart of hearts that I did everything to try to be fit.

"I was just unlucky at the time. I know the physio at the time, Grant Downie, and me were both pulling our hair out, constantly bouncing ideas off each other to get me fit. It didn't quite happen, but that was not for the want of trying.

"I have very fond memories and had a great relationship with the fans. But I feel as though it ended on a damp note, which is a shame, because of all the injuries.

"If I could turn back time, I'd like to have been fit for longer because the fans won't remember me particularly well because of all the injuries. But in the main, I loved my time there."

After heading to Boro from Derby with Malcolm Christie in a £3-million deal, Riggott made an instant impression, helping his new team earn a 1-1 draw at Liverpool before scoring twice in a 3-1 win at Sunderland.

Lest anyone forget, the centre-back also struck one of the goals in that amazing UEFA Cup semi-final comeback against Steaua Bucharest at the Riverside.

"I'll never forget what happened at Boro because I played alongside fantastic players. I count myself privileged to have been part of a few amazing years.

"When I reflect on my time at Boro, it is very much a mixed bag of emotions because of the injuries, but the memories are mainly good because I was very fortunate to be part of a squad with quality in depth.

"At the time it felt like the norm, but in hindsight there were some unbelievable players, especially in my position – Gareth Southgate, Ugo Ehiogu and Colin Cooper all vying for places in central defence. I didn't really realise what sort of quality was there.

"We had some brilliant games and to play in the final was phenomenal, but there were lots of other really special games as well - Roma and Stuttgart away and obviously Basel and Steaua.

"The final might have ended in defeat, but it was an amazing journey - bumping into fans and having a coffee with them when you were wandering the streets of some random European country."

Riggott played an important role in Boro winning silverware for the first time in the club's history.

And even though he had to settle for a place among the substitutes for the Carling Cup final in Cardiff, he still savours his Millennium Stadium memories.

"It was a bit of a shame because I played in every round bar the Tottenham away game when I was a sub, and I ended up sat on the bench in the final as well.

"Around 50 people had come down from Derby on a coach to watch me, so that was hard to take, but Steve McClaren made the right shout by going with Southgate and Ehiogu because we won, which was the most important thing.

"I couldn't argue at the time, but when you're a young lad and you've played in most of the games, it's bound to be disappointing but it was still brilliant to be part of such a momentous day."

After leaving Boro as a free agent, following almost 150 games, Riggott had a spell at Cardiff and then Derby before going off to coach in America and now calls Las Vegas home with his American wife and their two children.

"It's a pretty unique sort of place to live," he told the Evening Gazette. "When I retired, I'd had enough with injuries, so we said why don't we go and live over there?"

Pogatetz: Mad Dog Amid Englishmen

Emanuel Pogatetz was mad about Middlesbrough in more ways than one.

The Austrian defender was nicknamed 'Mad Dog' during his time on Teesside thanks to his wholehearted commitment to the Boro cause.

And Pogatetz believes it was that passionate approach to football that meant he and Middlesbrough were the perfect match for each other.

Manager Steve McClaren clearly felt the same because he brought Pogatetz to England in 2005 after he played against Boro for Grazer AK in a UEFA Cup tie.

It took a while to complete the deal, but it was threatened when Pogatetz received a 24-week ban from the Russian football authorities while on loan at Spartak Moscow for a tackle that left opponent Yaroslav Kharitonskiy with a double leg fracture.

The way was cleared for Boro to sign him when the punishment was reduced on appeal and so began tumultuous love affair, as Pogatetz became a talismanic figure on Teesside.

"I had a really strong connection with Middlesbrough people because they have to work very hard to make a living and that is what I had to do with my career," Pogatetz said.

"Going to Boro was the perfect move for me, because I always wanted to play in England and I fitted in very well in Middlesbrough, in terms of the club and the area.

"For an Austrian footballer it is very difficult to make a career in international football, so I had a very strong bond with the people of Teesside.

"I could identify myself with Middlesbrough as a town. We all know what other people in England think about the North East, and especially Middlesbrough.

"They think it's a rough town in a rough area, but they know nothing - I loved it there. I loved playing for the fans and that's why I always gave everything I had for the club and my teammates.

His fond memories were re-kindled during his summer holidays a year after leaving Boro as he met two former teammates in Las Vegas.

"I bumped into Andrew Taylor and Adam Johnson in a hotel in June in Las Vegas, where I was with my girlfriend, and it was great to see them.

"It was great to catch up with them and chat about our old Middlesbrough times. It was a big surprise. We had two really great nights.

"We were talking about the good times and all the funny things, but also what went wrong when we were relegated."

Pogatetz stayed put after Boro dropped into the Championship in 2009, but after a season trying to bring top-flight football he headed off to Germany to play for Hanover.

"Overall, I really enjoyed playing for Boro and, obviously, the first three years were the best.

"Then we were relegated and then the year in the Championship was difficult for me, because I had a knee injury that meant I couldn't play as many games as I wanted.

"It was frustrating and disappointing that I could not help Boro get back to the Premier League before I left.

"But overall, I loved my time at Middlesbrough because of the players I played with and all the people I met there inside and outside the club.

"On a personal level, I look back on it as a really great time in my career. I had a good relationship with the fans, the staff and the players.

"I wanted to stay a bit longer, but in the end it didn't work out, but I still feel it was the right choice for me to move to Germany.

"The last year was very difficult because I was injured, but also because of my private life, as I separated from my wife. That made things very tough.

"That was the worst year for me, for different reasons, but now things are going better and I have been with my girlfriend for two years.

"I am playing at a higher level again and everything is working out in my private life."

Pogatetz endeared himself to fans with his uncompromising passion plays that led coach Steve Harrison to nickname him 'Mad Dog' and he is struggling to shake it off.

"That still plays a part in my career. When I moved to Germany that was the first thing I was asked about.

"It was a nickname that suited me, but it made life hard for me with referees.

"Sometimes they did not treat me fairly because of the reputation that came with it, but overall it was a funny nickname and we all knew that Steve Harrison gave everyone nicknames, so it was okay."

He may have left the club on a low-point but he still has plenty of fantastic memories.

"The UEFA Cup run was very special, but also to score my first goal against Sunderland in the local derby was nice.

"Apart from that our big wins against Manchester United and Chelsea were very special occasions. I am still very proud to have played in those games.

"I still have DVDs of those games at home and I still watch them occasionally and they make me happy to think I played my part in those matches."

He has painful memories of Boro's second UEFA Cup campaign as he broke his nose, jaw and cheekbone in a clash of heads with Basel's Mladen Petric in Switzerland.

"I was sad to miss out on the rest of the campaign, but it was great to see the boys do so well to get to the final. It was a horrible injury, but it could have been a lot worse. They thought I might lose sight in one of my eyes."

His career may be flourishing (now in his homeland with LASK Linz) but he certainly misses the cut-and-thrust of English football.

"I had two good seasons at Hanover and we reached the Europa League quarter-finals, which was really good, and we did well enough in the Bundesliga to qualify again and I was enjoying myself there, but then the move to Wolfsburg came along and then I went to Hoffenheim.

"The Bundesliga is different to the Premier League and I have to admit that I prefer the Premier League. The Bundesliga is great because the stadiums are usually packed and the grounds and facilities are superb, but the style of the Premier League suits me more and sometimes I miss it."

Pogatetz, who played 61 times for Austria, is also hoping to return to Teesside – to watch his old team in action.

"When I have time in the winter break I really want to go to Middlesbrough and watch a game if it is possible. I would love to see a game over Christmas.

"I hope the fans still remember me as a very passionate player. I am still sorry about the year we were relegated, but hopefully they will be back in the Premier League next season."

Woodgate's The Real Thing

Playing for Real Madrid might be the ultimate schoolboy dream for young footballers.

And it may well be all downhill for those who do make it there once they leave the Bernabeu.

But, for Jonathan Woodgate, it was playing for Boro that saw the realisation of a childhood ambition – after he pulled on the Spanish giants' famous white kit.

"Not many people can really say they've fulfilled a childhood ambition, but I can safely say dreams do actually come true," Woodgate said.

"Playing for Boro and then captaining the side when George Boateng was suspended has to be one of the proudest days of my career.

"It's the club I've supported since I was a kid and nothing will change that. I'd always wanted to play for them. Plus, it's the club my dad, Allan, and mum Ann support."

Woodgate's career was resurrected after Boro boss Gareth Southgate persuaded him to head to the Riverside following a couple of injury-ravaged seasons in Spain and the centre-half hardly looked back.

"I badly needed to get my career back on track after being on the sidelines for so long.

"Once I met Gareth and Steve Gibson, there was only one place I wanted to go, even though there were a few other English clubs in for me.

"From my perspective, at least, it was the right decision. I've got no regrets at all.

"I really enjoyed my time at Boro, enjoyed the football, got on with everyone at the club because I'm not the sort of bloke that will have any airs and graces and I proved quite a few of my doubters wrong into the bargain.

"By that I mean those that thought I was an injury-prone crock. Thanks to the efforts of the Boro staff, such as the physio Nick Allenby, I managed to change a few people's opinions.

"I made 27 appearances in my first season and another 19 before I moved to Spurs. I also put in a lot of hard work behind the scenes as well."

After helping newly-appointed Boro boss Southgate find his feet while spending the first campaign on loan from La Liga, Woodgate's transfer to Boro was made permanent in a £7-million deal as the club's Premier League status was consolidated.

The former Marton Juniors star's endeavours evidently caught the attention of Spurs boss Juande Ramos, for he became the former Sevilla manager's first signing after he arrived at White Hart Lane.

"The transfer clearly suited both parties. Really it was a win-win situation.

"Spurs made a bid that was accepted by the club during the January transfer window and I wanted to play European football that was virtually within Spurs' grasp at the time, so it wasn't a particularly difficult decision for me.

"The transfer must have made sense for Boro because Gareth had an abundance of centre-halves such as David Wheater, Emanuel Pogatetz, Robert Huth and Chris Riggott and clearly wanted to be able to strengthen in different areas. It was good business.

"Newcastle were interested, but going there would have been the easy move. It would have meant not moving house or anything like that and going back to a club that I was already familiar with. Instead I chose to uproot.

"I have the utmost respect for Newcastle boss Kevin Keegan, but it was a case of wanting to open up a new episode in my career and looking for a completely fresh challenge."

Woodgate's decision was quickly vindicated as he scored the winner in Spurs' 2-1 defeat of Chelsea in the Carling Cup final at Wembley when he also scooped the man-of-the-match award.

"It was great to get my first winner's medal and score a rare goal with a fluky header past Petr Cech.

"It was a fantastic occasion for everyone connected with White Hart Lane and also made sure we had a place in the UEFA Cup to look forward to."

Woodgate's return to English football with Boro also helped him revive his England career and challenge John Terry and Rio Ferdinand for a place for a frontline place in the plans of England head coach Fabio Capello who, ironically, rubberstamped his move to Boro.

"I always said at Boro that if you do the right things at club level then international football will follow and that proved to be true when I was at Boro," said Woodgate who earned his sixth England cap – almost three years after his fifth - in a friendly against Spain in February 2007 at Old Trafford.

"Everyone wants to represent their country and I'm no different. I'm deeply patriotic and as a professional footballer you want to test yourself against the best in the world and on the biggest stages.

"Getting back into the international fold shows how much I progressed at Boro."

Had it not been for injury troubles, it is fair to say that Woodgate would have far more honours to his name.

"Sometimes people just aren't built for football," he told Guardian reporter Louise Taylor. "When I was younger Craig Bellamy told me I was a bit too quick for my own body. Maybe he was right."

As for playing in a Spurs shirt on Teesside, he was unfazed by the prospect of a hostile reception from the Riverside stands.

"I'm not sure how the fans will react to me, but they can boo me all they want," Woodgate said. "It won't make any difference to how I play. It will be water off a duck's back."

• *Jonathan Woodgate will go down as the one that got away by signing for Leeds rather than Boro and it was all to do with putting first Marton Football Club pals.*

The Nunthorpe School pupil was on Boro's radar but when his local club asked him along for a match he reluctantly turned them down to stay loyal to his Marton teammates.

And then Leeds swooped for a youngster who turned into one of the classiest defenders the Premier League has seen – before he ended up back at Boro.

"I was playing for Marton and we had a really good team and I loved playing with them so I put my teammates first," Woodgate said.

"When I was young a few scouts came to watch a few games and the reason I ended up heading to Leeds rather than Boro was because I wanted to play football with my friends for longer.

"Middlesbrough were keen to take me on back then. They called me one Saturday to say that they wanted me to play Sunday mornings, but I'd already made arrangements to play for Marton who were a good team.

"Then one thing led to another, Leeds spotted me and I ended up signing for them instead. I suppose timing was everything. Leeds just seemed right."

Woodgate surged through the ranks at Leeds as he excelled at the club's Thorp Arch training ground

"The Leeds academy was great and a lot of its success was to do with the standards set by the coaches, Eddie Gray, Robin Wray, and Paul Hart.

"Right from cleaning boots, wiping balls clean to clearing out the dressing room, they set high standards that were taken on to the pitch and the coaching they gave us – technically and mentally – really helped us kick on.

"I thoroughly enjoyed working with them and if you look at the academy players they brought through their record is amazing.

"There's the likes of Harry Kewell, James Milner, Paul Robinson, Alan Smith, myself and another Middlesbrough lad in Lee Matthews, Fabian Delph, Aaron Lennon. It was a conveyor belt of talent. It was just brilliant."

Woodgate, who joined the Boro coaching staff after his second spell with the club, sees similarities between the Leeds and Middlesbrough academies.

"Everything is built on really firm foundations thanks to the principles that are instilled in all the players at both clubs.

"Boro, year-in, year-out, produces talented players such as Stewart Downing, Lee Cattermole, James Morrison, Andrew Taylor and David Wheater and Adam Johnson and Danny Graham. They've all played in the Premier League, which says it all."

MIDFIELD TRENCHES – *Central Midfielders*

Masson - Misery To Mister Nice Guy

By his own admission, Don Masson wasn't the most popular figure in the home dressing room at Ayresome Park.

It had nothing to do with his ability because he could play all right but more to do with an unforgiving attitude to teammates.

"I was the world's worst person in my younger days - I was awful, especially when I was playing football," Masson said.

"I used to verbally abuse my colleagues so much that I now know they wanted me out of the club when I was at Boro.

"I went to a reunion at Boro of the 1967 Ayresome Angels and Gordon Jones told me then I was horrible and I was always moaning and he'd had a word with the manager (Stan Anderson) to release me.

"Looking back, I can understand why. I was terrible. I can't believe I was that sort of person. Gordon was spot-on."

But that was then and this is now and Masson reckons that he has changed for the better thanks to religion.

"I lost my mother, father and my first wife, Margaret, who was from Middlesbrough, and I became a Christian at the age of 40, so it felt as if I had wasted 39 years of my life.

"I feel as though the Lord has changed me and I'm so grateful. I treat every day as if it will be my last. It's as if I'm a different person now – but a much nicer one.

"I feel that I am the luckiest person in the world - like I've been given a second chance."

Masson is now running a busy bed-and-breakfast with wife Brenda in Elton on the Hill in the Nottinghamshire countryside.

"Brenda does the cooking; I'm the gofer and gardener, but it's fantastic for me.

"When you're a footballer, life is all take, take, take, but now I'm doing a service for other people and I love it.

"It's a bit more relaxing than when we had the Gallery hotel in the centre of Nottingham. It was very hands-on.

"I'm sitting outside with a view that reminds me of being back in Banchory where I was born.

"I can see for miles and miles around over all the fields, so it's not difficult to imagine I'm back in Scotland."

Masson headed down to Teesside as a youngster as his father searched for work.

"He wanted to be a bus driver, but a stringent medical revealed a hole in his heart and so he came to Teesside, which was the equivalent of going to Australia today."

He went to Marton Road School and was spotted by legendary Boro coach Harold Shepherdson playing for Middlesbrough schoolboys.

On leaving school at 15, he became an apprentice painter and decorator before being taken on by Boro at 16 and learning the football trade.

He turned professional at 17 and made his Boro debut at 18 against Charlton at The Valley when "starman" Ian Gibson was injured.

But he found his openings limited when Anderson brought in Johnny Crossan and would soon leave for lowly Notts County.

"I only made 50-odd appearances, but the first result I look out for is Boro's, even though I didn't play as much as I would like.

"The club gave me a good grounding in the art of being a midfielder and I'll always be grateful for that."

Some people have to go backwards to go forwards and that is what happened to Masson as Notts County were propping up the Football League, but under the wise guidance of Jimmy Sirrel the club "went from strength to strength."

So too did upwardly-mobile Masson. He moved to Queens Park Rangers who were soon challenging Liverpool for the League championship.

"We had a fantastic team and we should have won the league, but we were pipped at the post."

The 1977-78 season became the most eventful of Masson's career as his penalty against Wales helped Scotland clinch a place at the 1978 World Cup finals but he had a year to forget in club football after moving to Derby.

"I spent a year at Derby, which was a nightmare. I ignored advice from good friends in the game not to go there because Tommy Docherty was the manager.

"Bruce Rioch was there, which was great because it meant we had the captain (Rioch) and vice-captain of Scotland at the club, and we had proven internationals, but I just didn't get on with the Doc – it was a clash of personalities."

The World Cup finals were "disastrous" for Masson and his compatriots as he missed a penalty in the shock 3-1 defeat by Peru and Scotland crashed out at the first hurdle.

After contemplating retirement he returned to Notts County and "finished off the job Jimmy Sirrel started" by helping the club into the top tier of English football.

"I called it a day at 36, so I had 20 years as a professional footballer, which isn't bad by anyone's standards.

"After that I wanted to do something else with my wife, but unfortunately Margaret died when she was 39 of a brain tumour, which is so sad, but I feel grateful I had 20 years with her because she could have gone at any time.

"Then I was lucky enough to meet Brenda, my current wife, who was working at

Nottingham Forest on the commercial side when they won the European Cup."

They married at 43 and ran the Gallery Hotel near Nottingham's Trent Bridge cricket ground for 15 years before semi-retirement took the couple into the countryside and their B&B.

"It's great meeting up with people who visit the B&B, especially football fans.

"Keeping the place up to scratch keeps me fit, but I also play tennis three times a week and I play for the Nottinghamshire Over-65s, which I love.

"I wasn't the nicest person when I was a footballer, but I'd like to think I've done plenty of positive things with the rest of my life."

Stiles Cries Fowl In Yarm

Nobby Stiles has admitted he suffered a "culture shock" when he moved to Teesside.

He had helped England win the World Cup by driving opponents like Portuguese legend Eusebio to distraction.

But the tenacious midfielder got a dose of his own medicine when he moved to Boro – thanks to the local wildlife.

Stiles headed to Teesside after helping England win the 1966 World Cup and playing a key role in the Manchester United's European Cup win two years later.

However, the Toothless Terrier's hopes of picking up further honours with Boro back in the early 1970s were dented by a combination of injuries and local wild fowl when he was brought to Ayresome Park in a £20,000-deal by Stan Anderson.

"I had met Stan Anderson and I liked him a lot, and I knew his coach Harold Shepherdson from the England days, and he was great.

"The time had come to leave United and I wanted to play football, so I jumped at the opportunity, but unfortunately it didn't work out.

"I lived in Yarm for two years and it was an absolutely lovely part of the world, but I wasn't used to country life, so we didn't settle.

"It is a fantastic place, but the trouble was I just couldn't get used to the sodding birds waking me up and all that at seven o'clock in the morning.

"It was all a bit too much of a culture shock for me. I was brought up a mile-and-a-half from Manchester city centre on the main Rochdale Road in an area full of two-ups, two-downs.

"There were no gardens or anything like that. Even now I live in the thick of it – in the Stretford area of Manchester, near where I lived during my playing days."

Life in the midfield trenches had also taken its toll by the time Stiles arrived in the North East. He was appointed captain by Anderson but was a shadow of his former self.

"I wish I had more pleasant memories of my time at Boro, but sadly I was never the same after I'd had a knee operation.

"I played in the midfield, but I didn't have that same bite and sharpness that you need if you're going to dominate. Sadly, I wasn't the same player. My knee had gone.

"My job for England was to win it and give it to Bobby Charlton and Alan Ball and support the back four.

"My favourite position had been playing alongside Bill Foulkes in the centre of United's defence.

"When I went to Boro they wanted me as a midfield player, but to be perfectly blunt I just wasn't up to it. I felt as though I let them down a bit in my two years there.

"When Jack Charlton came in as manager, I told him that I had to get back to the North-West, which I did, and I joined Preston where his brother Bobby was manager."

Stiles became a player-coach at Deepdale before managing the club, which he guided to promotion to the old Second Division before relegation resulted in the sack.

After a spell in America, his career turned full circle when he went back to Old Trafford and coached a string of future England internationals.

"I ended up working with the likes of Paul Scholes and David Beckham and lads like that who are coming through the ranks.

"I worked as a coach with Brian Kidd and Eric Harrison which was great. It's always nice to try to put something back into the game."

He was then in demand as an after-dinner speaker with his glittering career the source of fascination up and down the country.

"I don't go to any matches and I haven't been for years because I have been doing the after-dinner speaking for the last six years.

"I'd always worked over the weekends since I left school, so when I did the after-dinner circuit I thought it would be better to relax at the weekends, so I could see my wife and spend some quality time with her and see our grandkids a lot more."

Souness' Career Crossroads

Graeme Souness believes the no-nonsense ways of Jack Charlton were the key to his success as a footballer.

Souness would help Liverpool dominate English and European football following a five-year spell with Boro.

And the Scot is certain that Boro boss Charlton got him on the road to success with a few choice words.

"Jack didn't beat about the bush and I count myself fortunate that he was very straight with me," Souness said.

"I can still remember his words clearly. Jack said this to me:

'It's quite simple - there are two doors for you.

'You can be a kid that has ability and does nothing with it.

'Or you can be a kid who works hard, becomes a decent player and has a good career.'

"That was a wake-up call for me because I really knuckled down under Jack."

Souness, who was born in Edinburgh, headed to Boro in 1972 after struggling to make the grade at Tottenham.

"I'd been brought to Middlesbrough by Stan Anderson when he was manager because the legendary Spurs boss Bill Nicholson put a good word in for me.

"I had been bought for £30,000 with a view to kick-starting my career, but I didn't have the most impressive of seasons under Stan.

"It wasn't the best of starts, but I still felt I had it in me to make it, which is probably because I've always had a ridiculous amount of self-confidence.

"I really rated Stan as a manager, but it's thanks to Jack that I put my money where my mouth was.

"It took a while for me to find my feet. I was only about 20 at the time and if I'm brutally honest I wasn't living as well as I should have been.

"I was enjoying myself too much off the field and under Jack I quickly realised I couldn't go down that road any longer and needed to buck up my ideas."

Souness initially found it hard to win over Charlton and struggled to get into his side following his arrival as manager in May 1973.

"That might have had something to do with him being jealous of all the curly hair I had at the time.

"But the fact I was unable to make my mark is more likely to be connected with Big Jack not thinking much of my attitude.

"In the end, it was lucky for me and unfortunate for one of my teammates that I managed to find my way into the side.

"I got a re-call and came on as a sub against Cardiff and I managed to make the most of it.

"Bobby Murdoch was playing in midfield, but our centre-back Brian Taylor, who we nicknamed Scoop Taylor, from what I can remember, got injured.

"Brian's misfortune meant Bobby had to move back into defence and I got my chance in midfield. I did well enough to stay there and the rest is history.

"I enjoyed being part of a wonderful squad. Like any team that is successful, you have to all be in it together and we certainly were.

"I took on board what Jack said, but I have to say that players at the time helped me as well.

"They would put me in my place, which was all good for me, and Jack's coaches - Ian Macfarlane and Harold Shepherdson - helped me begin to understand what senior football was all about."

That Souness and Charlton managed to hit it off is all the more remarkable because in many ways they were chalk and cheese.

Indeed, one tale from the dressing room says it all about their unlikely success.

"Me and a few of the lads were sitting in the communal bath and I had the shampoo and I had the conditioner.

"Jack is looking at me and I know he wants to say something.

"Eventually, after about 30 seconds, he could hold back no longer and out it came in his gruff way.

'What the eff are you doing with all that?'

"Then he turned to the lads.

'I've never used shampoo in my life.'

"There were none of us who dare point out that he had about six strands of hair on the top of his head.

"He pointed to the carbolic soap.

'I've only ever used that.'

"None of us were brave enough to laugh and certainly not brave enough to say anything to point out the irony of him taking the mickey out of me.

"But what did happen – and I'll always be grateful for this – is that Jack got me on the straight and narrow and my team made me realise just how sweet the taste of success was."

Charlton masterminded a 1973-74 campaign that would see the old Division Two title won in style and Souness was voted Player of the Season – "an accolade I am very proud of."

"We were a very powerful unit and we just used to simply steamroller teams.

"No one enjoyed playing against us because we were quite direct with our tactics.

"Also, in David Mills and John Hickton, we had two people up front who would terrorise opponents with their combination of pace, power and – especially in John's case - bravery."

Souness also managed to chip in with the odd goal and celebrated his first strike in Middlesbrough colours in a 3-0 over Preston on home turf.

"We were just too good for most teams and I felt privileged to be part of a great bunch of people.

"The team spirit was second-to-none. We had some fabulous individuals, but collectively we were a really strong bunch. There was a real camaraderie.

"We took some beating. We feared no one and I remember going to Anfield and knocking Liverpool out in the League Cup one night when I think Willie Maddren got our goal."

For Souness, a 1-0 win at Luton's Kenilworth Road ground that clinched promotion stands out, but so does the 8-0 trashing of Sheffield Wednesday at Ayresome Park.

"Although overall it was great to be part of something special, I can never forget scoring a hat-trick when we beat Wednesday towards the end of the season.

"It was our last home game of the season and we made sure we turned on the style. I hope the supporters enjoyed it as much as we did."

Once top-flight football returned to Teesside, Boro prospered but Souness believes that the club could have achieved more.

"Having been a manager, I know there's a lot of luck in it, because you've got to buy players and no one gets everything right.

"But if Jack had been a bit more adventurous with his buys and spent a few more bob, we might have got into Europe and finished fourth or fifth."

There was, though, no stopping Souness following his £352,000 move to Liverpool in January 1978.

He went on to captain the Anfield club to success in English and European football and represented Scotland in the 1978, 1982 and 1986 World Cups.

But he will always remain indebted to his former colleagues at Middlesbrough where he scored 22 goals in 176 appearances.

"Middlesbrough is very dear to my heart because it is where I felt as though I grew up.

"I went from being a boy to a man, if you like, when I was at Middlesbrough, although some people would argue with that and say I've still not grown up, which I'll take as a compliment.

"I thought I knew it all, but they made me realise I didn't know all the answers. I came up from London thinking I was the bee's knees and I was quickly put right.

"I was put in my place by the lads, the coaching staff and manager, which stood me in good stead going forward.

"I was lucky in that later on in life, when I was playing for Liverpool, I learnt that if we are 'at it' then we will go and win whichever game we played.

"That was the case with Middlesbrough under Jack Charlton. It was a wonderful time."

Otto's Dutch Of Class

Heine Otto has put four years of toil with Boro to good use at one of the world's most famous football academies.

Otto emerged with credit during his spell with Boro against the gloomy backdrop of a series of relegation battles.

They have served as an unlikely inspiration as he helps nurture up-and-coming talent at Ajax's celebrated De Toekomst academy.

At a place that has cultivated virtuoso talents like Johan Cruyff, Marco van Basten, Patrick Kluivert, Clarence Seedorf, Dennis Bergkamp and Frank Rijkaard, life in the trenches of English football has come in handy.

"The four years I had at Middlesbrough were really terrific and Boro will always have a special place in my heart, but that is not just because my youngest daughter was born there," said Otto.

"I learnt a hell of a lot about the importance of team spirit when I was there. It was what football people call grit and determination.

"It was about fighting when your backs are against the wall and never giving up, even when everything is against you.

"That has stayed with me. That is a quality I try to convey to the young players at Ajax.

"Our boys are often very technically gifted and great athletes, but without desire they will not go on to do what Wesley Sneijder has achieved for club and country, because life is not always easy."

Otto became a senior member of the coaching staff at the Dutch giants, where he oversees the youngsters on the club's books and the coaching staff.

This includes former Arsenal striker Bergkamp to whom he acted as assistant while they ran the Under-12s before his colleague was promoted to become Frank de Boer's right-hand man with the first team.

It is all a far cry from Otto's days with Boro when the midfielder moved to Ayresome Park after making his name while filling the void at FC Twente left by Arnold Muhren when he left for Ipswich.

"Even when I was playing, England was one of the top countries to play in and I was out of contract at Twente and went to Boro for a trial and played my first game at Spennymoor.

"I still remember it clearly. The game was played on a hill and if it was windy enough you placed the ball down in one 18-yard box and it would roll into the other box.

"I then played another friendly against Sheffield Wednesday and then Bobby Murdoch told me he wanted to sign me before we played Queen of the South."

Murdoch's team might have lost 3-1 to Tottenham when he made his league debut but he scored the goal that endeared him to Boro supporters who would see him play 139 games on the bounce for the club.

"The first game left me with good memories on a personal level, but all four years were great, even though we struggled, because I made a lot of friends there and everyone at the club was fantastic to me.

"We were in the old First Division and then we spent three seasons in the Second Division.

"It was a hard spell and it was tough every game because we were fighting against relegation all the time and then in my last game we had to win at Shrewsbury to stay up, and we beat them, which was not a bad way to sign off."

Otto returned to his homeland to play for Den Haag for seven years – during which he made 221 consecutive appearances - when his contract expired after Boro's relegation skirmish, but he still keeps a close eye on his old club.

"The last time I was there was in 2003 when I went there with my brother and some friends to see them take on Arsenal.

"It was great to see how much the club has progressed and I am looking forward to coming back over to see how things are.

"I can't wait for Boro to get back to the Premier League. I used to watch them all the time on television back home, but now I have to get on the computer and check out the club website to see how they are going on.

"When I looked at the training staff I saw people like Tony Mowbray, Mark Proctor, Stephen Pears and Colin Cooper, and they are all my old teammates. That is what we have at Ajax – the players joining the coaching staff."

Otto has a boyish enthusiasm for his work and is still going strong despite needing major heart surgery that cut short his spell in charge as manager of Haarlem before returning to Ajax where he spent two years as first-team manager Morten Olsen's assistant.

"Ajax is very special and is well known across the world. That is not only because Ajax has won the European Cup four times, but also because of the amount of young players that the club develops.

"There are seven or eight in the first team right now, but there are lots of great players at other clubs who have come up through our academy. It is very similar to Middlesbrough.

"Boro have a fantastic training ground and superb youth development system, which is well known even to people in Holland.

"I am sure we could learn a thing or two from people like Dave Parnaby and maybe vice-versa. I hope I can come over to pick his brains soon."

Proctor Makes Mark In Style

There was no way Mark Proctor would make a meal out of his Boro debut.

The teenaged midfielder had been gently eased into the first-team frame by manager John Neal.

But then, out of the blue, Proctor was served notice that he was about to take his Boro bow – after pre-match tea just ninety minutes before kick-off.

"We'd just lost 2-1 at home to Spurs and I was told to travel to Birmingham and I remember chatting to our physio about who was fit and that sort of stuff," Proctor recalled.

"It was a midweek game and we'd just had our pre-match meal and John Neal pulled me to one side and told me I was going to make my first-team debut at about six o'clock.

"I was full of the joys of spring, but he cleverly hadn't told me beforehand to stop me getting nervous or thinking about it too much.

"It was dropped on my toes, but then unbeknown to me, he had been in touch with my parents and got them to come down to St Andrew's.

"He had done a proper job. My dad was working, but my mum came down with my brother and a couple of relatives who drove down.

"There were tickets waiting, which was great, and we won 3-1, so it was a great experience and I played the full game and I was up and running.

"It was a shock even though I'd been travelling with the first team carrying kit, and that was probably them gently easing me into that environment around the bigger players and how the whole thing worked."

Proctor, who attended St Gabriel's and St Anthony's schools on Cargo Fleet Lane, had signed associate schoolboy forms with Boro at the age of 13 before turning full time as an apprentice after leaving school.

"Unbeknown to me, I was there in quite a productive period with lots of players coming through the ranks.

"There were the likes of Craig Johnston and David Hodgson the year above me and Billy Askew, and lads who had fleeting careers for Boro like Micky Angus, Jeff Peters."

Proctor scored nine goals in 33 appearances in his first season – not bad for a 17-year-old who credited Neal and coach Bobby Murdoch with his rapid rise through the ranks.

"I don't know how I did it. I was running on pure enthusiasm and didn't know what I was doing.

"The ball just dropped at my feet and I ended up putting it in the back of the net.

"I wasn't sure what I was doing, but it seemed to work. It dried up the following season, but I was marked more closely.

"John was very softly-softly and mild-mannered, nothing like the tough, abrasive types I came across later on in my career.

"He was perfect for me and very reassuring – ideal for a young player to develop under.

"Bobby Murdoch was my youth team coach and he was instrumental in my progression.

"Bobby was the first coach who didn't just say 'do this' or 'do that' but he would show you how it should be done.

"He could actually do what he wanted you to do - he had all the skills to drop the ball behind the full-back or play a diagonal pass.

"I'd worked with coaches who were great at giving information, but couldn't give you a visual. I thought, 'Wow!'

"I'd look at how he approached the ball and which part of the foot he struck it with. That finer detail I was privy to was a godsend.

"And then he got offered the manager's job the summer I was leaving, which made leaving even harder, because he had done a great job and we had a special relationship."

Proctor followed Craig Johnston and David Armstrong out the door by moving to Nottingham Forest after three solid seasons as a midfield mainstay.

"Boro was my club, but I was ambitious and the lure of working with Brian Clough was tough to ignore. It was a quicker transition into higher football and so the opportunity to further yourself was exciting.

"It was tough because I was a Middlesbrough lad. Brian Clough was like the Mourinho of his time - controversial, but also someone who masterminded European Cup titles.

"Nottingham Forest were the team of the day, so it was a massive attraction, but in hindsight I wasn't ready for it.

"I was 20 years of age with 100 league games under my belt, but I was playing with these massive international stars, like Peter Shilton, Trevor Francis and Viv Anderson, and I found it hard to settle.

"I was a bit of a home bird, a bit soft and naïve and it went okay – I played 60-odd games in a rarefied environment - but I didn't really enjoy it.

"It was a great experience but it was something I didn't entirely get the best of because I wasn't mentally in the right place.

"Brian Clough was the opposite of John Neal – abrasive and demanding. He had a unique way - providing very basic information, but good, simple traits.

"So it was a case of 'do this and that' or 'don't do this and that'. Nothing complicated and I always look back on that period and am so pleased that I worked with him. People are always intrigued.

"I regret not gravitating to the job a bit more than I did. I didn't apply myself. I didn't really have anyone I could turn to who could say you can apply yourself a bit more.

"It didn't help that there was a pull back to the North East. My mind was preoccupied with Boro when it should have been focused on Forest. I regret that now, but I was young and naïve.

"I should have been more switched on. I should have been pushing for England honours. My career rolled backwards. It didn't ignite."

Proctor ended up returning to the North East with Boro before joining Sunderland.

"It was great going back. I was brought back by Bruce Rioch and Colin Todd to be one of the senior statesmen in a young dressing room.

"I was one of the only players with any children and young players who were on wedges and were on a forward roll after three or four years coming through the divisions.

"They'd got into a great position and were then finding it tough going. It was very challenging because we were sitting just above the relegation zone in a precarious position when I arrived.

"They'd made giant strides since 1986, but the top division was unforgiving and they couldn't cope for nine months of constantly tough games and we went down.

"On a more positive note, we got to a final at Wembley. It might only have been the ZDS Trophy, but playing in front of a packed house at Wembley and being the first Boro team to appear in a final was a great honour and a great experience.

"We lost 1-0, but I thought I'd die a happy man because it seemed like such a big achievement."

After 273 games and 23 goals in a Boro shirt, Proctor eventually called it a day and entered coaching with Boro Under-18s.

He took on coaching roles with Darlington and Livingston before working as Tony Mowbray's right-hand man in his spell as Boro boss.

"It was difficult to call it quits as a player and set about making a transition from a closed environment where everything is done for you.

"It's such a regimented career and you think you'll play forever, but suddenly in your early 30s you get a reality check when you come out of that business.

"Suddenly you have got to formulate a new way to pay the bills and look after your family.

"Fortunately, I got into coaching with young kids at Boro and made a quick transition. I feel as though I've been very fortunate."

Who Dares Wins For Mustoe

He might not have been the most daring of midfielders Boro fans have seen but there is an undeniable spirit of adventure about Robbie Mustoe.

It is a quality that served him well both as a player on Teesside and now Stateside in his new career as a television pundit across the Atlantic.

Mustoe prospered in the North East after upping sticks to further himself by leaving local club Oxford for Boro.

And now he is doing the same in the United States of America where he is thriving as an expert analyst with broadcaster ESPN.

Mustoe certainly has plenty of experience to enlighten American audiences who like their English football.

That's because the midfielder saw almost everything in a 12-year stay at Boro that saw him make 367 appearances after a £375,000 move in 1990.

"Joining Boro was a big move for me professionally and personally, but it's got to be the best one of my life," Mustoe said, from his home in the Boston suburb of Lexington.

"I was nearly 21 and it was the other end of the country, which meant that after my dad dropped me off I was a long way from home with no family, so it was a difficult decision, but the right decision career-wise."

Boro were playing in front of meagre 6,000-strong crowds when Mustoe was signed by Colin Todd along with John Hendrie and John Wark.

But he went on to blossom in distinguished company during Bryan Robson's Riverside Revolution.

"I played with some of the best midfielders the Premier League has seen, such as Robbo, Andy Townsend and Paul Ince, which was great and for them to say they appreciated what I did meant a lot.

"Bryan taking over as manager gave me a huge confidence boost because he offered me a new contract.

"He pushed me out of the team, but then I forced my way back in and played with Jamie Pollock who, of all my midfield partners, I enjoyed playing with more than anyone else.

"We were both a bit unknown when we got promoted. Bryan put a lot of trust in us that we could shake up a few midfields and that's what we did. We shared the same type of desire to play for the team, energy and work-rate."

Mustoe appeared in all three Wembley cup finals for Boro, but the first game at the Riverside stands out.

"It's still embedded in my memory. It was August 26, 1995. We had a great 2-0 victory over Chelsea to mark the opening of the new stadium and then my first child was born that night, so it was an incredible day I will never forget."

Mustoe had made his mark with both goals in his Tyne-Tees derby in the League Cup against Newcastle at Ayresome Park which meant he "felt that I had arrived" and which friends in America have spotted on YouTube and use as proof that "I was actually a player."

He would experience the lows of relegation and the highs of promotion at Boro and saw the Riverside "bouncing" as Juninho, Fabrizio Ravanelli and Marco Branca excelled.

He left after rejecting Boro's offer of a one-year contract extension, having been "promised the deal of my life" by John Gregory at Derby.

"It's always a little bit sour to leave and sadly for me the Derby thing never happened because they went into the hands of the banks."

Mustoe was asked to join Charlton by Alan Curbishley, but a mystery back injury limited his impact before he returned to Boro for treatment and thanks to the physios he was back up and running within three weeks following months of frustration.

His final club was Sheffield Wednesday, which "finished me off physically," he says, "because Chris Turner ran us into the ground."

A hip operation followed and he took a year off back home in Wynyard and it was "contemplation time because a massive chapter in my life was over."

"I had three options. One was to stay around and do a bit of coaching and media work. The next was to go back to Oxfordshire, but I had no idea where I would go to work, and the final one was to try something completely different."

With his two sons - Ellis and Lewis who have "stuck with Boro through thick and thin" - young enough to be re-located, he fired off a few emails across to America and the Mustoes were on the move when he was invited over by Harvard head coach John Kerr who used to play for Millwall.

He jetted over the Atlantic, liked what he saw and next thing the whole family was on its way to Boston's Logan Airport.

His media career was launched with a little bit of help from former Sky Sports reporter, Dave Roberts, who was already over in America.

"I stayed in touch with Dave, who had covered Boro and he asked me to do some commentary work, so I did a couple of auditions and they started to use me more and more regularly.

"But things reached a crossroads after 18 months, because my new coaching work with Boston College was going great and I had a decision to make: full-time coach or full-time with ESPN.

"It was great working at Boston College because we went from the 30th-ranked side to No1 in the country, but staying there would have been being the assistant for another six or seven years, because not much changes.

"On the other hand, ESPN was a journey, which I didn't know where it could go. I took the ESPN contract and I've got no regrets because it's gone from strength to strength."

The self-effacing Mustoe plays down suggestions that fortune favours the brave in The Land of the Brave.

"People say it was a very brave decision, but I don't think it was because I had the opportunity to do this because I had made a little bit of money in football.

"My testimonial year enabled me to buy a plot of land and build a house and I was very careful with my money and that gave me breathing, so I could come to America and try and figure out what I was going to do for income.

"I didn't have enough money to sit on my backside and do nothing, but I didn't need a job straight away. So it wasn't that brave.

"If it had not worked out, I could have moved back to England, buy a small house and crack on, but it has worked out. Happy days."

Pollock Ready To Rumbel With Robbo

They say first impressions count and they certainly did as far as Jamie Pollock was concerned.

That's because he showed Bryan Robson what he could do long before the Riverside Revolution got under way.

Pollock and midfield partner Robbie Mustoe got stuck into Robson and his Manchester United team in a Rumbelows Cup semi-final in 1992.

Boro might not have made it to Wembley, but Pollock did so well that he was able to welcome Robson with open arms when he arrived on Teesside.

"What a game that was. It was only a fairly short time after that Robbie told me that Bryan had been impressed with us.

"It was a great cup tie and we gave our all in both games. We could both play a bit, we worked well together and we fancied our chances of going toe-to-toe with the big boys.

"We feared no one and didn't half upset them because we really got stuck in, snapping at their heels all the time, playing right on the edge, but we were also good on the ball.

"It was nice of Bryan to see good things about us, because he was one of the players I always looked up to – apart from when we played United, but they were just too good for us in the end."

Boro were heading towards promotion from the Second Division when they locked horns with high-flying United, who beat Brian Clough's Nottingham Forest in the final.

Pollock retired at the age of 28 and even though he quit playing at a relatively young age, he packed plenty into his career.

He was in the thick of it as a teenager when Boro gained promotion in dramatic fashion at Wolves – although Pollock is too modest to mention that his cross allowed Paul Wilkinson to nod in the winner at Molineux.

And later he was in the Manchester City squad that came back from the dead to gain promotion at Wembley against Gillingham. Those are two highlights of an extraordinary career.

"Just thinking about both of those games makes the hair stand up on the back of my neck.

"I broke into the first team as a kid at Boro before I knew I was at the centre of amazing drama when we clinched promotion at Wolves.

"We were losing when I caught Steve Bull late, he reacted badly and then Nicky Mohan stepped in and ended up getting sent off.

"That should have put paid to our promotion hopes but, roared on by thousands of travelling fans, there was no way we were going to go down without a fight.

"We staged one of those dramatic comebacks that become synonymous with Boro in the UEFA Cup and won promotion to the inaugural Premiership. It was fate."

Whilst he was a central figure there, injuries and suspensions meant he had a peripheral role in City's great escape, but still takes great delight in recalling that victory Wembley win over Gillingham.

"I'd lost my first-team place, so I was a sub and I will always remember the Gillingham players in front of the bench taunting me and Tommy Wright towards the end," said the former City skipper.

"Every City fan will know this, but we were 2-0 down with just a few minutes to go, before an astonishing recovery meant we won on penalties to get out of the old Second Division. It was brilliant – a day I will remember vividly for the rest of my life.

"It was great for the City fans. They're very similar to Boro fans. They are really passionate and have both got a great sense of humour. You've got to when your club is on such a rollercoaster."

Pollock left City for Alan Smith's Crystal Palace and Selhurst Park proved to be his last club before the former England youth and under-21 international midfielder called time on an eventful career that began at Boro.

"Leaving Boro has to be the only decision I sincerely regret because I relied too much on agent's advice.

"I ended up heading to Spain to play for Osasuna on a 'Bosman' as a free agent.

I was only a young lad and it wasn't the best career move. I shouldn't have gone there. The same probably applied to the manager.

"It was no less than Rafael Benitez. He ended up getting sacked, but I've only got good memories of him. He was a total professional and I wasn't surprised when he went on to greater things."

Pollock, who lives in Nunthorpe, failed to rein in Spain and headed back to England to play for Bruce Rioch's Bolton before being signed by then City manager Joe Royle in a £1-million transfer deal.

He helped Bolton to gain promotion, but still found time to help his close friend, Nicky Barmby, settle on Teesside following his £5-million move from Tottenham, "introducing him to our local delicacy, the parmo."

His move to Palace followed, but things failed to work out. After a loan move to Birmingham and what he calls a "carry on," he decided to call it a day and joined the family business, Polton Glass, which is based near the Transporter Bridge.

"I just felt that the time was right to start a new chapter in my life and for my family by moving back to the North East from London and for a fresh challenge," Pollock said.

"I'm lucky to have lots of great memories of the game and the camaraderie, but in hindsight I don't think I appreciated my career at the time.

"You don't get chance to look up to really savour things. In fact, you take things for granted. You get used to a five-star lifestyle and complain about luxury hotels.

"Things are certainly different now. Instead of working two hours a day, I'm grafting for at least eight. But I wouldn't have it any other way."

Pollock had a dabble with management when he took charge of Spennymoor United for two spells, and even though he regards non-league football as "too volatile" he is not ruling out a return to management.

"I'm taking my coaching badges and if something comes out of it in the future then so be it, but I'm certainly not going to worry about it. If it happens, it happens. Life's just too good at the moment."

Blackmore: Patience A Virtue For Boro

Clayton Blackmore followed Bryan Robson from Manchester United to Middlesbrough.

But Blackmore has revealed the former Old Trafford teammates would have ended up elsewhere had it not been for Boro owner Steve Gibson.

"Everyone knows what a huge impact Robbo had at Middlesbrough, but the funny thing is that Boro's history could have been so different," Blackmore said.

"Wolves really wanted Robbo as their manager as well, but they wanted him straight away, but couldn't wait until the end of the season which didn't suit him.

"It might have been a different case if Steve Gibson had come in for him mid-season, but the fact they were prepared to be patient paid dividends and Wolves' loss was Boro's gain.

"Who knows what might have happened if he'd gone to Wolves. In his first year at Boro he took the best out of Alex Ferguson, Ron Atkinson and himself and made a flying start to life as a manager."

Blackmore made his United debut alongside Robson before helping the club win the Premier League title in 1993.

And then he followed Robson to Teesside where he helped the rookie manager guide Boro to the Football League title and promotion to the Premier League.

"We'd agreed that wherever he went I would go with him.

"I just felt that it was time to move on and we had some great times at Boro, although it was an up-and-down time.

"Going down was awful, but we had some memories to treasure as well, like getting promoted and reaching the League Cup and FA Cup finals.

"Getting to the club's first major cup final was a testament to Robbo's managerial nous and with a bit of luck we'd have won the League Cup against Leicester, but injuries made life difficult against Chelsea in the FA Cup."

Football A Fine Art For Hignett

As farewells go, the way Craig Hignett said his goodbyes to Boro fans could not have been much sweeter.

After six years' sterling service, the skilful midfielder – who scored the first ever goal at the Riverside - left Boro with the perfect parting gift before moving to Scotland by making sure the club's promotion party did not fall flat.

Hignett had played a huge part in helping manager Bryan Robson steer Boro to promotion and signed off in style by scoring two goals as his team beat Oxford on the last day of the season as Premier League football beckoned on Teesside in 1998.

"It could not have been a better way to go," Hignett said. "I left on a real high having done my bit to get us promoted back into the Premier League ahead of Sunderland and scoring two in that game against Oxford - it was the perfect way to go out for me."

That Hignett should close a chapter in his distinguished career in such a way seems apt because he helped put Boro on the footballing map following the club's move from Ayresome Park to the Riverside after he had upped sticks and swapped Crewe for Teesside.

"There were a few teams looking at me and I nearly joined West Ham, but then everything fell into place when we played Boro pre-season and I scored twice.

"The season started well and Crewe manager Dario Gradi asked if I wanted to speak to them.

"So I went up and spoke to the then chairman, Colin Henderson, and Lennie Lawrence and ended up signing.

"I didn't know much about the area, but it felt right, even though we ended up being relegated."

Instincts proved to be spot-on for Hignett, who was on Liverpool's books as a youngster, and the appointment of Robson as manager galvanised the club.

"Steve Gibson had massive ambitions and when Robbo arrived he really lifted the whole club and the town.

"That last season at Ayresome Park was fantastic and then the move to the new stadium was just what everyone wanted.

"We made some good signings, people with experience, and we really gelled as a team. Everyone wanted to be there and the stadium was always full.

"Everything came together at once. With people like Juninho and Ravanelli coming in it was the place to be."

That Oxford game apart, the stand-out games for Hignett include the first Premier League game at the Riverside, when his opening goal put Boro on course for a 2-0 victory over Chelsea, and the League Cup semi-final wins over Liverpool.

Off the field as well things went well for Hignett as he embraced Teesside from the off.

"With the likes of John Hendrie and Paul Wilkinson, we had a great set of lads when I arrived, and then for six or seven years where we had great lads who all got on brilliantly, so there were so many funny bits.

"One of the things that sticks out, though, is down to Nigel Pearson and his artistic abilities.

"After the move to the Riverside we trained at Ayresome Park, and Nigel put up caricatures of the lads all over the dressing room. They were unbelievable - he was like Pablo Picasso."

Hignett, who agreed a pay cut following relegation in his first campaign, would eventually leave on a free transfer after being unable to agree terms over a new deal.

"I could have stayed, but I just felt the need to change. Although I loved the club they didn't show any great desire to keep me and a couple of clubs seemed desperate to get me.

"I loved the club to bits and I still do, but it was the time to move on then and I went to Aberdeen. My time at Boro was brilliant. Barnsley and Blackburn and Crewe the first time were all great, but everyone associates me with Boro.

"They thought I would never leave. People around the club knew that I loved the club and the area and felt I wouldn't leave, and they abused that, but I have told Keith Lamb that since, so it is all right.

"I still live in the area. Apart from being a Liverpool fan, which I always have been and always will be, Boro is in my blood now. It's a great place."

Hignett, who is now director of football at Hartlepool, helped nurture rising stars at Boro as a member of Dave Parnaby's coaching team at the Boro academy where he managed the Under-13s.

"I loved working at the academy, just teaching the kids how to play football and hopefully passing on a bit of my knowledge on a matchday to them and helping them understand the game a bit better.

"I did my bit trying to maintain Boro's tradition of producing young players, which they've been fantastic at for the last 15 years. It was brilliant to be involved.

"Just look at the players that have come through the ranks – Stewart Downing, Lee Cattermole, Chris Brunt, James Morrison - you could go on and on with the list of players now making a living in the Premier League."

Hignett has a lot of experience to draw upon.

"I played for 14 clubs in the end, so I have played for some duds and some really good managers. You try to take a bit from every one of them, because they are all good at different things.

"Some are good coaches, some are good man-managers and some are both. You try to put them into your own style."

Barmby In The Nick Of Time

Nick Barmby relishes the memories of his role in the Riverside Revolution.

The England international hit the ground running after swapping Tottenham for Teesside in 1995 for a club record-breaking £5.25 million.

And he proved to be worth every penny because he was instrumental in helping Boro acclimatise to top-flight football.

Indeed, Barmby immediately brought all his Premiership experience to bear when Bryan Robson's newly-promoted side made their bow in the big time.

That was on a boiling hot Sunday afternoon at Highbury when he netted on his debut and the new kids on the block were up-and-running.

"That game was supposed to be all about Dutch master Dennis Bergkamp because it was his first game for them," Barmby said.

"We were just the bridesmaids – or so they said. We were supposed to just turn up, get hammered and scurry off back home up North.

"But we went 1-0 up and ended up getting a thoroughly deserved point that set the tone for a fine season. It was a great day and the start of a great run."

Many eyebrows had been raised when he moved up the A1, but Hull-born Barmby insists the move was inspired by football factors alone.

"A lot was said about me being homesick and things like that, but that wasn't the case.

"The fact is I needed a fresh challenge. Looking back, I don't have any regrets whatsoever about moving to Teesside.

"Everyone maybe thought there was an ulterior motive, because I'd gone from Spurs, who were a well established Premier League club, to Boro, who had just gone up and weren't a trendy club.

"I thoroughly enjoyed my time at Middlesbrough. Everything was new – we were new to the Premiership and the Riverside was a brand new stadium.

"It was a fantastic place, the people were class and I really did enjoy it."

The Bryan Robson factor was also crucial as Barmby had played with him for England and seen him at work as a coach at Euro 96.

"I was really impressed with Robbo when he was on the England coaching staff.

"I was lucky enough to play a couple of games with him and I saw what a great player he was, even though he was 37 or 38.

"He had a phenomenal will to win that rubbed off on everyone around him. His man-management was good, but he demanded respect as well."

Barmby scored seven goals in his first and only full season at Boro as a mid-table place was secured by the new boys.

But he ended up leaving for Everton in a club-record £5.75-million deal after just 14 months in the North East as Fabrizio Ravanelli and Juninho arrived.

"Initially, the way we played with one up top and me and Craig Hignett behind Jan Aage Fjortoft worked really well.

"Rav came the year after. I got on great with him. He was a great finisher, as his 20-plus goals and his sensational hat-trick against Liverpool testify.

"But I ended up leaving for Everton because at the time it just wasn't working out for me.

"Juninho was fantastic, but he was playing in a similar position to me, so the balance of the team wasn't particularly right.

"But it wasn't a case of me spitting my dummy out or anything like that. It just wasn't working out and Everton came in for me and Boro got a record fee, so all parties were happy.

"I enjoyed working under Robbo and I still see him every now and again. He was unlucky in the way things unfolded for him, but he did a great job in terms of helping the club acclimatise."

Barmby, who remains firm friends with former Boro favourite Jamie Pollock, played for Liverpool before returning to Hull and helping his hometown club into the Premier League and then going on to manage the Tigers.

"There are lots of similarities between the two clubs. Both have new stadiums and they're both towns where people appreciate players who work hard for the cause.

"At Middlesbrough, that's personified by Steve Gibson, who laid the foundations for Boro to become an established top-flight club."

Stamp Duty

Phil Stamp went from playing football with his mates to rubbing shoulders with international superstars in next to no time.

The sudden elevation would be enough to get anyone quaking in their football boots, but Stamp took it all in his stride.

"For six or seven years, Boro fans were living a dream, and so I was I," Stamp said.

"I was a fan who was fortunate enough to be playing alongside these amazing players who really lit up the club and the town.

"I was playing against the likes of Frank Lampard, Steven Gerrard and David Beckham, and I was playing with people who were just as good as them.

"I look back now and you see old Premiership stuff and you think, 'Jesus! I was playing against them.'

"It was probably because I was young and maybe naïve, but it didn't really bother me."

A midfielder, the Teessider was at the heart of the Riverside Revolution that saw his hometown club enjoy the most exciting of journeys.

"We went on the biggest rollercoaster ride that you could imagine.

"We went from being an average First Division club to one of the most talked about clubs in the Premiership.

"That's because Bryan Robson took over as manager and the likes of Nick Barmby, Juninho, Emerson and Fabrizio Ravanelli arrived."

Stamp came through the ranks at Ayresome Park to rub shoulders with Boro legends.

"It was unbelievable. We were getting 30,000 fans a week and the majority seemed to have Brazil tops on because of Juninho. The town was really buzzing.

"Being part of that was unbelievable and I don't think a club of our size will ever see players of that stature on their books again. We had first-class internationals in our squad.

"It was not too daunting for me because I had mates there that I had grown up with, such as Ben Roberts and Alan Moore.

"It really hit home just what an amazing journey we were on when we signed Ravanelli, just after he had scored the winner in the Champions League final.

"For me Juninho was probably the most important signing. He was a brilliant player and he deservedly became a local hero.

"He was the catalyst. He could have signed for a bigger club, but chose us and things just lifted off."

Stamp fell out of favour when Steve McClaren replaced Robson, but there are no hard feelings towards the former England manager.

"Even though we didn't see eye-to-eye in football terms - because he wanted to sell me - I still thought he was the best coach I worked under.

"His man-management skills might have left a bit to be desired, but his coaching was second-to-none - it was out of this world.

"But first-team chances were limited, so after a spell on loan at Millwall I went to Hearts and played under Craig Levein who was excellent."

Stamp endeared himself to Hearts fans and is still a popular figure among Jambos in Edinburgh.

"It was so special because of the fans. We used to have big games every few weeks because we played our local rivals Hibs, Celtic and Rangers so often.

"Tynecastle reminded me of the old Ayresome Park, because the fans are unbelievably close to the pitch.

"Plus, we had a decent side and so I got to sample European football as well, because we were almost guaranteed a UEFA Cup spot.

"I've done a lot media work in Scotland because I'm still quite well known for scoring the winner for Hearts against Hibs in the last minute and then getting sent off for celebrating, so I've got my own place in Edinburgh folklore."

Unfortunately, injury curtailed his influence in his last season in Scotland and he ended up heading to Darlington where his career came to an end.

"I'd been struggling for six months with a bad calf injury and I could have signed a new contract, but I opted to join Darlington.

"I ended up being out for 16 months with a calf injury after a major operation and then when I came back I picked up another injury, so I didn't play as much as I would have liked.

"So I decided to call it a day. My calf was no better and there was no way I was going to have another operation on it, so I called it quits."

Now he is looking to build himself a new career as a football coach.

"I consider myself to have been very fortunate to have had the career that I had.

"Some people would give their left arm for it. It was a bit sad to retire early, but football has been very good to me.

"I was lucky because I was on that Boro rollercoaster and I ended up playing in the FA Cup final which took me to Wembley.

"That was incredible for a hometown lad. I just hope it happens to one of the local lads who are currently there, because it is amazing."

Townsend's Prime Time Regret

Andy Townsend has one major regret about joining Boro - that he didn't head to Teesside much earlier in his career.

Townsend was persuaded to head to the Riverside by then manager Bryan Robson, but still wishes he had upped sticks and sampled life in the North East a lot sooner.

He joined Boro for £500,000 in August 1997 following relegation from the Premier League and after helping the club to promotion he was made club captain following Nigel Pearson's retirement.

"I was nearly 35 when I came to Boro, but it would have been nice to have been there in my prime," Townsend said.

"I played all over the country before I headed to the North East, and in many ways I wish I'd had the opportunity to go up there a bit earlier in my career.

"But having said that, I shouldn't complain, because I played alongside some great players, such as Paul Gascoigne, Paul Merson, Gary Pallister and Emerson.

"And those so-called stars were all coupled with some real down-to-earth boys that I loved playing with, such as Robbie Mustoe and Steve Vickers.

"They all made for a great mix in the dressing room – genuinely top-drawer players together with your bread-and-butter professionals. It was a very good recipe."

Townsend, a solid all-round player, teamed up with Gascoigne in the heart of midfield as he helped Robson's side gain promotion back to the Premier League at the first attempt.

"It was enough to have been there with Bryan Robson, who I have a lot of time for, and despite what anyone will say I thought he was great and his motivational skills were second-to-none.

"Plus, there were some great players and he got everyone pointed in the right direction to get back up and then reach the League Cup final. We had some good days and I have very positive memories of Boro."

Boro fans also made a positive impression on the Republic of Ireland international.

"There's a very unique flavour to the North East. The fans are always really appreciative of players that go there and give everything they've got for the cause for the duration of their time.

"They're realistic fans. They don't think people head there to settle for the rest of their lives if they're not from round there. There's a lot of unrealistic supporters, but I've always thought the Boro bunch were pragmatic.

"They know their side won't be winning everything, but they want to see them competing. They want to see people roll their sleeves up for an honest day's pay.

"We were all very well paid and if we gave our all that was good enough for the fans. If you upped sticks 18 months or two years after, they realised that was part of the business.

"They want to see the club build stability and enjoy some relative success by staying in the division, going on some good cup runs and bringing the good times back to the Boro.

"I count myself fortunate to have played there for two seasons. I experienced a Cup final at Wembley, which sadly we lost, but I enjoyed some fantastic times and playing at the Riverside was brilliant because the place was buzzing."

Townsend jumped to the defence of former Aston Villa colleague Gareth Southgate during his ill-fated spell as manager that saw Boro relegated from the Premier League.

"I know Gareth's having a tough time, but things can change very quickly. He's working well within the budgets he's been set and working alongside Steve

Gibson in a sensible, controlled fashion.

"Some clubs are going crazy, but Gareth realises they've got to be selective and creative with the players they're finding. But always at the back of his mind will be the need to bring young players through like Josh Walker.

"Steve will give Gareth every opportunity to establish a strong foothold in the Premier League. Steve's as good a chairman as you'll meet. Between the two of them they have an excellent partnership."

Sadly, that did not prove to be the case, but Townsend, Southgate's skipper at Villa Park, was able to provide fascinating insight into the future England boss as Boro battled against the drop.

"Gareth will remain as calm and collected and as focussed where they are now as he would do if they were fourth-top.

"When you've got a young guy like Gareth in charge it should be cherished because he can relate to young players. They should do everything in their power to ensure he's around for a good few years to come.

"The players are working for a guy who is fair and reasonable, but isn't emotional, so he won't say one thing one minute and do the opposite the next. He's as honest, level-headed and assured as you can get.

"Gareth's a passionate man, but in an understated way. He doesn't have to bounce up and down on the touchline going ballistic.

"When you're dealing with modern-day players, if you are a turbulent and the emotional type, you will find that you lose players very quickly.

"In dressing rooms when things aren't going so well players wonder could someone else do this or that, but someone else could come in and rip the whole thing up and those guys are down the road."

These days the multi-media Townsend is busier than ever working as a pundit.

"I was never 100 per cent convinced management was going to be the way to go for me when I finished playing.

"I'd travelled a lot, but every time you change clubs you've got to move the family and at the end of my playing days I wasn't sure I wanted to go through the whole thing again as a manager.

"I'd been working on and off for ITV on a regional basis in the Midlands and that provided a platform.

"It takes a while to down your tools from being a footballer, but now I see myself as a broadcaster. I work hard just as I did at football. I've thrown myself into it 100 per cent and realise I'm in a privileged position."

O'Neil Down And Out

So, who says that footballers don't really care?

Gary O'Neil, for one, is living proof that such an assertion does not stand up to scrutiny.

It shows how much O'Neil still cares about Boro that he remains wracked with guilt when he looks back on his time at Teesside.

He came to the Riverside with sights set on European football, but ended up being relegated to the Championship in 2009 after an 11-year Premier League stay, and, he says, the demise still "hurts like mad".

"I enjoyed playing for Boro but that day we went down has to rank as the worst of my career," said O'Neil, who played 111 times for Boro between August 2007 and January 2011.

"The fans were great, and the staff were brilliant, so it really was awful that we couldn't stay up because we knew what an important place Boro has in the community."

After making a name for himself as a potent attacking force with Portsmouth, O'Neil headed to Boro to help Gareth Southgate continue re-shaping a squad that had reached the UEFA Cup final under Steve McClaren.

"I'd watched all the UEFA Cup games on television when Boro were going really strong in Europe with some fantastic players.

"It looked great and when the club approached me it felt like the right move and I've got no regrets. The facilities at Rockliffe Park and the ground are fabulous and the fans are superb.

"When I signed, the vision was to improve on the mid-table finish Boro had the previous season, as Gareth consolidated in his first season of management and when we clicked we were a match for almost anyone.

"There was the day we beat Manchester City and I scored my first goal in Boro colours, when they had the likes of Robinho and Vincent Kompany in their side, and then there was the 2-2 draw with Manchester United in the snow, which we deserved to win."

Boro were denied a memorable victory that day as Afonso Alves goals were cancelled out by Cristiano Ronaldo and Wayne Rooney.

Narrow margins between success and failure became even more pronounced the next season as a young Boro side was relegated.

"We produced some fantastic performances at the Riverside, like the time we beat Liverpool who were going for the title, and it really looked like we had what it took to stay up.

"We also beat Aston Villa away and we looked as though we'd have a good season, but injuries caught up with us when we were sitting comfortably in mid-table and things went against us."

Boro would not go down without a fight and the fight for survival went down to the wire.

"Right up until the end we had a chance, but there were very fine margins.

"In the penultimate game, we were 1-0 up against Villa, but let the lead slip and that took wind out of our sails.

"We needed to win by a few goals on the final day at West Ham, which would have been a tall order at the best of times. We gave it everything we had, but it was not enough.

"That was the only relegation I've been heavily involved in and it is still painful to think about. It's not something I would like to go through again."

Despite relegation, O'Neil remained loyal to Boro as the club plotted a way back to the Premier League.

"Even after we were relegated, I stuck at it and I firmly believed that we could go straight back up.

"I just don't think that it was right for people to automatically jump ship when they've been relegated. I wanted to stick around and put right a few of the wrongs that came with going down.

"My move away was a last-minute thing. Out of the blue, Tony Mowbray told me the club had accepted a bid from West Ham and he could do with me leaving to free up the wages, which was reasonable, but it was never driven by me.

"I've never left any of my clubs on bad terms. I managed to say my goodbyes to all the lads and all my friends and, every time I've gone back up there, I've been on good terms with everyone. So it's always nice to go back to Teesside."

SPEARHEADING THE ATTACK – *Strikers*

Proud Peacock Lives The Dream

Alan Peacock insists he doesn't have a highlight from his time leading the line with Boro – because every day was special.

"I have to admit there was no single high point, because every single game I played for Middlesbrough was great for me," Peacock said.

"I say that because I was a local lad, and all I wanted to do was play for Middlesbrough.

"It wasn't about the money. When we were in the first team we'd get £6 and that was it, but I never regretted it - it was great.

"I am Boro through-and-through and still am. I still want to see every Boro team do well and it hurts like hell when I see them lose."

Peacock was an England youth international, but had to wait until he was 23 years old before he signed for Boro full-time.

"I played for Middlesbrough schoolboys, and when I left school I signed part-time professional because I'd served my time as an engineer.

"I was playing part-time from 17 to 21, and I was then in the Army doing my National Service for two years till I was 23.

"When you were in the forces the club only had to pay you £1 a week to retain you, which seemed fine with me.

"We trained on Tuesdays and Thursday nights until we came out of the forces and then went full-time. It's all a far cry from what football is like now."

The future England striker, who attended Lawson Street School, made his Boro debut in 1955 alongside Brian Clough while playing part-time and together they struck up an impressive frontline partnership.

"One of the first things he ever told me was to put me in my place:

'I'm the centre forward, this is where I score my goals from. I don't go from one wing to the other, you do this and that, you do the running and I'll score the goals.'

"And because we were young lads, and he did score the goals, we went along with it, but the older lads couldn't handle it.

"He ruled the roost at the time because he'd got into the team and he was the eldest of our little group - two years older than me and Billy Day, and he more or less got us going.

"But the older guys in the team didn't appreciate what he was like. But because we'd grown up with him and knew what type of a bloke he was, we did."

Peacock and Clough remained firm friends after they went their separate ways.

"At first we only met on Saturdays while we did National Service, but we overlapped properly for three or four years and we got on really well together.

"We'd walk to Ayresome Park for training with Billy Day and Peter Taylor and have a right good old laugh.

"We kept in touch, but it was after he'd finished that we became closer because he'd invite me to his after-dinner talks and we got on really well.

"He never changed, it was always, 'Hey, you do this and you do that.' He was a one-off. There's been nobody like him.

"We remained friends afterwards and he was one of my first guests when I started doing hospitality with Boro.

"At that time he wasn't friendly with Boro and they said he wouldn't come, but he did for me, which was nice."

It was when Clough moved to Sunderland that Peacock's career took off.

"Brian left and everything fell into place for me as a forward.

"I sort of came into my own. I'd always been his sidekick, knocking balls down to him when he was in the team, but once he'd left I sort of took centre-stage.

"I was out of his shadow and I started to take more responsibility."

Peacock did so well he won himself a place in the England squad that contested the 1962 World Cup finals in Chile where he played against Argentina and Bulgaria.

He excelled at club level, but a burning desire to play top-flight football saw him move to Leeds, who were just getting going under Middlesbrough-born manager Don Revie.

"I did well for Don and we got promoted and I got to play in an FA Cup final at Wembley in 1965 which, sadly, we lost to Liverpool."

Leeds kicked on but Peacock suffered a huge personal blow when he suffered a serious knee injury.

"We went on tour and that's when I got my injury in East Germany when Checkpoint Charlie was in operation.

"I had to get back to England, but by the time I got back to Leeds it was too late to do the operation and I had to wait because of the swelling.

"I managed to get back to playing, but really I was more or less finished then (Plymouth was his last club). It wasn't long before the 1966 World Cup and I never made it into the squad.

"That was a pity, but you get over these things and the disappointments in life. You've got no choice."

Hickton's Striking Impact

By his own admission, John Hickton's time with Boro did not begin too well.

Boro were playing in the old Third Division for the first time when he made his debut against Workington Town.

"Everyone was thinking it couldn't get worse, but then I turn up and it looks as if it will," Hickton said.

"We were 2-0 down after five minutes and the centre forward I was marking scored both of them, so it wasn't the best of starts.

"Luckily, we got a penalty just before half-time and nobody wanted to take it, so I put my hand up and did the honours.

"Thankfully I scored and then Arthur Horsfield scored twice and we ended up winning 3-2, which was a bit of a turning point."

Hickton was playing at centre-back against the Cumbrian side – due to an injury to Dickie Rooks - but would go on to secure legendary status as a striker.

He scored 159 goals in 415 appearances for Boro, where his 20-yard run-ups for penalties became his trademark.

Hickton, who was born in Chesterfield, was signed from Sheffield Wednesday where he played as a full-back or central defender and centre forward.

"I think they thought I was one of those Jacks of all trades and master of none, so I thought it best to move on," said Hickton from his Chesterfield home.

"I should have played in the 1966 FA Cup final, but it wasn't to be which was really disappointing and that sealed it and I knew I had to leave.

"I was the reserve centre-back and our first-choice centre-half got injured and I'd played the game in the cup run, but I didn't get selected for the final and we lost 3-2 to Everton. It was very disappointing."

Boro boss Stan Anderson took advantage and moved to sign the unsettled Hickton in September 1966 in a £20,000 deal.

"Middlesbrough and Norwich came in for me, but my manager, Alan Brown, who came from the North East, recommended Middlesbrough because he said I'd like the area.

"He was right. Ayresome Park was a World Cup ground and that was the basic reason I chose Middlesbrough. It turned out to be the best decision of my career.

"I had a really good time there. I found my feet straight away. The pitch was awesome and there was lots of tradition about the club, which I liked.

"They called it the hotbed of football and I could see why. We attracted good crowds and we scored lots of goals.

"Stan was a very good manager. We were virtually bottom of the league when I arrived, but we gradually climbed the table and got promotion."

He scored 15 goals that season and would finish as the club's top scorer in his next six campaigns and three times he topped the Second Division goalscoring charts.

According to Boro bible, *The Who's Who of Middlesbrough*, Hickton became restless because he was desperate to pit his wits against First Division defenders.

He came close to joining Huddersfield (in a swap deal with Frank Worthington) and Queens Park Rangers, but the Boro board would not let him go.

He was desperate to play top-flight football after several near misses under Anderson and his ambitions would be realised after Jack Charlton took over as manager.

"I was always impressed by Jack - after all, he was a World Cup winner who knew everything there was to know about football.

"He knew how to get over what he wanted from his players and he got everybody playing as a team.

"Everybody followed his tactics. He brought in Bobby Murdoch and we all fitted in well together. It was a team effort.

"Jack was very forthright. He prided himself on being straightforward and honest.

"I wasn't very outspoken, but there were one or two who would argue with him, but they never won. He would take criticism, but always had the last word."

Hickton became more of a targetman under Charlton – a foil for David Mills and Alan Foggon - and it worked a treat with Wednesday reminded what they were missing as he scored in an 8-0 rout of the Owls on Teesside.

"We'd not had any success for a long time, so it was really exciting and the crowds built up and up and up.

"I count myself lucky that the fans took to me straight away and it's always nice going back because people still remember my goals and my penalties.

"I got married to my wife Rosemary when I was there and my two kids were born there, so I feel like an honorary Middlesbrough man."

Stephens' Senior Service

They say the old ones are the best and Archie Stephens showed that was very much true on one of Boro's landmark days.

Stephens was the elder statesman in Bruce Rioch's youthful Boro side, which revived a club on the brink in 1986.

And the striker led by example, etching his place in local folklore by scoring twice in the famous 2-2 'home' draw with Port Vale at Hartlepool's Victoria Park.

"That was a funny old day," said Stephens. "We didn't even know for certain where we were going to play until the last few hours before kick-off.

"You don't look upon it as going into the history books, but it is there forever now and it's something we should all be proud of.

"I have seen the clips on the telly of the players getting off the bus and they all look so young. I even look young myself.

"To go on and get a result that evening set the tone for the season because we hadn't prepared in the best circumstances.

"We were practising here, there and everywhere. There was so much uncertainty."

His goals on that opening day of the season were the springboard for a fairytale story as Boro overcame debilitating financial problems to jump from third tier to top tier in two years.

"It's an inspirational story because of what we did with the players we had.

"We did it with just 14 players. Nowadays, 14 players would not even get through a quarter of the season.

"There was a lot of determination. A lot of players, especially the young ones, wanted to prove to themselves they had what it took to be professional footballers while the older ones felt a duty to lead by example.

"A lot of players left before liquidation and the ones that came in did a great job. If we'd finished mid-table it would have been a success but it went way beyond that.

"We should have won the league, but we dropped some silly points, but the majority of the players that were there went on to achieve better things."

Before heading to Teesside, Stephens had made the leap from non-league football.

"I was a bit late coming into the professional game. Non-league players still come into the game at about 22 or 23 but I was 26 or 27.

"I suppose I was lucky that I was in the right place at the right time."

He was living in the West Country with wife, Julie and playing for Melksham Town in the Western League – the equivalent of the Northern League.

"I was happy as Larry playing for them. I was working for building firms, but I'd been scoring 25 to 30 goals a season for three or four years.

"Our manager Pete Carter was talking to Terry Cooper who was the Bristol Rovers manager at the time and was looking for a goalscorer. 'I've got one here for you,' and it went from there."

After former Boro defender Cooper moved on to manage Bristol City, he recommended Stephens to Ayresome Park counterpart Willie Maddren and the Liverpudlian was on his travels again.

"Everything seemed fine in the first season, but then things went pear-shaped on the financial front, the club went into liquidation and the rest is history.

"We still had experience in there, but the young lads came in and were brilliant.

"I was the eldest amongst them, but there wasn't too much responsibility on my shoulders because we had Brian Laws and Stephen Pears and a couple of other senior lads in the team.

"Plus, Mogga (Tony Mowbray) and (Gary) Pallister were only young lads, but made up for any lack of years and experience with tremendous character and talent.

"I was lucky because I had Bernie Slaven alongside me. Not only would he never shut up, but he never stopped running, so we hit it off well up front."

By Stephens' own admission, it could all have worked out very differently.

"It's funny because if I'd had my way I would have been long gone when we played at Hartlepool.

"Me and Brian Laws ended up taking the club to a tribunal with the FA for what we thought was a breach of contract because we had not been paid.

"We lost our case, but later Rioch – who I didn't always see eye-to-eye with – said we'd have won easily if we had got our own lawyers in to represent us.

"My intention was to see my contract out and move back down to Bristol, but my kids were young and one of them had started school, so we put our roots down.

"I played for Carlisle and Darlington and I was player-manager at Northallerton Town in the Northern League for a year. We just settled and we've been here ever since."

Slaven: Back From The Brink

I'd played part-time for Morton, Airdrie and Queen of the South before I walked away from football, writes Bernie Slaven.

I'd actually chucked the game in for a year when a mate of mine, a guy called Andy Ritchie who used to play for Morton and was a big hitter at the time, got me going again.

He went to Albion Rovers as manager and came round my parents' house and said:

"Listen Bernie, how do you fancy coming to Albion Rovers, playing in a free role - the role I'd played in at Morton? I don't want you defending or tackling, because you can't do that anyway, but I just want you to score goals."

I went to Albion, but Andy left after a couple of months and at the end of the season I ended up as Scotland's top scorer with 31 goals.

I was getting a bit of publicity in the *Airdrie and Coatbridge Advertiser* and the *Daily Record*, but on the back of that I ended up being offered the same money.

I said to the chairman, a guy called Tom Fagan, 'Listen, I ain't signing that, not for the same money when I'm Scotland's top scorer.' So I walked out of the game again.

I was really considering chucking it. I thought, 'If I cannae get a team even though I'm Scotland's top scorer, then I might as well wrap it.'

Anyway, a guy from *The Weekly News*, called Andrew Gold, who I didn't know from Adam, phoned and came to my parents' a couple of times, and suggested sending letters to teams in the top two divisions in England and the Scottish Premier League.

But I'm from a rough council estate, and reluctantly I said, "Thanks for the offer, but I ain't applying for a game of football." Surely I'd done well enough to attract something or somebody.

Nothing was happening, even though he was writing headlines asking why Scotland's top marksman could not find a club, and then he turned up without any notice, with stamped addressed envelopes and letters typed out.

They went along the lines of, 'Hello, I'm Bernie Slaven, I'm 24 years of age and I'm Scotland's top goalscorer.' When I read it I felt obliged to play along with it and sign because of all the effort he had gone to. Andrew did all the work and didn't ask for any money.

We sent them off and I got a host of replies saying clubs were full up with full-time professionals. Liam Brady signed one from Arsenal, Chelsea replied – and years later I played a part in relegating them - West Bromwich Albion, which was one of my favourite grounds for playing. The majority said, 'Sorry, but good luck with your career.'

The most disappointing aspect of the letters is that there was just one club in Scotland that did reply.

Even though it was well documented that I was a Celtic fan, they didn't have the courtesy to reply and, unbelievably, Rangers wouldn't sign a Catholic so I wasn't expecting a reply; Hearts were the only ones to reply and they said thanks but no thanks, out of courtesy.

Middlesbrough didn't reply, but they made a phone call. It was their chief scout, Barry Geldart, who phoned and I came down for one trial game and did okay and then returned to Glasgow and I got another phone call and they asked me down for a month.

But I had a part-time job with the local council, Glasgow Corporation, doing the gardening at the time and I wasn't overly keen on gambling with that.

Anyway, I called Willie Maddren, God rest him, and got through to his answer machine, which was the first time I'd come across one of those things, so I was panicking.

I said I wouldn't be coming down for the month and my late father went mad. He said, "You're going to blow it. Look, you're 24 and you'll never get another chance."

I went to work as normal on Monday morning, went back home and Barry called again. He'd heard about the message I'd left Willie and suggested I come down for just one game.

To cut to the chase, I trained a couple of days, played against Bradford City at Ayresome Park alongside strike partner Archie Stephens, who was an experienced campaigner. We didn't know each other, but everything clicked for us as a pairing.

There was a bit of luck, which you need in life, I scored two and made two and the following morning I signed a two-year contract with a two-year option.

The rest, as they say, is history - in the first four years I never missed a game.

My first season turned into a nightmare – Boro relegated, liquidated, bankrupt. It was like I'd gone to Hell.

That was the first time I'd sampled full-time football and I was at the crossroads. I had my first mortgage, which was 25 grand, and that was a lot of money if you've no got it, and we weren't getting paid, so everything was up in the air. I didn't know what I was doing or where I was going

But I'd sampled full-time training for the first time and I started enjoying it. I could feel my game coming on.

After three or four weeks, I phoned my father from a phone box and said, "I'm coming home – I don't like it, I'm chucking it."

"Be a man for once in your life and you're no getting in here."

His words were harsher than that, but he meant it. I knew what he was all about; he's from the notorious Gorbals area of south Glasgow. That's the best bit of advice I could have had. If he'd have said, 'Oh, you're not enjoying it, come back home, I'd have been back like a shot.'

But I had the mortgage, so I had responsibility. I kept phoning my dad. He said, "You'll be okay, somebody will save them," and he was right. In hindsight, it was the best thing I did. I could have cut my losses like Peter Beagrie, Pat Herd and O'Riordon because of the breach of contracts, as they'd not been paid.

Local lads were left who had a lot of pride in playing for their club and they didn't need to show that. They all stayed local and faithful, and seven or eight internationals, emerged from a squad of 14.

Without a man like Bruce Rioch at the helm, I don't think we would have come back. His nickname was Gaddafi. Some of the younger lads used to quake in their boots and I had many a bust-up verbally with him, but I loved him.

A couple of my mates didn't like him because they thought he was a dictator. I thought he went as near as he could.

But Bruce was a great motivator. He could make an average player feel 10-foot tall. He'd give you targets as a player – defenders were told to get three to five goals a season from set-pieces and midfielders eight to 10, and forwards 25-30.

We all knew each other's targets and it was up to us all to get them. That put the seed in our heads.

What he did is better for me than Jose Mourinho or Sir Alex Ferguson winning the Premier League. It was an unbelievable achievement and a unique period. That saying about putting jumpers down as goalposts was true for us - there were no big time Charlies.

I was confident and it was laced with a bit of arrogance, so Bruce was the perfect manager for me.

One story sums him up. He knew which buttons to press. He knew everyone had a different make-up. He knew I needed a boot up the backside. Not because I was big time, but he saw something that made him think, 'Give him a rocket and he'll respond.'

It was Christmas and I'd scored over 20 times that season and I got a call from the secretary, Karen Nelson, who said Bruce would like to see me - 1.30pm at Ayresome Park.

I headed there with a bit of swagger – 20-plus goals by Christmas, a new contract and more money and all those things floating round in my head.

I sat down and he was facing me and I was waiting for the new contract to look at and he put two pieces of paper in front of me. He said you've done okay, but there were ten things on each sheet of paper – which I've still got - and he said when you can do those things you'll be a good player.

He was always pressing buttons and I didn't think there was anything wrong with that. He knew my character. He might have thought about doing that to a frailer lad and then had a change of heart because he might not have responded.

Things like can't head the ball, only scores at home; release the ball when it's on, not when you feel like it. I came out of his office depressed. I never got a new contract, no rise, just 20 things I needed to do. I'd have loved to have known what Steve McClaren gave Michael Ricketts when he came in.

Bruce was ideal for me. I came down as an unknown, 25 grand to get me from Albion Rovers, and now I'm sixth top scorer in club history.

I came with goals and targets. I wanted to sample full-time football, and play top-flight football and I wanted to play at Wembley and gain international recognition. Thankfully with the help of the coaches and my teammates at Middlesbrough I achieved all those targets.

Relegating Chelsea in their own back yard was a highlight, but the downside was getting chased off the pitch by the nutcases and head bangers. We weren't allowed to come out and celebrate for 45 minutes.

Getting to the ZDS final was not the most glamorous of competitions, but it was still the first time we'd played at Wembley, so that stands out as well.

Wilf Mannion, the golden boy of football, and George Hardwick and Brian Clough - a host of players never got to the Twin Towers with Boro, which showed it was a great achievement as individuals.

I look at the money squandered since I arrived and it makes me wince. I was the last player to score 20 league goals and it's not as if we've been in the top flight all those years.

They've spent millions and millions of pounds on duds. I don't know who picks these strikers, but they should be shot and thrown in the River Tees.

We made it into the inaugural Premier League in 1992 after beating Wolves to win promotion. I finished that season, despite only starting 27 games, as the top league scorer, which was great for me because me and Lennie Lawrence fought like cat and dog. There was a clash of personalities.

In the Premier League, I still knew he didn't fancy me or like me or whatever and saw me as a strong character in the dressing room and he didn't want that.

In the first game I played at home I scored twice against Manchester City and then a couple of weeks later I scored against Aston Villa and things were going all right.

And then I scored against Man United, but I had been in and out of the team and had a few ding-dongs verbally. He pulled me into his office and said, "You're too strong a character in the dressing room – I'll have to move you on."

Then I was isolated, training with my boot boys and all that sort of carry on, to the extent that I was treated like a leper.

If I was on the radio at the time, looking at Middlesbrough FC letting a player like me go, with my goal record, no matter what you thought of me as a person, I'd have been up in arms. I'd have hammered the club.

There was only one recognised striker, and this was in the Premier League, when I went to Port Vale, and that was Paul Wilkinson.

John Hendrie could come in from the wing up the middle and he could score goals, but he wasn't prolific. It was square pegs in round holes. They never replaced me and inevitably they went down.

I'm not saying they would have stayed up with me, but it was a ludicrous situation. If I was boxing with Lennie, I could have understood it, but I've never punched anybody, although I'd verbally give it out.

I couldn't quite understand it for the top boys at the club to sanction it at the time. It was down to man-management like Bruce did, but not everyone is a good man-manager.

I spoke to Bruce, who came in for me at Bolton, and I spoke to Stuart Ripley, who said King Kenny Dalglish had been asking about me because Alan Shearer was injured, and I spoke to Ossie Ardiles who was at West Brom.

They were all talking short-term contracts, but Port Vale were offering two years, which was beneficial because I was 32-and-a-half.

I was still gutted that I'd been pushed out of Middlesbrough, and anyway I was ready to sign for Port Vale and board the bus to go to Leyton Orient when the manager, John Rudge, said we've got Keith Lamb from Middlesbrough on the phone for you.

John said Keith wanted me to sign a contract saying I wouldn't say anything slanderous about the club.

So I got on the phone and said, "Listen, you want shot of me, it's not the other way about, and regarding signing a clause saying I won't say anything detrimental about the club, you can shove it up your arse. I'll be back tomorrow. I'm no signing anything."

I put John back on and I never had to sign anything. I'd never have said anything negative about the club, but I would have said it to their faces.

But there was no way I was going to sign a clause saying I couldn't say anything. It was ludicrous.

Payton Turning On The Style

Andy Payton cringes when he thinks back to his time at Boro.

You might think that with his goal-scoring record there would be nothing that could embarrass the sharpshooter, but then you should think again.

Okay, he might not have been too chuffed that Boro was the only club where he did not end up head and shoulders above his colleagues.

But it turns out that it was his hairstyle rather than his lack of goals that will have him feeling a tad self-conscious.

"I was top scorer at every single club apart from Middlesbrough. I was on fire when I arrived and if I had not been crocked I would have done myself a lot more justice," Payton said.

"But one of my biggest regrets was my hairstyle at the time. I had a mullet and when I look back at the old photos, especially the ones where I was paraded on the pitch waving to fans after signing, that I think, 'Oh my God!' but then again I wasn't alone because half the team had them."

After being rejected by hometown club Burnley as a youngster, the so-called Padiham Predator ended up making a name for himself at Hull.

"I got 25 goals at Boothferry Park in what's now the Championship and we ended up coming bottom.

"I was attracting a lot of interest and the following season I scored something like eight goals in ten games, and to cut a long story short, they had to sell me because they were going under financially.

"I got a call from my agent, Eddie Gray, to say Middlesbrough were willing to pay £800,000 for me. That was a lot of money. It was a record for Boro and it went up if we got promotion to the Premier League, which we did."

Payton got off to a flying start on Teesside, but injury hindered him.

"What I remember from my time most is that I scored two minutes into my debut.

"I was flying at the time, so when Curtis Fleming put me clean through there was no way I was going to get my lines wrong.

"I rounded the keeper in front of the old away end at Ayresome Park and slotted the ball in.

"That was a fantastic feeling and we beat Bristol City 3-1. But the trouble is I got injured late on and it put me out for about a month and then I struggled to get going because of niggling injuries.

"I only started nine games in my time on Teesside and scored three, but I wonder what would have happened if I hadn't got injured in that first game.

"I could have been more of a success at Middlesbrough, because before that injury came I could hardly put a foot wrong."

Payton helped play a part in Boro's promotion party against Wolves as a substitute as Lennie Lawrence's ten-man side overcame the odds to go up at Molineux, which meant he would go out on a high.

"All in all, I have good memories of my time, but I was only there nine months.

"We had some really good players in that team. I always felt we were good enough for promotion and so it proved.

"Stuart Ripley, Gary Parkinson, Alan Kernaghan, Willie Falconer, Bernie Slaven and John Hendrie were great players and we had a cracking goalie in Stephen Pears, plus Jamie Pollock and Graham Kavanagh were coming through."

Payton failed to accompany them into the brave new world of the Premier League as he headed to Scotland instead in a move that saw Derek Whyte and Chris Morris join Boro.

"Celtic had already put a bid in for me when I was at Hull, but they only offered £500,000 and then Boro offered more, and obviously I headed to Ayresome.

"But after we got promoted, I remember playing in a pre-season friendly at Lincoln and we were done 5-1, even though they were Fourth Division, so they ended up getting desperate for defenders.

"I was happy at Boro, but when you go to Parkhead you are going to sign because it is such a huge club. They might not play in the most competitive league in the world, but Celtic as a club is absolutely massive.

"There was Charlie Nicholas, Frank McAvennie, John Collins and Paul McStay, but I still managed to finish off as the top scorer in the one season I was up there."

Fuchs' Cameo Performance

Uwe Fuchs will go down in Boro history as a cult hero.

The German striker was only on Boro's books for a short while, but his impact assured him of a place in club folklore.

A flurry of goals in a four-month spell secured promotion to the Premier League as the club bid farewell to Ayresome Park.

"It's amazing, but I still get letters from Boro supporters even though I only played for the club for a relatively short time," Fuchs said.

"I had an unbelievable few months at Boro. Every time the ball came to me it seemed to end up in the net - even if it hit my knee it went in.

"And there was a great atmosphere among the players – an amazing team spirit.

"It was really so special and I was very impressed with the fans because the whole region was behind the club."

Fuchs came to Boro's rescue midway through the 1994-95 season as the promotion campaign began to lose momentum.

"It all came about because (former Boro assistant manager) Viv Anderson was close friends with his old Nottingham Forest teammate Tony Woodcock.

"Tony had played in Germany and he contacted Viv because he had seen me playing for Cologne, which was his old club, and thought I could do a job because he thought I was a typical, old-fashioned English-style striker.

"John Hendrie was injured, the club had slipped out of the promotion places and they were under pressure so I was recommended.

"I came over in the middle of January, had two or three sessions with the team and Bryan Robson signed me up."

He would kick-start the faltering push for top-flight football with a burst of nine goals in 13 games that included a goal on his debut to secure a 1-0 win against Charlton.

Fuchs left a legacy that was enough for fans to vote him as the club's best ever loan signing in a survey by the Evening Gazette.

"To tell you all my special moments I would have to write a book because there were just too many.

"I will always remember beating Bristol City 3-0 because I scored a hat-trick and then a few nights later we played Watford at home and I didn't score.

"But, and I say so myself, I had a really good match and that performance was especially pleasing.

"I remember it so well because it sent us back to the top of the league and afterwards we had a drink together at Norton Hall.

"Before I went to bed I felt so happy to give something back to the team and the fans rather than just scoring."

Fuchs, whose father, Fritz was a professional footballer, may not have been signed on a long-term deal by Robson, but his farewell was the sort accorded to real heroes.

"I missed the last match at Tranmere because I was suspended (he was sent off for retaliation against Sheffield United) and when I stood up in the stands I was given a standing ovation and the fans started chanting my name.

"That was very emotional, but it got even more emotional at Stephen Pears' testimonial when I came out on to the pitch at half-time and I ended up in tears.

"I joined Millwall afterwards which was the worst decision of my life, but I went to Villa Park to watch Boro and some of the supporters recognised me and 200 to 300 queued up for a chat which made me feel better."

After Millwall, Fuchs headed back to Germany where he continued to ply his trade and eventually went into management as a head coach, but then, after being sacked by Osnabrück, he was considering a return to English football as a new chapter in his life loomed.

"I was really disappointed because we had a very young team and my job was to build up a new team after relegation and bring in new talent and I did everything they asked.

"We started the season with a very young squad and I had the youngest team in the league, but there was pressure and they did not have patience, but sometimes you cannot follow people's thinking in football.

"I am looking for a way back into football and my family would fancy a spell abroad – my son who is 12, my daughter who is seven and my wife are up for it, so it might be time to do something in England."

Fuchs came to watch Boro play at Leicester City where he was meeting up with former skipper Nigel Pearson before heading down memory lane at the Riverside.

"I am really looking forward to making a journey into the past because it brings back so many happy memories.

"Middlesbrough means so much to me in so many ways; it is difficult to put into words to show how special the club is to me."

Taking Flight With Fjortoft

Jan Aage Fjortoft gave Boro fans Premier League lift-off in more ways than one.

The Norwegian striker brought his inimitable aeroplane-style celebrations to Ayresome Park to help Boro get up into the Premier League.

And then Fjortoft scored the goal that secured a famous victory for Boro in the first ever game at the Cellnet Riverside Stadium.

Fjortoft, who joined Boro for a bargain £1.3-million from Swindon, helped his new club win the old Division One title before giving Boro the perfect start to life in their new home.

He followed midfielder Craig Hignett on to the scoresheet in a 2-0 victory over Chelsea as the Riverside opened for business in style following the move from Ayresome Park.

"The promotion season was great and then to score in the first game against Chelsea was extra special," Fjortoft said.

"It really was a fantastic experience and everyone who was there will have special memories of what a brilliant day it was.

"It felt like the start of an exciting new era. Everything was so fresh and I was just so happy to make the fans happy on such a big day for the club.

"I count myself very fortunate to have come to Middlesbrough when I did because there was fantastic optimism."

Boro fans had never seen anything like it as Fjortoft brought his aeroplane celebration to Teesside on transfer deadline day in 1995.

He moved after impressing with Swindon during their brief spell in top-flight football and then following relegation.

"In my first game with Swindon I got a small injury and played on with it, which was a mistake because things got harder and harder and I couldn't score, but suddenly I started scoring and I couldn't stop to be fair.

"I just did the aeroplane celebration when I finally scored because I liked doing silly celebrations, and when I walked off the pitch I saw an old lady doing it. I thought if it's good enough for her, it's good enough for me, so it stuck."

Fjortoft had no hesitation in joining Boro because of the way manager Bryan Robson sold his Boro vision.

"After we went down I was linked to a lot of Premier League teams, but as soon as I spoke to Bryan I knew Middlesbrough was the club for me, even though we were outside the top division.

"I was in the Championship with Swindon and then Boro came in for me when they were in the same division, but when I got a call from Bryan Robson my mind was made up.

"I spoke to him, saw the plans and I knew I could be a small part in something that was going to be big, and it certainly was. It was evident that we were going places."

He certainly relished life in the North East – on and off the field.

"When I joined Middlesbrough I had to launch a big search for a house and I was told there are factories all over the place and all that sort of nonsense.

"But I had a great time in the North East because it is such a wonderful place and the people are so warm and friendly.

"For the first eight months I lived in a castle because the owners were club sponsors, so how can I complain? It was great and I always enjoy going back there.

"I lived in Carlton and I once took my son – who supports Arsenal - back to show him where we lived and I couldn't believe my eyes because it was even prettier than I remembered."

Fjortoft was sold to Sheffield United after falling down the pecking order following the arrival of Fabrizio Ravanelli.

But being deemed surplus to requirements has not made him any less fond of the Boro.

"I played for many clubs, but when I think of the clubs I think of the people and so Boro means a lot to me.

"For some people, that is a cliché, but not in my case. The people I met there meant it was a great time for me to join the club.

"People ask me what was my best time and which club did I enjoy the most, but I always say football clubs are like women and you just can't compare them. But, saying that, I have been married for 25 years.

"I played for four English clubs and I loved them all. People might think I am kidding, but it's true. And that's thanks to the people I met at those clubs."

Nowadays, the father-of-three, who lives on a fjord in Norway, is a successful businessman and has built a media career, covering Champions League football as an expert analyst for Sky Sports.

It is a role in which he is able to put his knowledge of English football to good use.

"When I came to England it was a dream come true because of the connection we have with English football here in Norway.

"Since 1969 we have always had Match of the Day live on our telly and every Norwegian will have their favourite English team.

"When I arrived in Swindon it was incredible. A really fantastic feeling and I still have a great feeling about English football and always will have.

"A lot of people my age when they learned to love English football fell in love with Leeds, although nowadays most people seem to support Man United and Liverpool.

"I have four teams that I follow, but when I started at school at seven and I was growing up, the best team in England in 1974 were Leeds United. So that time I scored against Leeds in Juninho's first game was extra special.

"I worshipped the likes of Billy Bremner, Alan Clarke and Peter Lorimer and so to score against Leeds was very sweet – one of the highlights of my career.

"Things have changed a lot. I remember being interviewed by Sky on what it is like to be a foreigner in England and now it's a case of English players being asked what it is like to be English in the Premier League."

Beck For Good

Mikkel Beck turned down a string of leading European clubs to join Boro to "make history".

And now, looking back, the former Danish international centre forward remains convinced that his decision was vindicated.

Beck had become one of the hottest properties on the Continent in the mid-90s, thanks to his exploits with Fortuna Koln in Germany.

But he signed on for Bryan Robson's Teesside revolution and was a central figure over a three-year spell at the Riverside.

"I spoke to clubs all over Europe, but I chose Middlesbrough because I thought it was a young, up-and-coming club and I was proved so right," Beck said.

"They had Bryan Robson in charge and players like Juninho, Nicky Barmby and Jan Aage Fjortoft, as well as a lot of other good players throughout the squad when I arrived.

"So I opted to sign for, let's say, a smaller, more unknown club than one of the bigger ones that were interested in Europe, because I wanted to be part of something.

"I wanted to try to make history at Middlesbrough and that's what we did, even though we didn't win major silverware."

For some, Beck was Boro in microcosm as the club enjoyed thrilling highs as well as depressing lows that saw his spell in the North East marked by a relegation, promotion and two cup finals.

"I had a good time at Boro no matter what people might have thought.

"I was part of history and whenever I speak to people today they keep talking about those years I was part of, from 96-99, as being maybe the best years in the history of the club.

"I was part of a team that played some very attractive football and I managed to play alongside some of the greats of the modern game, such as Juninho, so I really enjoyed my time there.

"If only we could have won a major trophy sooner rather than later for the club.

"It was awful being relegated and losing those cup finals, but it was great winning promotion back to the Premiership in front of big crowds every week."

Beck may have had to hang his boots up early due to injury, but he certainly crammed a lot into his career.

"Apart from landing a big trophy with Boro, I achieved everything that I could have dreamed of.

"I got to become a professional footballer outside Denmark, I played for my country and played in the European Championships in 1996 in England and 2000, Cup finals in England at Wembley Stadium and the Champions League with my French club, Lille.

"The only negative things are that we didn't win one of those finals at Wembley and that I had to end my playing career far too early.

"That was a big blow to me and something that I was sad about, but until 29 I believe that I had a good career."

It says a lot about Beck's affection for Boro when he admits that he is desperate for Tony Pulis to steer the club back into Premier League.

In his new role as a football agent, he might spend his time these days jetting around Europe setting up deals, but would be happier if he could watch his old club on TV back home in Monaco, where he lives with his wife and two children.

"I am keeping my fingers crossed that Boro will get back into the top flight so that we can start following them again on the television and see them play in the big games again.

"That's all I hope for. I have fond memories of the club and I know how much it means to the fans who will stick by Boro through the good times and the bad times, like they did when I was there during those amazing ups and downs that you could not have made up."

Beck is doing well for himself as a FIFA-licensed agent and several of his clients graced the World Cup finals in Russia, such as Australian internationals Mat Ryan and Danny Vukovic and Denmark skipper Simon Kjaer.

"I quit in 2003 and took a year out to consider what I wanted to do, and then I decided to become an agent, working on my own, which is very different to being a footballer, but it's what I know best.

"Life is great at the moment and I have built up a good and successful business within that field, so I am happy that I have found something after playing football that is fun to do."

Nemeth Szil Crazy After All These Years

Szilard Nemeth faced some of the best defenders in the world during his four years at Boro.

But nothing could compare to the day the striker realised he had come up against a truly deadly opponent.

The Slovakian international had left Teesside and was plying his trade in Germany with Alemannia Aachen, when he was at the centre of a dramatic health scare as he came within hours of tragedy.

A seemingly innocuous football injury had been allowed to escalate into a life-threatening medical condition in November 2006 and the family man came within a whisker of going to an early grave.

"I had been feeling unwell and at first it was thought by the doctors that I had pneumonia and I was given antibiotics and so I thought nothing of it," Nemeth said.

"But the medicine didn't seem to be doing the trick and a few weeks later I went to hospital because I had bad chest pains and when they examined me they told me I was a very, very lucky man.

"They said I would have died within a couple of days if I had not come to see them because they spotted a pulmonary embolism – or blood clot – in my lungs.

"As you can imagine I was stunned but also relieved. It turned out to be really serious, but I think it started with something as minor as a calf injury.

"My doctor said I could have very easily collapsed in training and that would have been the end for me."

Nemeth spent ten days under the supervision of hospital specialists before being allowed home, but it would take a long, long time for his life to return to normal.

"It was a relief that they saved my life but afterwards things were unbelievably frustrating from a football point of view.

"My medication meant that I could not play football for a whole year because it would have been too dangerous.

"It meant that I could not do anything too heavy because physical contact could have been bad news for me.

"So I just concentrated on fitness work with the physios. It was annoying because I was fit enough to play football, but the doctors would not allow me to join in."

Nemeth is now married for the second time and has two kids as well as a step-child so has plenty to keep him occupied.

"I lost my place in the national side, but I don't let things like that get me down too much. If there is a little crash and we have a small dent on the car I do not let it bother me or my wife.

"After what has happened to me, I have now realised that the most important thing is health and making sure that you enjoy every day, because for me every day is a bonus."

'Szily', as his colleagues call him, still has fond memories of his time at Boro – even though he slipped behind the likes of Mark Viduka, Jimmy Floyd Hasselbaink and Yakubu in the pecking order for forward places.

"I loved playing at the Riverside, especially against great clubs likes Chelsea, Man United and Arsenal, but being there when the club won the Carling Cup and playing in the UEFA Cup are great memories.

"It had been an easy decision to join Boro. I was really shocked when I was asked to join the club. Terry Venables and Bryan Robson offered me a contract and straight away I said I would be coming to England.

"It was my big chance to play in one of the best leagues in the world. Boro might not have been well known to everyone back home in Slovakia, but for me I could not have joined a better club.

"I couldn't wait to get started. The only problem is that I signed a contract for Venables in April and then he left the club before I arrived. I hope I wasn't the reason he left."

His most vivid memory of the Riverside is the night he played for his country against England in a European Championship qualifier on Teesside in August 2003.

"That was an unforgettable occasion, although I must say it felt weird to be in the away team at the Riverside.

"The atmosphere was amazing because the ground was full and it was a really good game as well.

"I'd played in the home game in Bratislava against Gareth Southgate and scored before England came back to win 2-1.

"Even though no one gave us a chance at the Riverside we did really well and could have easily shocked everyone, but it wasn't to be and we lost, but we played really well."

Nemeth will always remain fond of the Boro.

"I want the fans and everyone I know at the club to know that I still follow Boro's results every week. It always makes me happy when I see Boro on the television."

Maccarone Savours Comeback Crown

Massimo Maccarone loves the fact he will go down in Boro history as the 'Comeback King'.

His prospects of making an impact on Teesside looked as bleak as Boro's European hopes when they looked down and out against Basel and Steaua Bucharest.

For Maccarone, who was once the club's costliest ever player, had been deemed surplus to requirements and ended up being loaned out to Parma and Siena.

That was because the Italian striker had fallen behind the pecking order as Mark Viduka and Jimmy Floyd Hasselbaink led Boro's attack.

But he returned to Teesside in 2005 and before the end of the season had turned himself into a Boro legend with last-gasp UEFA Cup goals.

His heroics against Basel and Steaua completed sensational comebacks as three-goal deficits were overcome in style and, as journalist Niall Hickman reported in the *Daily Express*, Maccarone showed lightning can strike twice in the same place.

"I remember in both games, watching from the bench as things looked bad for us and I knew that I could come on and do something," Maccarone said.

"I was confident. I knew I had the ability to score goals and I just needed a chance, but I knew I would get a chance because we had a strong spirit.

"It was lovely at the end of the Bucharest game when the fans and the team were all going wild because we had achieved something very special by getting to the final.

"I scored twice in that game, but the header from (Stewart) Downing's cross was beautiful. I can still see it in my mind. Wow."

Maccarone was unable to repeat the trick in the final against a very good Sevilla side in Eindhoven when he was again sent on as a substitute as Boro lost 4-0 to Juande Ramos' team.

He would play just eight more Boro games before returning to Italy on a free transfer to Siena, bringing to an end a remarkable journey.

Maccarone had arrived in a blaze of publicity in the summer of 2002 when he became Boro's record signing.

That was thanks to an £8.15-million transfer deal with Empoli following an impressive display for Italy against an England side featuring Boro defender Ugo Ehiogu.

Boro boss Steve McClaren was won over by the hard-working forward when he got a first-hand glimpse into Maccarone's finishing prowess from England's bench.

That was during McClaren's days as Three Lions manager Sven-Goran Eriksson's assistant at Elland Road and he saw Maccarone score a sublime winner in Italy's 2-1 win at Elland Road.

Before long the striker was on Boro's books.

"That England game was one of the best of my career because it is a big moment when you play for your country and to score the winner against England was amazing.

"I think that it was my performance in that game that made McClaren want to bring me to England, so it was very important to my career as well because playing for Middlesbrough was very special to me."

Maccarone also emerged as the leading scorer in the 2002 Under-21 European Championships with three goals, including two against England as he played in a team featuring Andrea Pirlo.

He looked every inch a star-in-the-making and things started off well for Maccarone in the English Premier League and 'Maccarone Tees' headlines sprang up in the national media.

He marked his home debut with two goals in a 2-2 draw with Fulham and he followed that up with another goal in a 3-0 home win over Sunderland.

In total, he notched nine goals in his first season in England, but he ended up slipping down the pecking order and missed out on a place in the 2004 Carling Cup final to Joseph-Desire Job.

"It was sad to not play in the final because I played in the other Cup games but I was very happy for my teammates, the club and the fans that we won.

"I know what had happened in the past in finals because everyone in Italy had been interested in Boro because of (Fabrizio) Ravanelli.

"So I knew how much it meant to everyone to win a first trophy for the chairman (Steve Gibson) and the town. That made me content. The team mattered more than individuals."

Eventually he would move on with plenty of special memories.

"I was sad to leave because I felt that I had made some very, very good friends at Middlesbrough.

"People like Szilard Nemeth, Bolo Zenden, George Boateng, Gaizka Mendieta and Jimmy Floyd Hasselbaink, Gareth Southgate and Mark Schwarzer were really good people.

"They were good friends to me and there were also a lot of very good footballers at Middlesbrough. I am proud to have played for the club. We did some really good things together."

Maccarone continued to enjoy his football again with Empoli, helping the Tuscan club to promotion to Serie A.

"I would like to say goodbye to the fans who were always very nice to me.

"I did not score as many goals as I would have liked at Middlesbrough but I always worked hard and the fans liked that.

"I will always remember those UEFA games because they were very incredible.

"The memories I have of those two games are really lovely and I want to come back to make everyone at the club know how important they are to me.

"I went back to Italy without being able to say 'thank-you' to everyone, but I hope that one day I can do that."

Christie: My Football Nightmare

Malcolm Christie lived the dream before his football career turned into a sporting nightmare.

The former Boro striker went from stacking shelves in a supermarket and non-league obscurity to the dizzy heights of the Premier League.

But then he suffered a broken leg during his time at the Riverside and his career was left in ruins.

"Joining Boro was a big move for me because when I joined Derby I was an unknown quantity who'd joined them from non-league Nuneaton Borough," Christie said.

"But then a Premier League club was paying big money for me, so there was a lot to contend with as well as leaving home.

"But it was a good opportunity because Boro were struggling with their goal-scorers and I thought I could be the striker they were looking for who could score 20 goals a season.

"I didn't know whether I would be that fella, but I was determined to give it my all."

Christie joined Boro in a £1.5-million move from Derby in January 2003 along with Chris Riggott and the England Under-21 international made a promising start.

"I played half a season and scored a few goals so I did all right and then had an operation to have my tonsils out and it went downhill from there.

"I wasn't really fully fit at the start of the new campaign. I wasn't really firing on all cylinders and that's when I broke my leg in training in November.

"After that I never got myself fully fit for the next three and a half years, which was a nightmare, a real nightmare.

"I was getting myself fit and then coming down with something else. There seemed to be a knock-on effect, which was unbelievably frustrating.

"There was just a catalogue of things and I lost all muscle definition in my leg because I was in plaster for so long.

"And I pretty much developed a limp because I was on crutches for so long. All sorts went wrong with my body because I broke my leg."

Christie was spotted banging in the goals for Nuneaton by Derby coach Steve Round - before he joined Boro - having already made an impression on Teesside.

His first two goals for Derby came in a 4-1 win at the Riverside in 2000 and he scored 35 goals in 129 games before moving to Boro.

He got off to a flying start with two goals on his full debut in a 3-1 win at Sunderland before a double leg and foot fractures.

Christie might not have played in the Carling Cup final, but he did help Boro on their way to Cardiff.

His solitary extra-time goal after coming on as a substitute saw off Brighton, but he was unable build on that cameo to take part in the showpiece game.

"I was really pleased we won the Carling Cup, but not to be involved in a showpiece event like that because of injury was very difficult to stomach.

"Helping Boro win their first major honour in the final would have been the highlight of my career.

"As it was, I sat in the crowd and watched which was hard to take because you want to play your part."

Christie clearly did not know whether to laugh or cry at Cardiff, judging by his reflections in an interview he did with the Derby County website.

"I wasn't even asked by the club to be in the changing rooms. I'd rather have watched it from my sofa at home.

"I was happy for the lads, but for me, the mental side of things, that was hard - wanting to be out there and wanting to celebrate.

"They had a celebration the night after. I said to Steve McClaren, 'I can't go'. Just something inside me said I couldn't face going and celebrating because I felt that I hadn't been part of anything.

"I felt that quite a lot with a lot of games. I remember eventually sitting down with Gareth Southgate. He said, 'We're not going to renew your contract.'

"I said, 'Tell me something I don't know - I haven't played any games. What are you going to do, offer me another five-year contract?'"

Christie struggled to find a club afterwards, but it wasn't for the want of trying.

"It's strange, but in a funny way my career has gone full circle and I'm back to square one even though I'm not even 30 yet," he said after he left Boro.

"It's a vicious circle. I want to prove I can still do the business for someone, but I can't get anyone to give me a chance, just like kids launching their career.

"It's all because there's a stigma attached to me because of the injuries I've had in the past. I seem to be in a no-win situation."

After eventually calling it quits after a spell with Leeds, Christie went on to work in an Aston Martin dealership in Houghton-le-Spring.

He continued to call Teesside home, living with wife Hollie and their young children in the Wynyard area.

"Things might not have worked out as well as I would have liked football-wise at Boro because it was very frustrating.

"But things could not have worked out better for me on a different level. That's because I met Hollie, who comes from Middlesbrough, here and we have two beautiful children.

"They pulled me through. If they hadn't been born I don't know what I would have done with my time since I left Leeds and I was without a club or contract. Anyone with kids will know it's a full-time job looking after them."

Viduka's UEFA Cup Final Agony

Mark Viduka was braced for a hostile reception when he returned to the Riverside.

He said he could be called every name under the sun by Boro fans when he went back for the first time since leaving Teesside.

But whatever the striker heard, Viduka insisted that it would neither deflect him from his duties with Newcastle United nor alter his affection for a club he served so well.

"Whatever reaction there is, negative or positive, nothing would change my feelings for the club or anything like that," said Viduka, ahead of the Premier League clash with the Geordies.

"I would love it if there was a positive reception from the fans, but if it's not, then so be it. I could be called all the names under the sun, but the Boro will always remain a big part of me.

"My kid (Joseph) loves the club because we spent three years there and they were really happy years.

"I loved my time at Middlesbrough. It was a really good set-up. I loved going to work every day, I loved playing there and I think the fans sensed that.

"I had so many good relationships with people around the club. I had a really enjoyable time there. I just wish we could have won a trophy."

Marking his Boro debut with a goal in a 2-0 win at Fulham, the Australian quickly established himself as a fans' favourite on Teesside following a £4-million move up the A1 from Leeds United in 2004.

And he signed off in style at the end of his third and final season at the Riverside, scoring the last of his 42 goals in a Boro shirt in a 3-1 win over Fulham when he made his 99th appearance for the club.

"I really used to appreciate it when the fans chanted my name.

"On that last day of the season when I was walking around the pitch after we beat Fulham, it was very emotional for me.

"I had my kids out there and when someone makes it public that they appreciate your ability, for me that is a massive thing.

"If they don't like you as a person or whatever, you've got to remember that first and foremost you're there to play football.

"But the fans appreciated my ability and I'm really proud of that in a weird sort of way."

Viduka headed up the A19 to be part of Sam Allardyce's Newcastle revolution in the summer of 2007 with the free transfer being hailed as the bargain of the year by many pundits.

Naturally, Boro supporters were sad to see him go, but with a £60,000-a-week wage deal on offer from the St James' Park chairman Freddy Shepherd, it was difficult to make sure he stayed put – as head ruled heart.

As well as a strong relationship with the fans, Viduka also built a warm rapport with his colleagues that he will cherish forever – notably with skipper-turned-manager Gareth Southgate.

"Gareth was the person I got on best with in the dressing room and also afterwards.

"I gave him a buzz before the first game of the season to wish him all the best of luck as manager and stuff like that.

"That's because it doesn't matter what happens when you meet people like that, you treasure those friendships and I'll always have a good relationship with Gareth. There is not a bad word I could say about him.

"Generally, I got on well with everybody at the club – the gear stewards (Elaine and Alex), and the physios Barnsey and Frenchy, the masseur, the players."

Viduka secured his own niche in Boro history thanks to his performance in the club's first ever UEFA Cup tie at the Riverside when he scored twice in a 3-0 win over Banik Ostrava on September 16, 2004.

Viduka played a pivotal role in Boro's two European campaigns and not surprisingly he particularly relishes the memories of the dramatic back-from-the-dead UEFA Cup ties against Basel and Steaua Bucharest.

Massimo Maccarone grabbed the headlines for his last-gasp goal against Basel that booked a UEFA Cup semi-final, but two goals from Viduka paved the way for an epic victory.

"I kept watching the highlights of those European games over and over again because they were unbelievable.

"They are the games I will remember for the rest of my life because matches like that, which are verging on the incredible, only very rarely come around.

"But then again, all our European games felt special because we were going into uncharted territory as far as Middlesbrough was concerned.

"It was great to travel to those new locations with the fans coming along too. It was a fantastic journey."

Sadly for Boro, Sevilla pipped them to UEFA Cup glory and for Viduka it was a case of what-might-have-been.

He saw a perfectly-struck volley brilliantly saved when the Eindhoven showpiece was still nicely poised with the Spaniards just 1-0 up.

"I might act laid-back and all that, but I killed myself after that final mentally.

"Most people would feel the same because it was such a big event and I'd had a great chance to drag us back into the game.

"For it not to go in was unbelievable. I did everything right, so I was really disappointed. In fact, if I'd mishit the ball, it would have gone in.

"And there could have been a penalty for us later on when I was pushed in the back. The result was 4-0, but it could have been very different.

"We were all deeply upset and to say I was unhappy afterwards was a massive understatement."

But it doesn't rank as the most disappointing game of his career.

"That has to go down as losing a World Cup qualifier against Iran (in 1997). That stopped us getting to the finals in France.

"After Iran, the Sevilla game would have to be up there with the most disappointing of my career because I was so gutted.

"It took me a while to deal with it, but I was meeting up with the international squad for the World Cup in Germany so I had to get over it quickly."

The UEFA Cup final was the nearest Viduka got to adding a major honour to a glittering CV.

"I haven't won anything in the UK, apart from in Scotland with Celtic when we won the League Cup.

"I was in great Leeds teams that got to the semi-finals of the UEFA Cup and Champions League. So I've been close, but there's still been no cigar."

Jimmy Worth The Hassel

Jimmy Floyd Hasselbaink was lured to Teesside because he was so difficult to handle as a striker.

But Hasselbaink found it difficult to handle life at the Riverside at first after swapping Chelsea for Middlesbrough in 2004.

"In the beginning, I have to admit I found it quite tough getting used to life with Middlesbrough," the former Dutch international said.

"When you play so-called big clubs like Chelsea or Atletico Madrid and Leeds and the Dutch national side you need to win games and when you lose the atmosphere is really bad.

"The pressure is there all the time and it is so intense. So I struggled a bit with it at Middlesbrough because when we lost it wasn't the end of the world."

Hasselbaink hit the ground running when he scored on his debut, netting a 90th minute equaliser against Sir Bobby Robson's Newcastle in a 2-2 draw at the Riverside.

Not long after, he scored a hat-trick in a 4-0 win at Blackburn, but what irked Hasselbaink were early-season defeats by Arsenal, Everton and Chelsea.

"It was just like it was expected - it was easier to forget and move on to the next game.

"I honestly couldn't handle that at the start because I was always so desperate to win. We had to change that mentality. And we did that together as a group.

"Slowly but surely, it became better and we pushed ourselves to the limit physically and mentally.

"And we put more pressure on each other so it was no longer just a case of 'We're playing Chelsea and we can't get anything out of the game.'

"It was no longer all right to lose against the top teams - we had to change our mindset.

"It was a steep learning curve, but we did well in the league and ended up seventh which was the highest ever Middlesbrough finish in the Premier League."

Hasselbaink first realised Boro were interested in signing him when he was on holiday in Dubai and got a phone call from George Boateng.

"George Boateng sold the club to me. He'd been asked to call me by Steve McClaren to sound me out because I'd just left Chelsea and I was looking for an ambitious new club.

"The next call was McClaren. He said he was going to pair Mark Viduka and me up front. It was a progressive club; they'd just won the League Cup and so were in Europe.

"He wanted to push on and aim for the top half of the Premier League and have a crack. It was getting better and better and me and Mark were the next step. That was music to my ears. I still wanted to win things."

Hasselbaink moved to Harrogate and would commute into training with his new neighbour, Mark Schwarzer.

"The Riverside was a proper Premier League stadium and the training ground was one of the best in the country. The infrastructure was absolutely magnificent.

"Plus, they had a really good youth set-up that was bringing in top players like McMahon, Morrison, Downing and Parnaby. Everything was really sound.

"We had a good team, with top players like Ugo (Ehiogu) and Gareth (Southgate), (Gaizka) Mendieta, Stewy Downing, Boateng, (Mark) Viduka, Mark Schwarzer and (Franck) Queudrue.

"It was a good, established team and all the players liked to play together - there were no conflicts in the team.

"Things were good and it was a very special time for Middlesbrough and for the players that were there."

Hasselbaink scored 34 times in Boro colours over two seasons as the club achieved back-to-back seventh-placed finishes and reached the FA Cup semi-finals in 2006.

He also played a key role in Europe, helping the club win a place at the 2006 UEFA Cup final thanks to those astonishing comebacks against Basel and Steaua Bucharest.

"They were the craziest games I ever played in. You'd be lucky if you experienced that sort of fight-back once, but to experience it twice is beyond incredible. You couldn't make it up.

"That just doesn't happen normally, the team caves in, supporters leave and they're angry, but they stayed and we repaid their faith.

"We got a fear factor in our opponents and we built up some kind of momentum and belief and what happened then was amazing.

"With Basel (when Hasselbaink scored) we were deeper in trouble. In the last 10 minutes we had six strikers on the pitch because we were really going for it.

"Against Steaua in the semi-final, the atmosphere was magnificent.

"Heads were down, but we found a way to talk to each other and say, 'Let's go, we can do this.' We were in the game even though they were in command.

"Everything clicked and we played with a certain arrogance and put Steaua on the back foot. They probably thought they were already there. But we didn't give up and everything just fell into place.

Friends re-united: Charlton's Champions take a walk down Memory Lane. Former Boro boss Jack Charlton was joined by the likes of Graeme Souness, Alan Foggon, John Hickton, David Armstrong, Stuart Boam, Gordon Jones, Jim Platt, David Mills and Frank Spraggon.
(Photos courtesy of Middlesbrough Former Players Association and Teesside photographer Doug Moody)

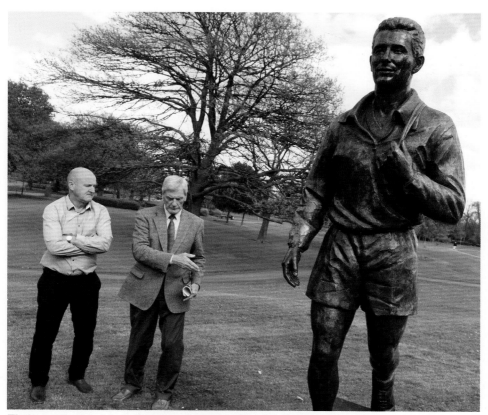

Fitting tribute: Mark Proctor and Alan Peacock remember Brian Clough in Albert Park.

Boro boys:
Mark Burke,
Dean Glover
and Gary
Hamilton;

Craig Hignett
and John
Hendrie;

Colin Cooper
with Alan
Kernaghan.

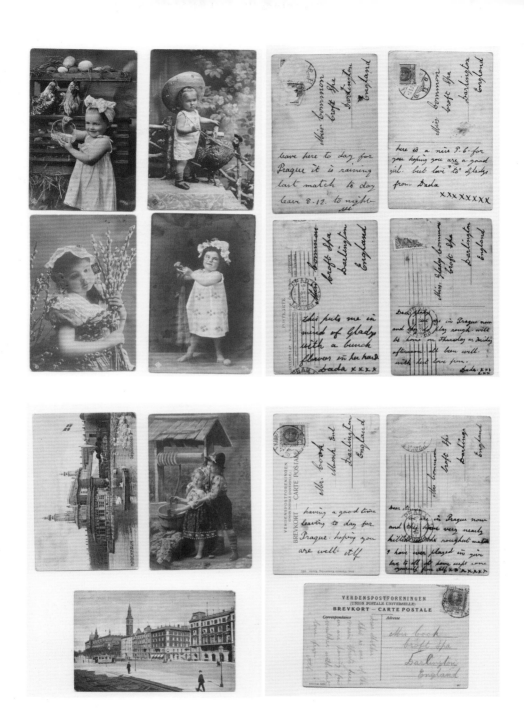

Off the post: Boro fan Harold Shepherdson, who lives in Crook, County Durham, shared these priceless postcards that club legend Alf Common, the first £1,000 footballer, sent to his family in 1908 from one of Middlesbrough's first European tours, to Denmark, and the Austro-Hungarian Empire.

Works of art: Boro stars, as fans had never seen them before, emerged thanks to artist Richard Piers Rayner.

Taking flight: former Boro goalkeeper Rolando Ugolini.
(Photos courtesy Ugolini family)

Raring to go: the Boro side in the 1950s. (Photo courtesy Ugolini family)

Best in class: Gordon Jones pits his wits against George Best at Ayresome Park. (Photo courtesy Gordon Jones)

Head-start: There was no stopping striker John Hickton.
(Photo courtesy John Hickton)

In command:
Graeme Souness
takes control in
his Boro days.
(Peter Robinson/
Empics Sport)

Red alert:
Bryan Robson
leads the
Ayresome Park
celebrations
with Derrick
Whyte.

Samba star: Juninho was a class act on and off the field, as the legendary Wilf Mannion discovered.

Midget gem: Craig Hignett led the Riverside Revolution.

Ab fab: Fabrizio Ravanelli sets the Riverside alight with a hat-trick against Liverpool. (Dave Kendall/PA Archive/PA Images)

Senior service: Colin Cooper shows teenager Wayne Rooney the old ones are the best.

Up close and personal:
Robert Huth marking
Liverpool striker
Fernando Torres.

Cup of joy: Boro skipper Gareth Southgate (centre) holds aloft the Carling Cup with Ugo Ehiogu, to the delight of Stewart Downing.
(Matthew Ashton/Empics Sport)

Cup of joy: Chairman Steve Gibson celebrates with players Ugo Ehiogu, Frank Quedrue and Bolo Zenden. (Matthew Ashton/Empics Sport)

"And it was one of my biggest achievements as a footballer to get through to the final. It was very, very special."

As well as developing a formidable partnership with Viduka, Hasselbaink also taught Downing a thing or two about attacking play.

"Stewy was a young boy with exceptional talent and an exceptional left foot and I'd put pressure on him because he provided the crosses for us strikers.

"We needed to get an understanding on what we wanted, how we wanted it and where and when we wanted it.

"He was a very important member of our team and if you look, quite a few of my goals came through him, especially the goal at Roma in the UEFA Cup.

"It was because there was a bond there that I gave him some stick, but it was good stick with lots of love and it's great to see him still doing so well."

Hasselbaink also sings the praises of McClaren and his backroom team.

"McClaren had a vision for the club which made me want to join Middlesbrough, but he also had good people around him.

"His main strength was as a coach, but he got all his staff into position and they really complemented his strengths.

"Steve Round was the younger and more serious one who worked with the forwards and Steve Harrison was the joker, but was definitely very good with the defence.

"Then there was Paul Barron, who was one of the best goalie coaches in the country and we had a fitness coach in Chris Barnes who was ahead of his time.

"Bill Beswick would come in and do his stuff in terms of sports psychology.

"When you're young you don't see the benefits of psychologists, but when you get a bit older you're more open to that support. We had quite an older group so he did benefit us.

"But McClaren was the main man and he was a very, very good coach. We loved to train and the sessions were always with the ball. That's why we did so well.

"It would have been nice to have finished on a high in the UEFA Cup final, but Sevilla were just too good for us on the day. It was one match too far."

WIDE BOYS
– The Wingers

Delapenha The Boro Trailblazer

Lindy Delapenha's cheerful disposition stood him in good stead for the rigours of professional football.

It was the pioneering Jamaican's jovial nature that ensured he dealt with everything thrown at him while navigating the ups and downs of the game.

"Overall, I got on with the people and when they decided to get a bit nasty at times I just laughed about it," the former Boro forward said.

"I had a joke because I knew everyone plays badly at some point and they ended up laughing with me. That is how I got through my career.

"I had a good sense of humour that I developed there in England and it has stayed with me ever since.

"It's the famous English sense of humour - the ability to be able to laugh at yourself.

"For me, if you can't laugh at yourself you don't have a sense of humour. A lot of people here in the Caribbean don't have it which is a shame."

The trail-blazing Delapenha became the first Jamaican to play top-flight English football during his time at Boro and the first black player to play for the club.

"There will always be a special place in my heart for Middlesbrough, but I had a soft spot for the North East as a whole.

"You name it, I loved the people from Middlesbrough, Sunderland and Newcastle, South Shields, North Shields, Redcar.

"They are very friendly and they had the same sense of humour as myself, so we used to get on very well. I was made to feel very welcome.

"And there was none of that nasty racism from the terraces you heard about when people like John Barnes came on the scene.

"I only had a couple of experiences of that sort of behaviour, like when I was at Mansfield and someone came and apologised after a game for being abusive."

As well as falling in love with the whole of the North East during his time at Boro, he also met his wife on Teesside.

"I am lucky that I am able to cherish some wonderful memories. I met my wife, Joan, because I came to Boro.

"Her father was a big builder in Middlesbrough who didn't agree with the relationship because of the colour of my skin.

"So she left home and went to live with her aunt. Unfortunately I lost her in January 2009. She died of a heart attack, but we had many great years together.

"Meeting Joan was the single best thing that ever happened to me – and it wouldn't have happened if Boro hadn't signed me."

Delapenha left Jamaica to pursue his football dreams in the 1940s.

He had a spell at Portsmouth before heading to Boro after finding first-team opportunities at then Football League champions hard to come by.

"Before the season started we used to have two practice matches between the first team and reserves and we'd swap teams around.

"I played in the reserves, but I was concerned that I would be back in the same boat as I was at Portsmouth.

"They said Wilf Mannion is in your position in attack and I was informed I wouldn't displace him so it wasn't looking good.

"Then, 'So', they said, 'how would I like to play on the wing?' I'd never played there before but I would try anything.

"And then Wilfred and myself struck up a partnership that brought the house down.

"I was mainly a winger, but I played in all five forward positions and they said my name was stuck to the team sheet for six or seven years."

Mannion was not the only player to benefit from Delapenha's skilful wing-play - Brian Clough also profited.

"Cloughie was a loveable rogue - he was big-headed and a little too sure of himself, but a likeable character all the same.

"He was very funny, but he would offend a lot of people with his arrogant attitude and he had Peter Taylor, our goalie at Middlesbrough, as his side-kick.

"Peter made the bullets and Brian fired them. Peter never had any luck as a career, but Brian was able to speak to the manager in a very arrogant way telling them 'this has got to happen' and they would do it."

Delapenha played for Mansfield and non-league Burton Albion under Taylor before heading back to Jamaica.

There he landed a top job with the Jamaican Broadcasting Company and even into his 80s was still involved in television as a horse-racing pundit – a role that ensured he could mix business with pleasure.

"I have become a figure of fun because I used to have a reputation of picking the wrong boxer even though I tipped Leon Spinks to beat Muhammad Ali.

"Before that I chose a lot of losers. I like the underdog so would stick my neck out when I was presenting the sports news.

"So everyone would say, 'Pick the other one.' But I am doing well with the horses. I am doing a bit of horse-racing commentary and analysis with a doctor who is an owner and breeder."

"Horses are in my blood. My father owned a Jamaican Derby winner - Master Jack just before I left for England.

"When I was playing for Boro I used to visit York, Redcar, Catterick, Thirsk, Ripon and hardly missed a race meeting."

As well as the horse-racing punditry, he keeps tabs on English football when not playing golf.

"I'm suffering with arthritis, so it can be very painful for the first five holes because I am little but crippled with the arthritis in my hands.

"But I keep fighting and working at it. If there is one thing that I am it is a fighter.

"When it comes to sports, even if it hurts, I will continue until it stops hurting. But whatever happens, nothing stops me laughing."

Lindy Delapenha died at the age of 89 in January 2017.

No Spiking Armstrong's Guns

David Armstrong left school without a qualification to his name.

But he still ended up a Middlesbrough hero thanks to what they call an educated left foot.

Armstrong worked hard to earn himself a place at Durham Johnston Grammar, yet ended up quitting earlier than his classmates to pursue a career in football.

While he may not have an O-level to his name, it was a move that yielded impressive results off the field as he made a record 359 consecutive appearances (305 in the League) in Boro colours.

While it is fair to say it would not go down well with current educationalists, the decision to finish school early has been vindicated, as Armstrong enjoyed a distinguished football career and is now prospering in the commercial sector in Hampshire.

"The school was predominantly football and cricket-orientated, but through the fact we had very good footballers in our year we became very successful at football," Armstrong said.

"I was never particularly good academically, although I was quite conscientious and I was quite good at sport and then come 15, Boro coach Harold Shepherdson came up to see my headmaster to get me to leave early.

"You weren't supposed to be able to leave until you were 16 unless you had a job to go to, so Harold pleaded my case and said that I did have a job to go to and my future was in football, so I never ended up taking my GCEs and the rest is history."

Armstrong had been on Boro's books for six years when Shepherdson headed to the headmaster's office.

"Word must have got round that I could play a bit and the Boro youth team manager then, George Wardle, who lived in Durham City, came round to our house and invited me to training.

"He used to pick me up on Tuesday and Thursday nights from the age of nine and take me to training along with Malcolm Smith, who also made it with Boro.

"Sadly, George has died now, but he was everyone's mentor and I've never seen nor met anyone who knew as much about football, and throughout my career he is the best coach I have ever seen and met.

"We recognised the way he helped nurture and develop children not only into footballers but people who have good morals and good ethics and knew everything about self-discipline."

It was under the management of Jack Charlton that Boro really kicked on as Armstrong's career took off as the club won the old Second Division.

"When you become successful as I did with Jack, you tend to look at things through rose-tinted spectacles and think that this can happen every year.

"But that particular side was blessed with such warmth and camaraderie because there was a closeness between each and every one of the players.

"We did well because we knew each other's strengths, we knew each other's weaknesses and we worked very hard.

"We had a stellar team made up of players who worked their socks off not only for themselves but also for each other. That was the key to our success."

Nothing lasts forever and Armstrong would eventually move to Southampton in a Boro record £600,000-deal.

"I left because I felt I needed a change. I asked to go on the transfer list and the club told me that Southampton were interested, so off I went to meet Lawrie McMenemy in London.

"He sold me the club although it didn't take much selling with England internationals Kevin Keegan and Mick Channon on their books and World Cup winner Alan Ball there as well.

"There was also a number of up-and-coming youngsters like Steve Moran and Stevie Williams because they had a good youth set-up as well like Boro and they still do.

"The biggest attraction was that they were a side that enjoyed playing football and because of that – as I found in my time at Middlesbrough – that showed they valued the importance of fans going home feeling they'd been entertained. For me, that is what it was all about and still is."

It certainly wasn't about the money for Armstrong.

"The fee didn't bother me at all - I have never been in football for the money.

"Numerous clubs were after me, but I didn't get close to talking to anyone else apart from Southampton.

"It was about going to a club where I could express myself. If I was able to do that consistently as I did at Southampton as well as Boro then the rewards personally came my way.

"When I watch football I want players to go out and show how good they are, try things and to go out with an attacking mind-set and to entertain and that was always a big factor for me."

The run of consecutive games between March 1973 and September 1980 is an extraordinary achievement, but Armstrong plays it down.

"There were times when I played with knocks and had injections and nothing as trivial as a cold would stop me playing.

"But I suppose the bottom line is that I looked after myself and got myself ready for every game in the best possible way.

"I had two older brothers who played local football and I also got involved in coaching them and a number of local sides so that gave me a different perspective on football.

"What I mean by that is that these were lads who would go out to work day-in, day-out, but also wanted to play weekends because they loved football.

"I just wanted to play as much as I could and I still can't understand people who get jaded after playing two or three times a week.

"I would much prefer to play three times a week rather than training and going on an eight-mile run.

"You have to be strong mentally and physically, but I never ever forget that people played for nothing and their jobs were on the line.

"I got paid for it and got good physiotherapy as well from our medical staff. It was better than working for a living.

"Things have changed a lot since I left the North East, but my wife is from Sunderland, I'm from Durham City, and when we come to the North East and get past Scotch Corner, the hairs on the back of the neck stand up on end.

"We have lots of friends still in the North East and lots of happy memories of Teesside and the region in general."

• *David Armstrong used to play football against future Boro academy manager Dave Parnaby and they teamed up at cricket together as well with Durham City.*

"We were very successful at it as well," Armstrong said. "I was an all-rounder but mainly a batsman, David a very accomplished bowler."

It seems apt that the pair should go back such a long way because there are so many similar traits between a regime that helped Armstrong make it as a footballer and the one that Parnaby oversaw at Rockliffe Park.

"I had a fantastic time at Boro because it was – and clearly still is – a fantastic club for helping youngsters along and everything we did there stood us in good stead both on and off the field of play.

"Not everyone made it, but we produced an awful lot of players who had good careers and enjoyed it, which is the main thing.

"At places like Boro's academy, and the one closer to home at Southampton, you can't help but learn the right things in terms of how to approach the game and life in general."

Foggon: Title Tilt Trauma

Alan Foggon believes Boro's long wait for major silverware should have ended almost 30 years before the 2004 League Cup final win in Cardiff.

According to Foggon, Boro were just one player away from reaching the very summit of English football and winning the League Championship during Jack Charlton's reign as manager.

He played a vital role in helping Boro win the old Second Division by a record margin and then Charlton's team took the top flight by storm, only for their title challenge to fade late on.

"It was a golden era for the club, but it could have been so much better," said Foggon.

"We'd won the old Second Division and the year after that, if we'd had someone else to score goals for us, we'd have won the League Championship.

"We finished sixth and that was after losing a couple of games we should never have lost. We lost 1-0 to Brian Clough's Derby at Ayresome Park and they won the title.

"If we'd won that we wouldn't have been far away. We just didn't score enough goals. We had some really good players, but we just lacked one last player and the rest of the team would tell you that."

The club's upward mobility mirrored a remarkable upturn in fortunes for Foggon who was brought up in Craghead, County Durham, and attended the old Bloemfontein Secondary Modern School.

He had made a name for himself as a teenager with Newcastle by scoring in their 1969 Fairs Cup Final win, but was "too young to fully appreciate it."

The former England Youth International left Tyneside for Cardiff at the age of 21, "because he had no one to advise him", but confesses the spell in Wales was "a disaster".

So he was grateful to then Boro boss Stan Anderson and his coach Jimmy Greenhalgh for coming to his rescue.

"I was over-the-moon to get away from Cardiff, not because of the people, because it is a lovely place, but it's because I was rubbish there."

Anderson resigned shortly after his return to the North East, but Charlton's arrival invigorated the club and Foggon excelled.

"Jack didn't really do anything that extraordinary, but he achieved extraordinary results.

"Jack came in the close season after Harold Shepherdson had a spell as caretaker manager.

"He re-organised the side, signed Bobby Murdoch on a free from Celtic and the rest is history."

Boro won the old Second Division with eight games left to restore top-flight football to Teesside for the first time since 1954.

"Jack didn't suddenly make us a great side because we were a good side already. He just put everything together. Him and Bobby were the two final pieces in the jigsaw.

"Jack is still a pal now. He is a brilliant guy. We had great respect for him because of what he'd won with England and Leeds.

"He knew what he was doing. He had a good team around him. His coaches got the best out of the players.

"Unfortunately, the two players who first spring to mind when you think about that team are Willie Maddren, who was formidable alongside Stuart Boam at centre-half, and Bobby Murdoch in midfield, who sadly are no longer with us.

"I used to room with Bobby and he was a great player and a great guy.

And then there was Graeme Souness who couldn't even get in the team at first and then went on to lead Liverpool to the European Cup."

Foggon was regarded as the key player in the promotion season and was the 19-goal leading scorer that season and the following campaign thanks for his position just behind Charlton's two frontrunners.

He did, however, fall out of favour with Charlton and would eventually leave for Manchester United.

"It was a wrench to leave Boro, but I hadn't played much the previous season because Jack felt the other teams had sussed how we played and I was the one who suffered.

"They stopped the balls coming to me and I found myself getting caught offside and Jack felt as though I could only play one way.

"I was playing in the summer in America because I used to struggle to get fit for the start of the season.

"Then I got a call from Man U manager Tommy Docherty saying he wanted to sign me. At first I thought it was not real, but we met up in Montreal and I was on my way."

Foggon, who lives in South Shields, made just three substitute appearances for United - including games against Boro and Newcastle – before he headed back to the North East to sign for Sunderland.

"Sunderland played Man U in the League Cup and I was summoned to Tommy Docherty's office and there was Sunderland manager Bob Stokoe whom I knew vaguely.

"He wanted me to join them and I just thought, 'Why not?' Sunderland was fine, but after 14 games Bob resigned, Jimmy Adamson took over, and things did not work out for me."

Tongue-in-cheek, Foggon says his "career went rapidly downhill" but he went on to play for Southend and Hartlepool before gracing the Northern League for Consett and Whitley Bay.

Foggon – who worked in the security business after he quit playing football for a living - has the distinction of being one of the few players to represent all of the big three North East clubs.

"I've always felt that to play for all three of the big North East clubs is an honour and a privilege."

'Roo' Johnston Bounces Back in Style

The phrase 'bouncebackability' entered the Oxford English Dictionary in 2005 as Crystal Palace boss Iain Dowie described the club's journey from relegation fodder to play-off winners.

But it is a term that could easily have entered the football lexicon in the 1970s or 1980s, thanks to any football sages who had the good fortune to watch Craig Johnston in his pomp with Boro and then Liverpool.

That is because the inspirational tale of Johnston's voyage from his sickbed in an Australian hospital to pinnacle of English football epitomises 'bouncebackability'.

It was while he recovered from an acute illness in an Australian hospital that Johnston would tell anyone who was prepared to listen of his ambitions to become a professional footballer.

But Johnston became the laughing stock of the children's ward as he dreamed of becoming the first Aussie to make it big in English football.

This son of a part-time player, Dundee Johnston, he was mocked and his plans were derided as something of a sick joke by fellow patients, but Johnston was determined to prove the cynics wrong.

And he had to do the same to then Boro manager Jack Charlton when he arrived at Ayresome Park.

"I had been in hospital for six months and I said, 'I'm gonna get out of here and be a pro footballer,' and everybody started laughing at me," Johnston said.

"I could see why, because I'd had a really bad polio-like disease, but it was the thought of making it in football that kept me going because it was a really tough time being stuck in hospital.

"I was 15 years old and I got my mum and dad to write me letters to Chelsea, Man United and Arsenal and, last but not least, the Boro, because they had toured Australia in the mid-70s.

"Middlesbrough were the only ones who responded. The late Boro coach Harold Shepherdson wrote back and said if you pay your fare and board and lodging we will give you a trial like everyone else."

His parents could not afford to pay his plane ticket and so they sold their house to finance the trip halfway round the world.

He was desperate to make a name for himself, only to be told by Charlton to hop it just days after arriving in England.

Yet Johnston, born in South Africa but raised in Australia, and nicknamed 'Skippy' or 'Roo' by his Boro colleagues, defied scorching disappointment to bounce back in style.

"On the first day I got there, we had a trial match and at half-time Jack told me I was the worst footballer he'd ever seen and he didn't even let me finish the game.

"He told me I was rubbish and that I should cut my losses and get on the first plane home.

"So I had to lie to my parents that Jack loves me and asked me to stay. I wouldn't go back a failure."

Johnston got lucky as his senior colleagues rallied round him – and he was allowed to stick around in the shadows of Ayresome Park.

"Some of the established pros heard about this, such as Graeme Souness, Terry Cooper, John Craggs and Willie Maddren and they came to my rescue.

"Someone clearly saw there was a footballer in me trying to get out somewhere and they said if you clean our boots then we will give you enough money to stay in digs."

Johnston knuckled down, with Charlton's blessing, and spent every spare minute trying to raise his game.

"Jack Charlton was right – I was rubbish, but I knew I could get better and I think he did too, but just showed it in his own, uncompromising way.

"I knew I still had a chance and every day I woke up I was able to say, 'Okay, after the work how do I get better at the football?'

"Apart from my jobs I had one thing in my life and that was to be a better footballer, each night, then when I woke up in the morning.

"Jack was never wrong and maybe he felt I had the raw talent, but that was the kick up the backside I needed. So I thought, 'How do I learn this stuff and how do I learn it fast?'"

When he wasn't cleaning boots, Johnston would be found kicking a ball against the wall of the Ayresome Park car park.

"I was very fit and very fast and I would run all over the place, but my skill was all over the place as well.

"So that's why I spent, four, five and six hours a day in the car park, practising to develop my touch and technique when everyone else had gone home.

"It was the purest time of my life from 15 to 19. It was just a football and me after my jobs and those moments I will always remember.

"After I retired I have met Jack many times since and I like and respect him and I still owe him in a funny sort of way. He got me to push myself to the limit."

Johnston got yet another lucky break due to the misfortune of others when John Neal had taken over as manager from Charlton.

It meant he became the youngest Boro player to appear in an FA Cup tie when he played against Everton in January 1978, two months after his 17th birthday.

"One day there was a flu epidemic and everyone was sick and they didn't have enough players to get a team together so they put me in and I did really well and after that, but purely by accident.

"That was down to the coaches, Harold Shepherdson and Harry Green, who had faith in me. Plus, it was at Christmas and a lot of the lads, who were above me in the pecking order, went home."

Johnston thrived as an attacking midfielder alongside two other rising teenage stars in David Hodgson and Mark Proctor.

Johnston made such an impression with Boro that he earned a move to then dominant Liverpool.

According to their official website, it was Johnston's 'consistency and battling qualities' that brought him to their attention and he moved to Anfield in April 1981 at the age of just 20, but with over 60 league appearances under his belt.

And even though he reached the pinnacle of European football with the Anfield club he almost blew his chance of joining Liverpool.

"I'm still eternally grateful for the experience I had at Boro - the people at Middlesbrough were very kind to me.

"When Graeme left for Liverpool he fixed me up with his digs that were owned by a lovely lady called Phoebe Haigh right near Ayresome Park.

"Souey said he'd put a word in for me at Liverpool and lo and behold two years later I got a call from Bob Paisley thanks to Graeme who must have said this kid is worth a look.

"It was nearly a disaster because I thought it was one of the Boro lads taking the mickey, pretending to be Bob Paisley and I told him to get lost.

"I was convinced it was one of the Geordie lads - Billy Woof, David Hodgson, Billy Askew or Graeme Hedley. Then he argued with me and remonstrated and started stuttering like only Bob Paisley could."

Such was his progress at Boro, Johnston had been spoilt for choice as two managerial legends vied for his signature.

"At the same time Brian Clough was phoning me asking me to go to Nottingham Forest.

"Having both Clough and Paisley on the phone was bit heady given what Jack had said just four years earlier. But I was a joke. I was keen and I loved it but I couldn't control the ball or pass it or dribble.

"Somehow, I went on to be part of a golden era for Liverpool and one of the most successful eras. They were all smart guys. No idiots in the team. They were all captains who have gone on to do really well. It was a unique dressing room.

"People still rave about that team. Everybody that is old enough will know how good we were. Even if we were losing 2-0 you knew we were going to come back and win."

In his seven years at Liverpool, after a sticky start to life on Merseyside where he was described as 'frustrating' by the Reds' own website, Johnston won five championships, the European Cup, the FA Cup, three League Cups and four Charity Shields.

Johnston became a crowd favourite as he ran until he dropped, but described himself as "the worst player in the best team in the world", but there was clearly no end to his talents as he also wrote hit song, 'The Anfield Rap'.

Johnston was hampered by a back injury, but then shocked the football world by quitting Anfield at the age of just 27 to go back to Australia to look after his sister who had been badly injured in an accident in Morocco.

He made it clear there would be no sentimental return to football – not even to Teesside: "I'd never play for anyone else than Liverpool. The only other team I'd play for would be Liverpool reserves."

After hanging up his boots, Johnston designed the famous Predator boot for Adidas but was then declared bankrupt before reinventing himself as a photographer.

"I am a very natural designer and photographer. I don't have to think about it, but everything I did at football I had to think about.

"It just comes out of me like football comes out of Glenn Hoddle or Kenny Dalglish or Ian Rush.

"What I would have given to be like Bernie Slaven, David Armstrong or Juninho or Graeme Souness or Stan Cummins, who are natural footballers with my enthusiasm.

"I was never a natural, but I made up for that with boundless enthusiasm. I was like Kevin Keegan – everything I did was due to practising and rehearsing."

• *Craig Johnston, whose long-term partner is Vivienne Lewis, the daughter of billionaire Tottenham owner Joe Lewis, has had to face plenty of business challenges since masterminding the Adidas Predator boot with a football skills project ending in bankruptcy.*

But he has also had to face serious health issues having been diagnosed with three types of skin cancer – melanoma, squamous cell carcinoma and basal cell carcinoma – due to his upbringing in the 'melanoma capital of the world'.

"I must have had 30 or 40 bits of skin removed - one on my left cheek kept coming back," he told the Newcastle Herald *newspaper in Australia.*

"I deal with it as it comes along, like a lot of people of my generation but I've never been able to sit still and thankfully my brain is still incredibly active and creative.

"When I was really sick with the radiation, I thought about the struggle in Middlesbrough to be a player – the struggle for acceptance, the bullying I had to endure, the hardships."

Beagrie Hits Back

Peter Beagrie lived the dream by turning out for his hometown club before his own fairytale turned sour.

But, in his most forthright interview since leaving Teesside in acrimonious circumstances, he revealed "an extra tenner a week" could have made him stay put.

Beagrie had made the seismic jump from North East Counties League football with Guisborough Town to Boro, but then headed off when the club faced bankruptcy in 1986.

Rightly or wrongly, he was cast as the villain of the piece by Boro fans for apparently jumping ship following relegation to the old Third Division, but has insisted that he was more sinned against than sinning.

"In the early stages it was fantastic, but it was soured a bit because I was a local lad and people used that to their advantage," Beagrie said.

"I'd been on the same contract for two years and I'd just won the young player of the year and (manager) Bruce Rioch said he would look after me.

"I went into his office and he offered me a new deal, but said he couldn't offer me a rise. I was on £60 a week, so I was absolutely devastated after finishing on a high that season.

"I was disappointed. Even if he'd offered me a tenner rise, being Boro-born-and-bred, I'd have accepted it, but in the end I left with a nasty taste in my mouth.

"Close friends and family and the lads at the club knew the full story, but the fans didn't as the fairytale of playing for my local club ended on a bit of a sour note."

Beagrie had something of a love-hate relationship with Rioch.

"We had a few confrontations and not many people did that with Bruce. Even though I was only small I never shied away from anything and he respected me for that.

"Plus, he knew he'd let me down because a month later, he said, 'Because of the financial situation at the club I can't offer you anything in writing, but what would you like?' But it had gone too far down the line as far as I was concerned.

"The manager had to do what he thought was right and bully me into signing a contract there and then and not giving me a rise. I understand now. That's the way football works.

"The irony is that Bruce has tried to buy me back five times since and I was with him at Wigan."

Beagrie's love affair with Boro began when he was a young boy.

"Before health and safety regulations were tightened up, we used to get a squeeze down in the Clive Road end at Ayresome Park, not having to pay in," Beagrie recalled.

"And then we'd steadily work our way in to the Holgate End where the way the sound reverberated was as incredible as the way we crashed forward whenever anyone scored.

"With me being a winger, I'd focus on Stan Cummins and David Armstrong and then Graeme Souness, Mark Proctor and ones that were brilliant like Craig Johnston, thinking I would live to be part of that.

"I'd tell my parents I was just going to my pals because they weren't too keen on me going to games on dark nights. That was when we were ten and 11 which is never heard of these days because kids get less freedom."

Beagrie was on schoolboy forms at Hartlepool and was also tempted to join Grimsby until fate intervened.

"Gary Pallister and myself were offered contracts at Grimsby, of all places, but I wanted to bide my time to see if I could win a Boro deal.

"Malcolm Allison watched me playing for Guisborough Town and offered me a contract and Gary, who was at Billingham Town, followed suit.

"Pally got his wages sponsored by a lad called Stephen Corden's dad, who ran a scaffolding company, because money was so tight.

"Finally, on a cold night at Oldham, I made my debut against Mal Donaghy who was an experienced international. It was a marvellous night for me in front of a great travelling support who were vociferous because I was a hometown lad.

"Boro rarely had a player from outside the area in those days. There was Tony

Mowbray, who was my best pal and best man at my wedding, and we had the likes of Stephen Bell who I played with at school, Stuart Ripley and Gary Gill.

"There was also Colin Cooper who weighed three stone dripping wet but read the game fantastically well. It was no surprise he went on to have a fantastic career.

"The only ones from beyond the Boro, were Gary Hamilton and Alan Kernaghan, who were from Scotland and Ireland respectively. It was a very close-knit group."

Beagrie enjoyed a 23-year career playing for a total of ten clubs, including Bradford City, Everton, Manchester City and Scunthorpe United.

"I've got fantastic memories of Everton. Even though Boro's my local club, because my three children were born over in Merseyside and it was my first taste of top-flight football, Everton means so much.

"The people on Merseyside were incredible. They were similar to Teesside people in the respect that everything is based on hard work, and the sense of humour with people taking the mickey out of themselves as well as other people.

"I played some of the best football of my career there with the likes of Maurice Johnston, Duncan Ferguson and Peter Beardsley. Evertonians are passionate, but you can't fool them.

"You have to put in a proper shift. Even if you're what is classed as a flair player they liked you to get your foot in as well.

"Although Boro is my hometown club, I probably class Everton as my team. It's funny looking back - if I hadn't moved I might not have ended up having a career spanning 25 years into my 42nd year."

Hendrie's Parting Gift

John Hendrie has etched his name into both Boro and Premier League history thanks to his goal-scoring prowess.

The Scotsman became only the third player behind Eric Cantona and Mark Robins to score a Premier League hat-trick as Boro beat Blackburn in December 1992 at Ayresome Park.

But it was a brace against Luton three years later that has more significance on an emotional and practical level, because his winner was the last ever goal netted at Ayresome and secured Bryan Robson's team promotion back to the top flight.

"That hat-trick against Blackburn stands out because it was a dream come true, as they were managed by 'King' Kenny Dalglish who was my boyhood hero," Hendrie said.

"And I didn't think I would better that until that game against Luton. That really was the stuff dreams were made of because it was the end of an era.

"The club was moving out of Ayresome to the Riverside and we really made sure that the fans, staff and players all went out on a high with Premier League football in the bag."

Despite being born in Scotland, Hendrie started his career with Coventry, but things really took off when he headed to Bradford on a free transfer.

The winger – who became a striker - helped the Valley Parade side win the Division 3 title when the Bradford Fire Disaster brought the Yorkshire club to its knees.

Hendrie spearheaded the club's recovery and made 173 consecutive appearances as the Bantams went to the brink of top-flight football before being beaten in the end-of-season play-offs by Boro.

Short stints followed at Newcastle and Leeds before Hendrie headed from Elland Road to Teesside and helped Boro into the inaugural Premier League.

"When I came to Boro it was a matter of finding my feet and settling down and it turned out to be a very good move for myself and I would look at that as a very high point in my career.

"I was at Newcastle when the club was in turmoil and I was running out on a Saturday not to chants of 'Newcastle United' but to chants of 'sack the board'.

"I just tried to focus on playing and I didn't leave Newcastle thinking I have got doubts about my career, far from it.

"I was one of Newcastle's only saleable assets, so I joined Leeds and helped them achieve promotion to the top flight. So I wasn't thinking my career was falling apart.

"But then I had my worst season at Leeds injury-wise. That is just one of those things. It was very much stop-start at Elland Road.

"I wasn't the apple of Howard Wilkinson's eye and it was likewise from me. It was circumstantial. I had enough confidence in my own ability to say I would show Howard was wrong."

The same applied when Hendrie left the Riverside for Barnsley following the arrival of Juninho and he added the Player of the Year award there to the ones he collected at Bradford and Boro.

"Barnsley were sixth in the Championship when Boro were eighth in the Prem and I remember Robbie Mustoe turning round to the lads in the dressing room and saying this is a big mistake and we'd regret this for the sake of £250,000.

"It was a wrench leaving, but I just wanted to play. Robbie's words were true because they were relegated that year. Do I think I could have helped them stay in the Premiership? 100 per cent absolutely.

"The same year Barnsley got promoted to the top flight for the only time in their history and from October to the end of the season I got 17 goals and won Player of the Year and our final game was against Bradford ironically.

"I had two-and-a half brilliant years there. The fans used to sing, 'It's just like watching Brazil.' We played some fantastic football even though we weren't a big team. I linked up with my old Boro teammate Paul Wilkinson again and it worked a treat."

While Hendrie enjoyed a fine playing career he does not have a single Scotland cap to his credit.

"When I was playing there was an anti-Anglo sentiment in Scotland and because I'd left home at 16 and didn't come back it went against me.

"When Alan Hansen could only get 23 caps, and he was the best defender in Europe at the time, then you see there is something wrong.

"I never kicked a ball in Scotland, but you make your bed and you lie in it.

"I've certainly got no regrets. I was at Boro for six and a half years which tells a story in itself, because to be at a club for that period shows how happy I was.

"We had ups and downs with promotions and relegations, but I made a lot of good friends and I've got loads of great memories".

Ripley Takes It On The Chin

Stuart Ripley insists his time in a Boro shirt was the happiest of his career even though he reached the pinnacle of English football with Blackburn.

The Middlesbrough-born winger helped Boro battle back from the brink of extinction with what then manager Bruce Rioch called his 'Band of Brothers'.

And for Ripley that spell in the mid-1980s still surpasses his achievements at Ewood Park for all-round satisfaction on and off-the-field.

"It might sound strange, but my time at Middlesbrough has to rank as the happiest spell of my footballing career," Ripley said.

"Yes, winning the title with Blackburn has to go down as the single highlight of my career, but overall those years at Boro were the most enjoyable years I had.

"I say that because we had a bond and a camaraderie that was amazing and we overcame the odds to achieve something truly special.

"There was a special connection with the community because our club was in grave danger.

"That brought us all together – the players, the staff, the management and the fans – which was extraordinary."

Merely playing for Boro was, by his own admission, a "dream come true" for the promising schoolboy footballer.

He played representative football in his pre-Boro days with future Boro teammates Gary Parkinson and Lee Turnbull as well as Phil Parkinson who went off to make his name at Reading.

"It might sound a bit corny, but I can honestly say that I fulfilled a childhood ambition by playing for the first team," said the former Oaklands School pupil who helped the Boro Boys team share the old English Shield in 1983.

"From what I remember I was spotted by the Boro scout John Jennings and I got a letter through the post inviting me for a trial and things went from there.

"The thing is, though, I could not have believed how it would work out with the club almost going to the wall because of all the financial problems with the Inland Revenue and the padlocks on the Ayresome Park gates.

"But, ironically, that is what made it so special because we went through the season with a squad of just 14 players and yet we managed to win promotion from the old Third Division.

"We were a bunch of young, local lads with a couple of exceptions, and that whole backs-to-the-wall mentality galvanised us.

"We had a really brilliant team spirit and we got on well on and off the field and we played some really good attacking football which suited me down to the ground as a winger.

"We had some great players in the team as well and, according to my calculations, seven of us went on to play international football."

Ripley, a qualified solicitor who went into lecturing in sports law at the University of Central Lancashire, puts the club's renaissance down to Rioch.

"We didn't always see eye-to-eye, but above all Bruce was and probably still is a fantastic coach and a fantastic manager," said Ripley, whose son Connor is on Boro's books.

"We had our differences, but they weren't serious. He came from an army background and he wanted us to be smart and clean-shaven, but I was a stubborn so-and-so, a bit of a rebel, and so I grew a beard.

"It put me on a collision course with Bruce, but there was a lot of mutual respect. "He kept fining me, but in the end, in private, he let me off, but only after telling me he liked people who stuck to their guns.

"Bruce was very astute tactically and was a disciplinarian, but that was probably what we needed because most of us were at the start of our careers and so we needed to be kept on a tight leash."

Ripley, a member of the FA's independent disciplinary panel, helped Boro to promotion to the newly-formed Premier League before upping sticks and moving to Blackburn in a £1.3-million move in 1992.

"It was a wrench to leave, but it was, in a way, the perfect time to go because I'd made my mind up that it was time to go and what better time to do it than go after we'd gone up.

"It turned out to be the perfect move because the club got a fair amount of money for me and I joined a club that was heading towards the Premier League title under Kenny Dalglish."

Ripley, who won two England caps, was a key component of a team bankrolled by Jack Walker with his pace and ability to pick out teammates with crosses and pull-backs.

"Rovers had a potent mixture of young and experienced players and a simple plan which worked a treat because we won the title in 1995," said Ripley, who now lives in the Ribble Valley.

"It involved me getting crosses in from one wing and Jason Wilcox doing the same from the other side and Alan Shearer, Chris Sutton, Mike Newell and Kevin Gallacher applying the finishing touches.

"I'm lucky, though, because despite leaving I always got a warm reception whenever I went back to Boro. The fans were always superb with me, which isn't always the case when old players go back to former clubs. That always meant a lot."

Moore The Merrier

Alan Moore left quite a legacy at Boro by teasing defenders and thrilling crowds with cunning wing-play on Teesside.

And it served as an inspiration for another leftie in Boro academy product Stewart Downing, who idolised Moore and Ryan Giggs as a schoolboy.

"That's the ultimate compliment," said Moore, during his spell as a coach at Bury.

"Stewart is a cracking player who has done Middlesbrough proud by being so consistently good.

Dublin-born Moore headed to Teesside after being spotted by Boro talent scout Ron Bone in his homeland.

"I was playing schoolboy football in Ireland and Ron came over to watch a game and spotted me as a 15-year-old.

"Then he brought me over as a 16-year-old on a YTS (Youth Training Scheme) and I ended up spending ten mainly happy years at Middlesbrough.

Moore was playing Sunday League football with Dublin-based Rivermount and having trials with Manchester United when he was persuaded to join Boro.

And he was hailed as the new Ryan Giggs when he burst on to the scene with Boro, scoring twice on his debut against Notts County in 1993.

He was named Ireland's Young Player of the Year and went on to play for the Republic of Ireland eight times.

"I loved the whole thing; living in digs in Thorntree and just enjoying football and learning about the game.

"That was thanks to the likes of (coach) John Pickering and (manager) Lennie Lawrence - plus we had a strong Irish connection with Graham Kavanagh and Curtis Fleming, which helped."

Moore also had a thing about Ayresome Park.

"For me, Middlesbrough will always be Ayresome Park and proper, old-style football, people standing on the terraces.

"The playing surface was excellent and the atmosphere was so good you even got a buzz when you turned out for the reserves.

"You just knew that when you went there it was to play football, but it's different now because the big grounds are more commercial and it's not always geared towards football. Other things are more important on a matchday.

"Ayresome was all about football. People went to watch football there, stood up for a couple of hours and sang their hearts out.

"Sometimes they sang just to keep themselves warm on a cold night and that's what got the players going when it was freezing. That's got to be my fondest, most abiding memory of Middlesbrough."

Moore helped Boro win promotion to the Premier League in 1995, but in the latter stages of his time with Boro he was hit by a litany of injuries before re-launching his career at Burnley.

"The fans were always very good to me but we had a very good team.

"We tried to play decent stuff and when we went up I became a central midfielder which helped me develop and become an international.

"The club wasn't in a great state at the time when I arrived, but the club really took off when Bryan Robson was brought in as manager by Steve Gibson.

"It went global when Juninho, Ravanelli and Emerson signed and then Paul Gascoigne and Paul Merson.

"I ended up getting a lot of injuries and after ten years, with new managers and stuff, it was time to move on and set my sights on a new challenge.

"I enjoyed it there as well and it felt great to be part of Burnley because it's a club steeped in history and it was – and still is – a hot-bed of football.

"Like Boro, they had a nice pitch and a nice stadium at Turf Moor and it was a chance for me to make a name for myself again because I had about four years without football because of bad injuries."

Moore spent a few years playing back in Ireland after that, but returned to England as a coach with Bury where he hoped to unearth a new Stewart Downing.

"It's a new challenge for me trying to spot players and educate them and it is very rewarding.

"Small, family clubs like Bury should always be producing players. We just need to find a new Stewart Downing, hopefully sell him for £12 million and that would keep the club going for a decade."

Cochrane A Local Icon

Some footballers have kids named after them, others have pet animals named in their honour, but Terry Cochrane is the subject of an altogether more powerful mark of respect.

Thanks to his exploits when he was plying his trade at Boro, the residents of his former hometown of Killyleagh in Northern Ireland have paid homage to him and other local boys made good in a giant painting.

Cochrane is featured on the mural along with Sunderland striker David Healy thanks to international exploits that saw the pair score goals against England.

"It was the stuff of dreams," Cochrane said "You could have killed me after that because I just couldn't believe I had scored to join an exclusive club of footballers to have scored against England in front of the Twin Towers.

"Scoring for your country at Wembley takes some beating and our old neighbours have recognised that.

"That mural is something that makes me feel immensely proud. I went to school with David's family and his father lived about seven doors away from me.

"Far more people will remember his goal against England in Belfast because mine was in the pre-Sky Sports days."

As well as that momentous strike at Wembley that secured Cochrane's country the Home Championship crown for the first time in 66 years, he also has a collection of spectacular goals to his credit.

"A goal I got against Swansea will stay with me forever because it was a spectacular overhead kick.

"It was the last goal in a 5-0 win, but they say save the best till last and that's what we did. Plus it was an FA Cup tie, so it was broadcast nationwide on a day we really clicked and the nation saw us in full flow.

"The Swansea goal was unusual because it was in the days before lots of other players started trying overhead kicks. I got the first and all of a sudden others started to try it because it was on Match of the Day."

Cochrane, who still lives on Teesside, spent five years at Ayresome Park following a club-record £233,333 move from Burnley in 1978.

It meant he was quickly making up for lost time, having only joined the Lancashire club at the age of 23 following spells in his homeland with Derry City, Linfield and then Coleraine.

"I really enjoyed my time at Boro and even though we didn't win any major honours when I was there we did well and finished about sixth in the old First Division.

"One of the games that really stands out was when we beat Chelsea 7-2 – yes honestly 7-2 - at Ayresome Park. Again, everything clicked and I managed to get on to the score-sheet.

"I loved playing at Ayresome Park. The surface was excellent, the crowd was appreciative of the skilful and committed players and the fans on the Chicken Run seemed to warm to my efforts to beat opponents on the wing."

Parlour Games

If local tourism officials are looking for a Teesside ambassador to spread the word about the region in London they should look no further than Ray Parlour.

The 'Romford Pele' headed to Middlesbrough with a little trepidation when he left Arsenal, but now admits the North East proved to be better than he could have imagined both on and off the field.

Not only did he relish playing alongside some of the greatest players in Boro's history during his two-year stint at the Riverside under Steve McClaren, but when he was off-duty he savoured life after making Yarm his home.

"It was a bit of a culture shock, but it was a move that filled me with excitement because they had qualified for Europe and we had some really good players on the books at the Riverside," Parlour said.

"I had a great time at Arsenal and I was there for such a long time, so it was always going to be a wrench to leave the place, but because Boro were going places it seemed like the right move for me.

"I really fancied a new challenge and I really enjoyed my time there and wouldn't have a bad word said about the club or the area.

"It is a fantastic club with excellent fans who feel really passionately about their club and I really enjoyed living up there in the North East. I didn't know what it was going to be like, but it exceeded all my expectations.

"I loved living in Yarm. It had a brilliant High Street. Everything was there and the countryside was beautiful. I enjoyed it so much that I can honestly say that it wasn't easy to move back to the London area."

Parlour spent 14 years with Arsenal. He made 339 appearances for the club and won three Premier League winner's medals as well as helping his team win the FA Cup on four occasions and the 1994 European Cup Winners' Cup before leaving for Middlesbrough in 2004.

The former England midfielder was brought to the club to bring European experience to the Boro ranks as the club prepared for a first tilt at continental competition.

"The club was on the up-and-up in those days and I wouldn't have gone there otherwise because I felt as though I still wanted to win things and play European football.

"I took a gamble by leaving Arsenal for Boro, but it paid off because they were really exciting times for the club.

"It was great playing and working alongside great players like George Boateng, Jimmy Floyd Hasselbaink, Mark Viduka, Gareth Southgate, Ugo Ehiogu and even a young Stewart Downing. It was a really strong squad and they were really helpful in terms of helping me settle in.

"In the second season I picked up a few injuries and didn't play as many games which was a real shame because I wanted to contribute as much as humanly possible, but it wasn't to be."

He would eventually move to Premier League rivals Hull City in the search of regular first-team football.

"I ended up getting frustrated after a while and at the age of 30 I thought it might be time to move on if I am not playing regularly, and so I ended up moving down the road to Hull.

"I trained with Arsenal during the week and travelled up to Humberside to play in the games. But I had a good time there as well, even though it was a different scenario and we were involved in a relegation battle."

That was a far cry from his time with Boro when the club was pushing for honours at home and abroad.

"I enjoyed working under Steve McClaren. He is a good coach and a good manager even though he got a bit of stick when he became England boss.

"What I liked about the way Steve and his coaching team worked is that they were always looking out for ways to improve the players on the practice ground. Most of all no one should forget what a success he was at Middlesbrough.

"Apart from the Carling Cup final win, just getting to the final of the UEFA Cup was a brilliant achievement even though we were beaten 4-0 by Seville who were a very good team, with players of the quality of Daniel Alves on their books.

"It was real rollercoaster on the way there as well, especially with those amazing comebacks against Basel and Steaua Bucharest. He pushed the club towards another level."

Nowadays, Parlour is busy with media work and runs his own business, Spirit Events, but is considering a return to football in a coaching capacity.

"I do all sorts of work now," Parlour said. "I work for TalkSport with my own show every weekend, but I've got my own company called Spirit Events which is going very well and is keeping me occupied during the day.

"I am trying to keep fit as well which is the hard bit. Go to the gym most days to keep myself ticking over and I have a game of football every now and again if I can, especially charity events.

"I still love that sort of stuff because not only is it generally for a good cause, but it's still great to sample a bit of dressing room banter because that is the thing you miss most when you have retired.

"The day-to-day business of football is something you can't beat. As well as working hard, it's good fun because of the dressing room camaraderie.

"When you're playing you want to make sure you have no regrets at the end of your career, and that certainly applies as far as Boro is concerned for me. You want to say you've done your best. That's how I look back on my career."

Downing Streets Ahead

They say some things are worth waiting for – and that certainly applies to Boro as far as Stewart Downing is concerned.

Boro were made to play a waiting game when it came to securing Downing's signature when he was a schoolboy being brought up on the Pallister Park Estate.

Most Teesside parents would jump at the chance of seeing their son signing for the Boro – but not Downing's mum and dad.

Having been spotted by Boro head of recruitment Ron Bone and trusted scout Keith Noble while playing for Marton Juniors, the club were keen to get him on their books before rivals moved in – but had to bide their time.

"Ron and Keith got on well with my dad (Stewart senior) and they approached him about signing me, but he didn't want me to sign when I was a kid," said Downing, who also played for Seaham Red Star.

"My dad asked me at the age of about 14 or 15 what I wanted to do and there was only one team I wanted to join and that was Boro.

"He wanted me to enjoy my school and county football, playing with my mates and stuff like that, but always promised them that ultimately I'd join Middlesbrough.

"It was on a handshake with Ron that I signed. Dad always promised Ron and he's not the type to go back on his word. He said, 'Let him do his thing and when the day comes he will sign for Boro,' which I did.

The Keldholme Secondary School pupil's childhood heroes were Juninho, Emerson and Alan Moore, along with "role model" Ryan Giggs, but no one was more influential than his dad.

"My dad didn't drive so the bike was our main form of transport for home and away games here, there and everywhere. We'd just hop on the bike and then head all over Middlesbrough.

"My dad was really supportive, but he'd never shout and bawl at me. He'd keep quiet and leave the coaches to get on with giving out the instructions."

"He always taught me that when things aren't going well you should never point the finger at other people, it is up to you to take personal responsibility.

"You have to look at yourself and make sure you're doing things right before anyone else.

"Football is always up and down. You just have to keep working hard when things are not going well and hope things turn. That's stood me in good stead as a footballer and as a person.

In a *Daily Telegraph* interview with Henry Winter, Downing also explained how he had to overcome family tragedy, losing sister, Vicki, to leukaemia.

"She contracted leukaemia when she was about two. We lost her when I was eight or nine and she was about four. I think about her every day. I have photographs of her all over my house. I have talked to my mum about her a lot."

After working under then Under-17 coach Dave Parnaby ("who taught me how to adapt to playing in different positions, which meant I learnt a lot") he then kicked on under Under-18s coach Mark Proctor.

But that didn't last long as Steve McClaren was soon alerted to Downing's potential when he took over as manager at the Riverside in 2001 and he was fast-tracked towards Premier League football.

"It went a bit quickly because I played for the reserves and then Steve told me that by the end of the season I would play in the first team, which is exactly how it panned out.

"I kept my head down and before I knew it I made my first-team debut at Ipswich.

"It was a huge jump. It was nerve-wracking. He didn't tell me until the last minute so I didn't have time to think.

"Unfortunately, I hit the post in the last minute and we lost 1-0. But afterwards the gaffer complimented me and just told me to keep going."

That's what happened, but Downing was sent up the A19 for a six-week loan spell at Sunderland, where Mick McCarthy was manager, and that accelerated his development.

"I went in to see Steve with my dad and there were lots of clubs wanting to take me on loan such as Chesterfield and Queens Park Rangers.

"But they were in the Second Division then and okay I might have flourished there, but I wanted to play in the Championship in a good footballing team and Sunderland were perfect. I played every three or four days and loved it.

"That loan move to Sunderland really helped me out and that move kick-started things for me. I didn't look back when I returned to Middlesbrough until the day I left for Aston Villa."

He came back from Wearside and was rewarded for his progress with a place on the bench in the Carling Cup final win over Bolton at the Millennium Stadium.

"With it being my hometown team winning its first ever major trophy, it was great to be part of history.

"It was just a little bit disappointing not to get on because I was desperate to get out there.

"But I count myself lucky. Some of the lads who'd played almost every round had not made it even on to the bench.

"If I'd just got on for five or ten minutes I would have counted myself very much part of it, but it was still an extra-special experience."

He has certainly made up for lost time, ending up as a losing finalist with Villa before winning the man-of-the-match award when Liverpool beat Cardiff in the Carling Cup final at Wembley.

"On a personal level it was nice to get that accolade, but the most important thing was for the club to win the trophy.

"Andy Carroll mentioned it to me on the pitch that it had been announced, but I didn't have a clue because there was that much singing and dancing and cheering going on around me."

Downing relished life at Anfield. "They will do anything for you. It is a family club very much like Middlesbrough.

"The fans are great and playing at Anfield is brilliant. I dreamed of going to a really big club like Liverpool and making the most of it."

After a spell with West Ham, Downing returned to Boro where he continued to add to the memories of the days when Boro gave the game's biggest clubs a run for their money.

"People might not believe me, but when I got into the England squad I found out a lot of the senior internationals disliked coming to the Riverside.

"I took that as a back-handed compliment. They reckoned it was always cold and windy and we were always in their faces.

"That's the type of team we were – we made life hard for people – and that means I've got some great memories of the Riverside and always will have."

Downing played 35 times for England, but his UEFA Cup heroics will stand out for Boro fans.

The memories of the way the winger curled over a cross for Massimo Maccarone to nod in the winning goal in the heroic comeback against Steaua Bucharest are bound to bring a smile to anyone's face.

It was a magical occasion and, like everyone associated with Boro, Downing still remembers that fightback in the UEFA Cup semi-final at the Riverside as if it was last night.

"Other games still feel special like beating Manchester United at home and at Old Trafford and beating Chelsea 3-0 ("Jose Mourinho shook every player's hand in the tunnel afterwards") but the Bucharest game stands out a mile because of the sheer drama and prize at the end of it.

"Winning the Carling Cup at Boro was good, but for me personally the UEFA Cup run topped even that. It was absolutely brilliant. How many times could what happened to us happen to anyone else?

"We might have been a small town in Europe, but we made the sort of impact the biggest clubs would have been proud of, beating Roma (Remember Downing's inch-perfect cross for Jimmy Floyd Hasselbaink's headed goal in Italy anyone?) and Stuttgart and getting to the final after those amazing comebacks against Basel and Steaua.

"We did ever so well considering we didn't have that big a squad and we did well in the league as well. That was a massive achievement. Even though we lost 4-0 against Seville in the final it wasn't a 4-0 game. We could still hold our heads high."

• It is when you hear about Stewart Downing from his former teachers that you realise why Boro were so keen to secure his signature.

It was at Pallister Park Primary School where teacher Mick Waterfield first saw the 'wow' factor.

"I remember his dad, who I used to call 'Big Stewy', would have 'Little Stewy' perched on the crossbar of the bike," Waterfield said.

"Other people from opposing schools turned up in flash cars and then his dad would arrive on two wheels with Stewy's boots around his neck and he'd be the best player on the pitch by an absolute mile, which was great because he was a Pally lad.

"The boys were seven and we went outside for a kickabout for my first PE lesson and I saw Stewy beat one player, then another, then another and then another and just slotted it into the net. Then he did it again, and again and again.

"It reached a stage where schools rang up and said, 'Please don't let him play, or just

put him in goals.' Otherwise there was no point playing because he'd just score five or six easily.

"He'd beg me to let him play in goals or we made up rules to stretch him where he could only score with his head. In the hall, his dad made him take his left shoe off to encourage him to use his right foot. If he didn't shoot with his right then the goal wouldn't count.

"I didn't like hammering teams seven or eight nil, so Stewy would say, 'I'll get two and come off,' and I'd reply, 'You can have three if you score with your right foot.' He accepted without hesitation because he's such a nice lad.

"He was also a good tackler. He'd work backwards and forwards and possessed unerring balance. Plus, I've never seen a kid run as fast with the ball at his feet. Teams were in awe of him. 'Oh my God, it's Downing!' they'd say when they saw him."

THE MAVERICKS

Old Big Ed Proud Of Humble Roots

"Middlesbrough born-and-bred," my dad used to tell almost everybody whenever he was introduced, writes Simon Clough.

Dad, who was better known as Brian Clough, or Old Big Ed, said that because he was so proud of his roots – he thought he had a fantastic upbringing.

He had a great deal of affection for Middlesbrough. Some of the happiest years of his life were spent growing up as a carefree kid.

Even though he 'had nowt', as he used to say, and he was sharing a big bed with three of his brothers, he loved every minute of it.

Dad came from a good family, but one that didn't have much financially. They were hard times, but they weren't alone - most big families in the North East lived on the edge.

My granddad worked at the local sweet factory, and I always remember my dad saying, "We were very popular on our road because he used to bring home all the misshapen ones and all the damaged ones."

By all accounts there was always a queue of kids that formed outside their house of kids hoping for a little treat.

Dad's mum, who we lost when I was seven (Pop went a few years later) was the dominant one. She completely ran the show in every aspect of their home life.

She was an incredible woman. She was the one who left the biggest impression on everybody.

There were nine of them. They lost one at a young age. She hurt herself on a fence and died from the infection.

There was a lot of competition football-wise in the family and that always helps.

One of his elder brothers, Desmond or Dessie, was considered by many to be a better player than Dad – although my dad used to say they were all wrong.

Dad played for a couple of local clubs with a few of his siblings. One of the team photos we've got shows five of them together, but he was the one who did well enough to get signed up by Middlesbrough.

He had to do his National Service and the club paid him £1 a week as a retainer, to keep his registration.

From what I remember, he was based in Somerset for some of it, and he wanted to be closer to home. But his boss down there, a senior officer, liked him playing for the Army team, so he was kept down there for as long as he possibly could be.

Once he got back, his aim was to attract the attention of the manager. He didn't hit the ground running, it took him a period of adjustment to get up to the required speed, but once he gained a foothold he never came out of the side.

Peter Taylor had come up to him in the dressing room, just a week ahead of him getting in the first team squad, and he said, "There are only two people who know how good you are at this club. I think you do and I'm the other one."

My dad never forgot that. Peter always made him laugh and that was one of the occasions when Dad said he got him going.

That was before he became a regular, but that gave him a big boost that someone thought so highly of him.

He didn't know Peter very well, but after that they became almost inseparable and he became as close with Peter as he was with his brothers and they went on to form a managerial team.

There is an unbelievable television interview that Peter gave in 1967 when they left Hartlepool to join Derby County and he was asked about his working relationship with Dad and the response was remarkable.

"It's been everything I expected it to be and more. I'm going to stay with Brian Clough and the two of us are going to go right to the very top."

They actually did that. They put their money where their mouths were by twice leading Nottingham Forest to the European Cup, which is something that will never be repeated.

They were great times, but his Teesside upbringing certainly always kept Dad grounded. Even to his dying day, he and my mother never changed at all.

Their values were still the same and the way they approached life was very much the same. He made a few bob, but they were very simple folk who remained very true to where they came from in so many ways.

He didn't let anything go to his head. He met Muhammad Ali and Frank Sinatra, but he never became too full of himself.

That's why he used to call himself 'Old Big Ed'. It came about because he was awarded the OBE and he came up with 'Old Big Ed'. He said he called himself that to remind himself not to be one.

Whenever he did get too big for his boots, he just used to say that when he did go back to Middlesbrough his brothers used to bring him back down to earth very quickly.

There is a statue of Dad in Middlesbrough that means a lot to our family because the town was so important to us all.

My parents met in Middlesbrough at Rea's Café – Chris Rea's family's place – around the corner from Ayresome Park.

Dad had seen Mum a couple of times when he was walking through Albert Park on his way to training.

My mum said that statue of Dad there with the boots over his shoulder was exactly as she first saw him on his way to training.

That's why it's such a special statue. In fact, of all the statues of Dad, that one, in my opinion, is certainly the best. It's brilliant.

When your mum and dad come from a place it will always stay in your heart.

We've got relatives there, so we always regard it as a lovely place to visit to see where they grew up and see family.

I've been to the Riverside at least a dozen times - practically always in a working capacity as a scout for my brother Nigel for Derby and latterly Burton, and they always make me feel very welcome.

But I make a point of walking down the corridor there which has got all the team photos going back to the 50s and to see Dad and Peter on them gives me a lovely feeling.

I've been back and met people I've never met before who saw my dad growing up and they always said he was a little bit different and always had something about him that they couldn't quite put their finger on.

They say he was always a bit bossy and always had something to say, even when he was 13 or 14. That makes me think my dad never really changed.

As my mother used to say, 'He said too much, too often,' and that's why he never got the England job or several other jobs he maybe should have had a chance of getting.

I'd liked to have had him a few more years than we did, but that apart I wouldn't have changed him for the world because we're massively proud of him and that goes for my kids as well and hopefully they'll pass it on to their kids as well.

He never forgot his roots. In some people's eyes he tainted it little by going to Middlesbrough's bitter rivals up the road at Sunderland, but that's football.

Every time we go up to Middlesbrough we go and visit the statue – which should go without saying - because it is absolutely fantastic.

My first grandson (Harrison Simon) has just come into the world and as soon as he comes of age, if I'm still around, the first thing I'm going to do is take him up there to have a look.

I've got a few years to wait, but I'm being deadly serious about that. It's so special. When my mum saw it, she said they had got him to an absolute 'T'. That was exactly how he used to be and it's in a nice place too.

I'm not sure how many people notice it these days, but we certainly do, so hopefully they'll keep it there for a good while longer.

Brian Clough died at the age of 69 in September 2004.

Taylor-Made for Success

Middlesbrough Football Club has plenty to shout about, but one of the things it can really boast about is that it changed the course of football history, writes Wendy Dickinson.

For it was Boro that brought together one of the most successful double acts that English and European football has ever seen in Brian Clough and my dad, Peter Taylor.

My mum told me she could remember the first time she ever heard Brian Clough's name when Dad had been at the club a week or so.

Brian had just been de-mobbed after National Service, and had returned for the 55/56 season. Dad had been there for pre-season training and there was a match between the 'Possibles' and the "Probables'.

He came home that night and said:

"I've seen a lad playing in the reserves and it's an absolute crime because he should be in the first team."

"What's his name?"

"Brian Clough."

Looking back, that was probably the most important day of their lives. The start of it all.

But Brian struggled a bit to be accepted. He was – to put it politely – outspoken. Even as a young man he said what he thought and often it didn't go down too well, but my dad always fought his corner.

Brian liked it that someone who was much older then him clearly rated him. Brian said he felt valued and supported by Dad and from my dad's point of view it was great having a young man who looked up to him.

They spent a huge amount of time together. I remember Brian coming to the house several nights a week and my mum said he'd knock on the door standing there, "Is Peter came in?" and they'd just talk about football, they were obsessed.

From what I'm told by his old teammates, when they went on away trips, which was usually on the train, with long corridors and separate compartments, they didn't mix with the others. They'd go in and pull the shutters down and that was it.

What made me laugh is how they worked together. My dad had a reputation for throwing the ball a long way. He was a big guy – about 6ft 2in – and he had this thing where he could hurl the ball beyond the halfway line and often to Brian's feet because he was incredibly strong.

Brian used to say your job is to get the ball to me and my job is to put it in the back of the net.

We lived in Saltwells Crescent, in a club house. Nobody had a car and nobody had a big mansion. Home was a two-up two-down we rented off the club. I went to Marton Grove School, which Brian went to a few years before me.

We were nomads. We lived all over the place and Middlesbrough was the start of lots of travelling.

When the men weren't playing football or talking about it, the players would be playing snooker or gambling while Mum had me as a young child and then my brother.

Mum said she couldn't have coped had it not been for the warmth of people, of Middlesbrough and she genuinely meant it.

Brian's family were really supportive, but local people made sure she didn't feel far from home. We always had a soft spot for Middlesbrough. We feel very affectionate towards the town and its people.

We were in Middlesbrough for five years and my brother, Phillip, was born there. We went up there recently to have a coffee at the club with Dad's former colleagues - Billy Day, Alan Peacock and Gordon Jones.

They were absolutely fascinating and hilarious.

Billy says Brian was incredibly goal-hungry. He'd be the one who'd barge people out of the way to score. And that's what my dad loved about him.

A 19-year-old telling senior players wouldn't have gone down terribly well, especially with Bob Dennison who was the manager.

There weren't any tactics and training was minimal. It was a completely different world. I'm not sure if it was better, but certainly different.

In those days players weren't the kings, unlike now, where the player is king. They all used to walk to work from where they lived, not far from the ground. Just like most ordinary folk.

They were merely club employees and they were all frightened to death of the groundsman.

According to Billy, the groundsman said, 'You do anymore sliding tackles you're in for it'. But they got him back and nailed his sandwich to the wall in his hut.

We left Middlesbrough when Dad joined Port Vale and we moved back to Nottingham. Then he went to Burton as a player and was offered the manager's job and so we moved to Burton there for four years.

He did really well at Burton. They won the Southern League Cup and they had an up-and-coming team.

Then one night he got a call from Brian. It was my brother's birthday, so we had a house full of boys celebrating when the phone went, and it was Brian, who said he'd been offered the job at Hartlepool, but 'would only take it if you come with me.'

Dad's career was on the up so he consulted his brother and everyone in the family said you must be mad going back up North when you've got a great job here. He took a day and then said, 'I'm on my way,' and he took a cut in wages.

Alan Peacock said he wasn't surprised that they got together at Hartlepool. He reckoned that Dad had a maturity and knowledge of the game that Brian needed.

They were quite different characters, my dad was confident but he wouldn't have been out there doing a TV interview with all the swagger that Brian showed.

But they did complement each other; they brought different skills to the partnership.

They didn't live in each other's pockets – it was purely football that brought them together and kept them together. They had the same views on how the game should be played.

What they achieved was very unusual. Winning the Football League with Derby and then Nottingham Forest – two relatively small provincial clubs – and then winning back-to-back European Cups with Forest was extraordinary.

They did it with tremendously talented players with the odd misfit thrown in.

I was very privileged to have lived through it and I went to all the European Cup matches – home and away – and both finals, so it was a fabulous time.

I was listening to Gareth Southgate saying they were trying to create a family atmosphere among the England squad in Russia and that's really what it felt like at Derby and then Forest - everyone pulling together.

One of the things that gets me is the picture that was painted of them in the *Damned United* book and film, which focuses on Brian's time with Leeds.

They portrayed the age difference as much bigger than it was, as if Dad was a lot older, but they were actually contemporaries and played in the same Middlesbrough team.

They made my dad out to be a dimwit and Brian to be a complete nutter. Neither was true, so I thought I needed to do something and tell the truth about what they were like and the nature of their relationship in my own book, *For Pete's Sake*.

The book went down well and people said it was nice that a daughter had written the book. It was a lot of hard work, but well worth it.

Peter Taylor died at the age of 62 in October 1990.

Stan – A Little Man With Big Reputation

Stan Cummins was tipped to become the first ever £1-million player during his Boro days by manager Jack Charlton.

And as a teenager, he was also likened to legendary goalscorer Jimmy Greaves by Boro's former England coach Harold Shepherdson.

Yet the 5ft 4in forward relished the heightened expectations that came with being praised by football icons who helped England conquer the world in 1966.

"Jack certainly gave me a lot to live up to in the eyes of the fans and the press with that one," Cummins said from his home in the United States.

"The transfer record in those days was only about half that amount, but that was just the way Jack was – and I honestly wouldn't have wanted it any other way.

"He was a great man-manager and for him to say that about me was a terrific compliment, because he obviously knew a thing or two about football having won the World Cup."

The *Evening Gazette* would describe Cummins as the 'Little Man with a Very Big Reputation' which neatly summed up his situation.

"It was great to be at Boro at the same time as Jack. When he said things like that stuff about me being worth £1 million you knew it came from the heart because he never ever said things that he didn't mean.

"He even had a bet with me when I was pushing for a first-team place that he'd give me a fiver if I scored 50 goals in the juniors and reserves in one season and I got 40, so his money was safe, but he got me going."

Cummins' potential was first spotted when he was playing for Ferryhill Grammar School at the age of 11 by honorary Boro scout Ray Grant.

The retired headteacher, who also brought Brian Clough, Tony Mowbray and Mark Proctor to Boro, said Cummins was blessed with "the sharpest footballing brain."

The left-footed Cummins also had trials with the top English clubs, but signed for Boro as an associate schoolboy when he was 14 years old.

"I used to go and train with Boro every chance I got because it was a great place to play your football.

"The camaraderie was great and that is why I was happy to stay there, even though I had trials with Man United, Arsenal and Chelsea.

"It just felt right and Jack Charlton saw enough in me even though I was a pretty diminutive striker to give me a debut when I was still an apprentice at the age of just 17, so I owe him a lot."

His debut took place against Ipswich Town at Ayresome Park in November 1976 and at the end of the season Cummins headed over the Atlantic to further his education.

That was with the Minnesota Kicks in 1977 in the North American Soccer League against the likes of Pele and George Best.

And when he returned to Teesside the move seemed to have paid off as he scored his first league goal in a 1-0 win over Aston Villa and then he struck twice in a 4-2 win over Newcastle in January 1978.

However, Cummins lost his way after suffering a knee injury the following pre-season.

And after losing his place in the Boro front-line, following the arrival of Micky Burns and Bosco Jankovic, he was tempted up the A19 to Sunderland in a £300,000-move at the age of just 20 in November 1979.

"It was a bit of a wrench to leave Boro, but life moves on and footballers do.

"I was a professional footballer and I had a living to make. Sunderland came in with an offer than suited everyone and I became their club-record signing.

"Things worked out really well at Sunderland to start off with and it is a club that is also really close to my heart."

But it is Charlton who has certainly left him with unforgettable memories because of his unorthodox ways.

"I am sure that everyone who ever played under Jack Charlton would look back on their time at Ayresome Park really fondly.

"When it comes to special memories, Boro is right up there at the top because of Jack.

"Not only was he an inspirational manager, but how many footballers can say their manager set their dogs on them?

"That is what happened with Jack and his Labradors in training. That was a strange way to work on fitness. You couldn't make it up."

Nowadays, Cummins is an American citizen, having done his bit to help spread the soccer word in a country dominated by basketball, baseball and American football.

It was the sale of Trevor Francis from Birmingham City to Brian Clough's

Nottingham Forest in 1979 that meant Cummins failed to live up to Charlton's billing.

So a player described by *Northern Echo* journalist Mike Amos as a 'boy wonder' may have struggled to fulfill his potential, but football transformed his fortunes.

"I grew up in an area that was so rough that the kids bit the dogs, but I did well at all the clubs I served.

"Now I am living in a beautiful part of the world where the weather is gorgeous, in Kansas, so it's fair to say that I haven't done too badly.

"I know it's a cliché, but it really is the land of opportunity and a great place to live.

"I might not have become the £1-million footballer – possibly because football became too physical.

"But, I tell you what, I just have to look out into my back garden and look at the swimming pool and then I feel like a millionaire."

Best Pub Side Bar None For Ashcroft

Billy Ashcroft says it was like being in a pub team when he played for Boro.

It might sound like ridicule, but for Ashcroft, who used to run pubs for a living, it is meant to be flattering.

"In a way it was like being in the best pub team you could imagine, but I mean that in the nicest possible way," Ashcroft said.

"It's not supposed to mean we were just a set of cloggers and hoofers - it's because we were all good mates.

"There was no backbiting or anything nasty. If someone said, 'Let's go down the pub,' every single one of us would be there.

"There was a tremendous camaraderie, which is why my time at Boro feels so special. We were so close – just like a team you'd see down the park on a Sunday. All for one and one for all."

Ashcroft became Boro's first six-figure signing when he moved to Ayresome Park from Wrexham for £135,000 in 1977.

"That move was the highlight of my career because it was my dream to play in the top flight," said Ashcroft, now a driving instructor on Merseyside.

"I was awestruck in my first day at training because I was surrounded by internationals, but people like Graeme Souness, David Armstrong and Terry Cooper helped me settle. They were top-class."

That Ashcroft arrived at Boro as a striker, but ended up flourishing as a centre-half, puts into perspective how hard he found goals to come by on Teesside.

"I wanted to be the most successful goalscorer Middlesbrough ever had, but it didn't pan out that way. People still talk about a sitter I missed against Orient in an FA Cup quarter-final.

"But I'd been used to playing alongside Graham Whittle with Micky Thomas and Bobby Shinton as wingers at Wrexham and between us one season we scored 86 goals because it was cross after cross after cross.

"It was incessant, but at Middlesbrough it was a different style of play. I ended up at centre-half and they sold Stuart Boam, which was a big compliment to say they thought I could fill the void he left.

"In the end, I had two happy years playing at the back and it was all down to being alongside Tony McAndrew who was one of the best in that division.

"He had an amazing never-say-die attitude and talked to me all the time which was vital because I'd gone into the unknown."

Ashcroft – who described his distinctive hairstyle in his Boro days as being "A cross between Shirley Temple and Village People" – has fond memories of the day he scored a belter against his beloved Everton.

"You just couldn't have made it up. I scored what I thought was an amazing winner – picking up the ball from Jim Platt and then thumping a 25-yarder past George Wood - in a 1-0 win against Everton at Ayresome Park.

"I was high as a kite, but then I came back down to earth with a bump. I went back to Liverpool that night to see family and friends, walked into my local, saw my mum and dad and he completely shunned me.

"He wouldn't talk to me all night because he was dyed-in-the-wool Blue, while all the Liverpool fans were shaking me by the hand, congratulating me. Still, I was still on Cloud Nine for a week afterwards."

After five years with Boro, he was released after relegation and following a recommendation by ex-colleague Heine Otto, he headed to Dutch side FC Twente where he became a cult hero.

"Over there I was known as the 'crazy Englishman', but in Grangetown and Eston it was just normal behaviour. If someone said, 'I bet you can't do this,' it was a case of just watch me.

"One night out someone said I sounded like the late comedian, Tommy Cooper, because my voice was getting croaky and funnily enough he was a friend of mine and I'd spent my stag night with him.

"Anyway, I did an impression of him, one thing led to another and I ended up on Dutch television dong this Tommy Cooper act.

"Other Dutch teams didn't like me because I was bustling and they were used to skilful players, so I got a lot of stick, but then everywhere I went everyone loved me, even at Ajax and Feyenoord. I even went to Country and Western bars and got my guitar out and played.

"That was great, but I still feel a pull towards Middlesbrough. It's probably why I got the only three points on my licence that I've ever had when I was driving to the Riverside a few years ago. It happened on the A19 because the closer I got the more excited I felt about being there and the more my foot went down."

Kennedy: Getting A Kick Out Of Football

Tough-tackling Mick Kennedy served Boro with gritty determination for two seasons in the 1980s.

But he is the first to admit he would have to change his ways drastically to last two minutes in the current game.

Kennedy developed a reputation as one of the most combative midfielders around during his spell on Teesside and believes there is little place for his aggressive tendencies in the English game these days.

"I'll always proudly remember being compared to Nobby Stiles during my time there and that was as big a compliment as a midfielder could get," Kennedy said from his home on Ireland's Atlantic coast, where his parents once lived.

"But people like him and me would really have to curb our natural instincts to have a chance of prospering in top-flight football. I'd never survive these days because you can't tackle.

"I loved getting stuck in and although I could play a bit I knew my limitations and that meant winning the midfield battles.

"The game was a lot more physical in those days, which suited me down to the ground, but ball-winners such as myself and Gary Hamilton wouldn't last long at all in the current climate because referees have clamped down on those who love a tackle.

"For me, that's a crying shame because fans love seeing a strong challenge or two, but I can only see things becoming less and less physical in the Premier League at least."

An uncompromising approach endeared him to Boro fans and teammates, but occasionally even his colleagues saw red thanks to a Salford-born player who, ironically, idolised George Best as a schoolboy.

"I'll always remember one training-ground incident. For some reason our goalie, Jim Platt, was an outfield player in practice and I accidentally caught him.

"The game was allowed to continue and the ball was on the other side of the pitch when I heard the stamping of footsteps behind me. I thought it was odd.

"Next thing I know I was hauled to the ground in a headlock. It was Jim. I thought I was being murdered and I've still got the mental scars to prove it."

Kennedy launched his career at Halifax and rose to prominence at Huddersfield before moving to Ayresome Park for £100,000 in 1982 and making 68 appearances in Boro colours.

"I had a great time at Boro and we had good up-and-coming players, such as Stephen Bell, David Shearer, Gary Hamilton, Darren Wood, Paul Sugrue and David Currie, as well as old heads like Jim Platt, Kevin Beattie, Terry Cochrane and Irving Nattrass.

"It's incredible how many young players the club has produced over the years and it's amazing that they keep churning them out. Boro show the North East still is a hotbed.

"They even put Man United to shame because they've done precious little since Fergie's fledglings came through, whereas Boro are still as productive as ever as

Ben Gibson has shown."

Kennedy was initially signed for Boro by Bobby Murdoch and he still regrets only working with the legendary Scot for a few months before Malcolm Allison was hired to revive the club's fortunes.

"Malcolm was one of the most flamboyant characters you could wish to meet and he had us playing some good stuff in the old Second Division.

"It was after we'd beaten Arsenal 3-2 in the FA Cup at Ayresome that he revved things up. He appeared for his post-match interview smoking a huge Cuban cigar and sporting his trademark Fedora hat.

"He told reporters he only got them out when he knew we had the makings of a really good team, but sadly that proved to be the ruination of us. We got ahead of ourselves.

"We could have done with reinforcements, but there was no money in the kitty and his comments made people sit up and take notice of the talent at his disposal and soon players were on their way – including me to Portsmouth."

• *Mick Kennedy does not have many honours to his name despite playing in 536 senior games over a 16-year period, which is why he cherishes his two international caps.*

They were won for Republic of Ireland when Kennedy's former Boro boss Jack Charlton was running the national side.

"Jack's still regarded as a God here in Ireland and rightly so, especially by people like me," Kennedy said.

"I'd joined Portsmouth, but was back up in Middlesbrough helping the lads celebrate promotion in 1987 when I got word that I was in Jack's squad.

"I rang him and headed back to Portsmouth to get my passport. Those were the days when it was difficult to get hold of cash, so when I turned up at the airport I had to cadge £50 off Jack.

"We landed in Iceland and were still on the Tarmac when he asked for it back. I thought he was a laugh, but really he was deadly serious."

Summerbell Spurred On To Success

Mark Summerbell went from serving Boro as a ball-winning midfielder to serving pints in a Durham pub in a painfully short period of time, but you won't hear him complaining.

His football career almost failed to get off the ground and may have been cut short by injury, but he still insists that he lived the proverbial dream in a Boro shirt.

The Durham schoolboy was rejected as not good enough by Newcastle, but was rescued by Boro scout Ron Bone and when he ended up playing for Bryan

Robson it meant he was working for his childhood hero.

"When I was a kid I used to idolise Bryan Robson, so it was like a dream come true to play with him and for him," Summerbell said.

"He was the ultimate role model. I tried to base my game on his as I was growing up, because he was the best player in Britain in his pomp at Manchester United and it was brilliant to watch him in action close-up, because he could do everything brilliantly.

"I loved every minute of my time at Boro. We finished in the top ten and I played with some fantastic footballers from the manager down including Juninho, Paul Ince, Branco, Paul Gascoigne and Fabrizio Ravanelli.

"It was a great to play with them and it was a pleasure to play against the Premier League's top players, such as Paul Scholes and David Beckham. It was a challenge I really enjoyed."

Had it not been for Bone, Boro's legendary chief scout, he might not have realised his childhood ambitions after he failed to win over Newcastle coaches.

"I ended playing for a local Sunday league side in Chester-le-Street called Hilda Park as a kid and Ron Bone was running the team. Luckily enough for me he was a Boro scout and he got me on the books at Ayresome Park.

"I signed the old-fashioned apprentice forms as a 15-year-old and became professional at 18, but between those points there was a lot of hard graft, but I thoroughly enjoyed it.

"We had to do all the cleaning, but it was great and I had some good times there with the rest of the lads because we really bonded.

"I used to clean the boots belonging to Stephen Pears and Jamie Pollock, and coach Ray Train's as well, but we were all very close.

"We were in and around the first team each and every day. Cleaning their boots and putting the kit out for them and then sorting all their stuff out afterwards."

Summerbell, who attended Framwellgate School, was second-team captain and rose through the ranks swiftly, but he took his first-team debut against Tottenham at White Hart Lane in his stride because he had no time to fret about his entry on to the big stage.

"My first-team debut came as a shock and it all happened so quickly that I didn't have time to panic.

"It was great to play, but it was unexpected because there were others on the bench that I thought would get the nod before myself, so for first-team coach John Pickering to give me a shout when Robbie Mustoe got injured in the first half was stunning.

"I even thought I had scored because my effort went over the line, but the goal wasn't awarded to me – the goal went down to Phil Whelan instead, who put the rebound in after it was scrambled off the line.

"The main thing is that it meant we drew 1-1, not whether or not the goal went to me. Unfortunately, I missed a sitter as well, but I'd like to think the ball took a bobble before I connected."

Summerbell ended up leaving Boro following the arrival of Steve McClaren, but injury problems prevented him enjoying a long career post-Teesside.

"I suppose all good things have got to come to an end. Bryan left, the new manager came in and he had different views and I left the club and ended up at Carlisle, which is a really good club.

"I really enjoyed my first season there, but I picked up a couple of injuries and I came out of the game after that. I just couldn't get to the level of fitness that I wanted to play my game and I stopped enjoying it.

"I was a ball-winner and I just couldn't put myself about as much as I would have liked. So that's when I decided to quit.

"I went on to do my first coaching badge, but I knocked the second one on the head. I didn't really enjoy it very much because, and I'll be honest, I didn't really enjoy being coached myself. I just liked to go out and train."

After retiring from professional football, he went into the pub trade.

"I used to play for my mate's team at South Moor, but since we moved there is a lot more travelling so I haven't bothered since.

"There are people here who want me to go and play for the local team, who are a young side and they want someone with a bit of experience, but I've had to play it by ear with a pub to run and everything."

Karembeu's The Real Deal

It was something of a culture shock for Christian Karembeu when he swapped Real Madrid for Middlesbrough.

He went from the most successful club in world football to one that was fighting relegation, but soon found out there were more similarities than first met the eye.

"We were not one of the biggest clubs, so it was very different to my time at Real Madrid," Karembeu said.

"At Real we were the biggest and the best team who everyone wanted to beat, but it was fine with me at Middlesbrough because there we had a similar mentality as we knew we had to give everything in every game or we would lose.

"It was that mentality that made me love English football. It was a lot more physical than in Spain and there were more close games, but I enjoyed it, especially when the fans got behind the team."

The most decorated player in the club's history may not have added to his haul of medals, but insists his year with Boro remains invaluable.

A former teammate of future Boro boss Aitor Karanka at Real Madrid, Karembeu headed to England after helping the Spanish giants win the Champions League and World Cup holders France win Euro 2000.

"I was ready for a new challenge and so helping Middlesbrough establish themselves in the Premier League was the perfect move for me.

"I'd had an amazing journey with clubs and country and I came to Middlesbrough because it was evident after meeting Bryan Robson and Steve Gibson the club was going to very interesting places.

"They were very ambitious and I liked that. I knew they were desperate to win something really special for the first time. That was how I felt when we won the World Cup. That is why Middlesbrough will be special to me, always."

Karembeu hardly missed a game during his solitary season on Teesside after a £2.1-million move from Madrid in the summer of 2000.

"I wanted to come to Middlesbrough because the club was a fascinating project due to the chairman and to find out for myself what it was like to play in England.

"I liked the passion and the pride for the club that Steve Gibson had because it meant so much to him. He was a fan and I felt inspired by him.

"I really wanted to do everything I could to help him make the club do something special. We all felt the same in the dressing room. There was a fantastic spirit.

"I will always have happy memories of playing for Middlesbrough. The Riverside atmosphere was magnificent. It is a beautiful stadium and the fans always made it feel good for the players."

Karembeu was accompanied to Teesside by his now former wife, the supermodel Adriana Sklenarikova.

"One of the things I most liked about Middlesbrough was that the people in the club and the fans were so friendly.

"Everyone I met was so nice to me. They made me feel very welcome which is important when you are in a new country.

"There were some very good players like Paul Ince, Alen Boksic, Ugo Ehiogu and Gary Pallister.

"And there were some great characters as well, like Dean Windass, who always made me laugh even though I could not always understand what he was saying."

Karembeu scored one of his three Boro goals in a 1-0 Boxing Day win over Liverpool at the Riverside.

He left for Greek side Olympiakos after a season on Teesside, but only after signing off in style with a goal in his last Boro game – a 3-1 home win over West Ham.

"I did not score many goals, so I remember them all. I scored when we lost 2-1 against Manchester United at Old Trafford.

"But my goal against Liverpool, which was a simple goal after a goalkeeper's mistake, was great because it meant we won three important points and then that last game was good because it showed we were a good team.

"It was difficult to stay up and I was worried we would be relegated, but when Terry Venables came in to help Bryan Robson we became a better team."

Windass' World At His Feet

Dean Windass' time on Teesside was sealed with a kiss.

That is because his key role in Boro's successful fight against relegation was caught on camera as Christian Karembeu gave him a smacker – on his foot.

"It's funny looking back, but that kiss sort of epitomised what we were all about," Windass said.

"It all happened because just before kick off at the Riverside I realised my boot had split and so Christian lent me his spare pair.

"Because he was a World Cup winner from Real Madrid, they were top-of-the-range, the most comfortable I'd worn, and when I scored he was straight in there to give me a kiss on his boot.

"Sadly, we lost the game (against Ipswich) after I put us ahead, but that kiss really showed what incredible team-spirit we had and we all had a right laugh about it.

"Christian had won the World Cup with France, he was a superstar and his (now former) supermodel wife (Adriana) was one of the most beautiful women on the planet and here he was kissing my foot. You couldn't make it up."

The same could be said of the Humbersider's football journey that saw him go from Hull City reject to Boro saviour under ex-England boss Terry Venables.

"I was shown the door by Hull as a teenager because they didn't think I had it in me to make the grade.

"I was gutted, but deep-down I knew it was the right thing to do at the time by the club.

"I wasn't good enough or strong enough, so briefly you think you might never get the opportunity again.

"But it turned out that I was a late developer. I went to work for a living, played non-league for North Ferriby, and worked on my weaknesses.

"I came back a stronger person in more ways than one and I had to get a proper job in a fish factory which spurred me on."

Windass savours his time with Boro following a surprise move from Bradford.

"I was Terry Venables' one and only signing which was a real honour in its own right because he's one of the best managers in the business.

"I say that because he was a top manager and Boro are a top club that had come on leaps and bounds under Bryan Robson.

"My remit was to help keep Boro up in the Premier League because we were struggling. We finished 14th (Manchester City, Coventry City and Bradford City went down) which was a great achievement."

Windass insists that joining Boro in 2001 was "one of the highlights of my career."

"Terry was absolutely fantastic – probably the best coach I've worked with, so my game really came on."

"I wasn't the quickest player around, but I had a very strong football intelligence and that's what he saw in me and brought out in the same way he did with Teddy Sheringham.

"He played me with Alen Boksic who was the best finisher I ever played with, plus we had Paul Ince in midfield leading everyone and it just clicked. It was a great effort.

"It was a shame that Terry left because if he'd stayed and signed a two or three-year contract then I would have stayed.

"That would have suited me down to the ground because I really enjoyed myself at Boro. But things happen for a reason."

Windass left Boro as Steve McClaren rang the changes, but went on to prosper elsewhere before eventually retiring at the age of 40 when he was a player-coach at Darlington under former Boro manager Colin Todd.

"My philosophy after I reached the age of about 35 or 36 was to play as long as I could.

"It was also to treat every game and every training session as if it was my last. I was fortunate, too, with injuries as well, which stood me in good stead.

"I was always a good trainer, but as you get older you get more disciplined and that helped me play on so long."

Having already secured his place as a Tigers hero during the club's Boothferry Park days under Terry Dolan, Windass returned to the club following its move to the KC Stadium in fairytale fashion.

For, with the sweetest strike of his career, he volleyed home the Wembley play-off final winner against Bristol City at Wembley in 2008.

And with it, Windass, who is now a Hull City ambassador, brought top-flight football to his hometown for the first time in the club's 104-year history.

"Brian Horton was the Hull manager when I was released and he was the assistant manager when I scored at Wembley. I was 39 when it happened.

"I was making up for lost time. And if that doesn't show that things happen for a reason I don't know what does. It was the stuff of dreams."

Merson's Case For The Defence

Paul Merson was left wondering what he had let himself in for when he joined Boro.

His first impressions after swapping Premier League big-hitters Arsenal for Championship promotion hopefuls had him fearing the worst.

But Merson stuck at it and not only inspired Boro to promotion, but was also rewarded with a place in England's squad that contested the 1998 World Cup.

"It was an eye-opener at the start, leaving a massive club like Arsenal and going to Boro," said Merson.

"And I'm not going to lie – the first couple of months were a shock, really, in all kinds of ways.

"In pre-season, I signed when the club was in Italy and I got to the airport and there was no car waiting for me.

"I had to find my own way to the hotel, which was two hours away, in a cab. That would not have happened at Arsenal in a month of Sundays."

That was not the only thing that took Merson aback.

"When we got back we played a pre-season friendly at York and Bryan Robson was giving his team-talk in the dressing room.

"All of a sudden, Gianluca Festa's mobile phone went off and he started talking to someone in Italian.

"He would have been thrown out of the club if that was Arsenal. It was so disrespectful to Robbo and to his teammates.

"I couldn't believe what I was seeing. I thought, 'Wow! This can't be right. What have I done?' At first, I thought I'd made the worst decision of my career."

It was in the summer of 1997 that Merson was signed by Boro in a £5 million five-year deal which was reportedly worth a princely £20,000 a week to spearhead the club's bid to bounce back from relegation at the first attempt.

The Bryan Robson factor was key to the attacking midfielder signing on the dotted line and ending his 12-year association with Arsenal.

"Bryan Robson is a legend and the word is used too loosely in football, but it definitely applies to Robbo.

"So when someone of that stature likes you and thinks you're a good player it really means something.

"Plus, Middlesbrough was - and still is - a big club. Juninho had left and so I really fancied the challenge.

"It had gone a bit sour for me at Arsenal where we weren't really challenging for anything and I just thought, 'Let's go for it.'

"The club really lived up to my expectations. The Rockliffe training ground was just getting done when I was there, but the Riverside stadium was right up there with the top Premier League grounds."

It took a while for Merson to find his feet, but once he did there was no stopping Boro's new talisman.

"I had a nightmare debut. It was a real shocker. We were real fortunate to win. We beat Charlton 2-1 thanks to a couple of late goals even though we were at home.

"It was hard going at first. There was a lot of travelling; I was going up and down the A19 and M1 from home in Hertfordshire all the time so it was tough because I didn't move up for a long time.

"There were times when I thought, 'This ain't working at all,' and I felt really homesick, but in the end it did work out really well."

Merson scored just one league goal before mid-October and then when he got going there was no stopping him.

He ended up with 16 goals to his name as Boro finished second behind Nottingham Forest.

"One of the main reasons it clicked for me is because of the fabulous support we got from the fans.

"The Riverside was packed for every home game and it was really hard to get a ticket.

"But the travelling support was even more incredible – I don't think I've ever played in front of away fans like Middlesbrough's.

"Oxford on a Tuesday night and the away end is packed to the rafters – that just said it all. To travel there on a Tuesday night was just phenomenal for me. That was another eye-opener."

Boro won 4-1 that night with Merson completing the scoring in the 90th minute to cap a memorable evening.

"We had a really good team. Andy Townsend was a great signing and then Gazza (Paul Gascoigne) came and we already had Craig Hignett who was a very underrated player.

"It was a massive deal for me to help Boro get promoted. You set out to do a job. I was up there to bring the club back into the Premier League, which is where they belong. To be part of that was great."

Merson, of course, also helped Boro overcome Liverpool to reach the League Cup final where they lost to Chelsea at Wembley.

"Scoring and beating Liverpool at Anfield and then beating them 2-0 at the Riverside is still my standout memory.

"There's a decent chance for anyone to beat anybody over a one-off game, but to beat a club of Liverpool's stature over two legs takes some doing.

"To beat a team a division above you in a cup semi-final is a big ask, and so it has to go down as a major achievement.

"And the atmosphere as well that night when we finished them off was the best I experienced in my time there."

Merson did so well that he was picked to represent England in France in the World Cup finals by Three Lions boss Glenn Hoddle.

"Getting selected for France 98 was the icing on the cake. I was so proud to get the call-up and play out in France.

"I don't think anybody has been to the World Cup who's not been playing in the Premier League since then.

"We had a really good squad and were unlucky to go out on penalties against Argentina which was so, so disappointing because I honestly thought we'd win the competition if we'd got past them."

After coming off the bench against Argentina, Merson scored in the penalty shoot-out that followed a 2-2 draw that was best remembered for Michael Owen's sensational solo goal and David Beckham's sending off.

That game in St Etienne also marked the end of Merson's international career, which saw him score three times and win 21 caps.

The clock was also ticking on Merson's spell with Boro and he would soon be off, joining Aston Villa in a £6.75-million deal in September 1998.

It was a move that was surrounded by acrimony with Boro left fuming as the club's ambition and his teammates' attitudes towards alcohol and gambling were called into question – something Merson quickly disputes.

"I had nothing to do with that. That was a load of rubbish.

"That was majorly distorted. That wasn't what I said at all, not at all.

"No one drank and gambled more than I ever did. I wouldn't say that at all."

Merson insists he left Teesside following an eventful 14-month spell with his head held high.

"I left under certain circumstances where the fans don't like me anymore, well certainly a lot of them don't.

"But I think that's a bit wrong. I don't think they understand. Things were blown out of all proportion at the time.

"It was no secret that my family didn't move with me to Teesside. It was hard for me because I didn't want to be without my wife and kids.

"But I still did my job. What makes me laugh is that Juninho is a hero to Middlesbrough fans and he jumped ship when they were relegated.

"I left one of the biggest clubs in Europe to join Middlesbrough and I dropped down a league.

"I had a four-year contract at Arsenal if I wanted it and yet I went up to Teesside, did my job and ended up getting cast as the villain of the piece.

"That's what makes me feel a bit miffed when I get stick from Boro fans.

"People need to understand that I left Middlesbrough for family reasons, not football reasons.

"If I'd not done what I set out to do I'd have been fairly criticised. My job was to be part of a team that got promoted back to the Premier League. I was a big part of that.

"I could have understood the fans having a go if I went up there, we failed to get promoted and I turned round and said, 'Hold on, I'm not having this'. Not one bit.

"The fans were not too bad at Villa Park for the play-off final, but there were a few banging on the studio window calling me every name under the sun."

His season outside the top flight also gave him a fresh perspective on life outside the fast lane of English football.

"You soon get fed up with losing every week in the Premier League if your team isn't up to much.

"It soon gets disheartening if you're paying a lot of money to follow your team away from home and you're getting beat all the time.

"You see teams in the Premier League and half their fans are thinking, 'You know what, if we could guarantee bouncing straight back up, I'd take a season in the Championship.

"I'm certainly glad I did with Boro. It was a great season - there was an amazing feel-good factor.

"The fans were brilliant. After the first couple of months when I settled and started scoring goals I loved my time 'up there', as we say down South."

THE SPECIAL ONES
– FA Youth Cup Joy

Parnaby's Academic Success

It had been the dream of Newcastle United owner Sir John Hall to field a side of Geordies in a Premier League game.

But Middlesbrough owner Steve Gibson got there first when a team full of Smoggies took on Fulham at Craven Cottage.

That is the reason why Saturday, May 7, 2006, will surely go down as one of the greatest days in Boro's history.

And, for Dave Parnaby, that red-letter day will go down as the proudest in his distinguished career.

It was, of course, the day when 11 homegrown players represented Boro in a Premier League game.

Steve McClaren's team might have narrowly lost 1-0, but for Parnaby - and club owner Steve Gibson – it was more than just a game.

"The Fulham game is the one everyone remembers – and football in general remembers it," former academy manager Parnaby said.

"When we got news that it was going to happen, that Steve McClaren was going to rest all the first-team players because of the UEFA Cup final, Stephen Pears and myself drove down there.

"We got lost in London which was a nightmare. We arrived late, but it was worth the stress because the boys played ever so well and possibly should have won.

"In terms of the bigger picture it felt like a cause for celebration. I suppose every youth development organisation wants to achieve that. It's the ultimate dream for people like me.

"That's what you do. You spend hours and hours and hours of your time educating, pushing, probing, admonishing, congratulating as part of the everyday cycle. That's why Fulham meant so much."

Parnaby, the son of a miner, was brought up in the County Durham village of Kelloe where he dreamed of becoming a professional footballer.

He played alongside Bryan Robson's brothers Gary and Justin at Gateshead while teaching and then went into coaching.

At the same time, he completed his UEFA 'A' Licence and took on a role coaching with English Schools, but declined an offer to join the Football Association full-time before heading to Boro.

Parnaby was appointed as Boro's academy manager in 1998 and the production line of talent he oversaw – with more than 100 professional footballers emerging from Rockliffe - will be a constant reminder of the fact that Middlesbrough's gain was neighbours Sunderland and Newcastle's loss.

"Sunderland were the first club that came knocking and had a chat with me and then Newcastle.

"Sunderland couldn't offer me enough enticement to leave teaching and then I spoke to Kenny Dalglish when he was Newcastle manager.

"I was really taken by Kenny, really impressed, but he was sacked two weeks after I'd spoken to him so that was short-lived.

"Eventually, Steve Gibson and Keith Lamb – through Ron Bone who recommended me – asked me if I'd be interested in what at that time was the role of academy director.

"Steve was very clear about what his aims and objectives were because he has a great faith in the people and the area of Teesside.

"I talked it through with my wife, Jean, and we thought this was the best opportunity I will ever get to go into football on a full-time basis.

"Jean and I were in agreement because of Steve's values and what he wanted to achieve was what I firmly believed in, so there wasn't much persuasion to be done.

"It was about me believing in the product and theory behind it and most of all believing in Steve, that and knowing Ron helped because he was way ahead of the game in recruitment terms."

Parnaby left teaching, started a new job on September 1 1998 "and off we went".

"My brief was a lot simpler than it was for a lot of other academy managers, thanks to Steve.

"He made a statement as I joined the club about the academy, which brought clarity to its role, along the lines of:

'Giving the children of Teesside and surrounding areas an opportunity to become professional sportsmen.'

"That said it all. It was about local boys from the local area and giving them a good coaching programme; it was about finding good coaches and finding good recruiters and we had the best in the country in Ron.

"Our mission statement and core values of humility and honesty stood out like a sore thumb.

"It's all right putting things on paper, but you've got to live them and I do believe the one thing we did at the academy is that we lived our core values.

"The attitude was all based around Teesside kids, being humble, working very, very hard, making it a fun, enjoyable programme and doing our best to produce first team players."

Parnaby had a reputation for being a disciplinarian among his former charges, but he was clearly no dictator when it came to the academy.

"It wasn't so much as me creating rules – it was more like you go back to 'What do we stand for?'

"I always used to ask, 'What does class look like? Define class.' Class on a football field is somebody who makes a lovely cross-field pass.

"But class off the field is conducting yourself the right way. It's looking at role models – people like Gareth Southgate – and saying that's how I want to do it.

"As soon as you sign on the dotted line you're a Middlesbrough player and that entails personal responsibility.

"You are representing Steve Gibson, the club and everyone associated with it.

"If you're not prepared to do that then action has to be taken. Either you suffer the consequences or we make a decision on what those consequences are.

"I didn't think it was about rules - it's standards of behaviour, core values, the difference between right and wrong.

"Everything goes back to our core values of humility, respect and honesty so, for instance, we emphasised good manners.

"It's about respecting referees. If someone swore on the pitch in our early days we used to withdraw them and put them on the sidelines.

"That set the standard. One of the nicest things that anyone said to me is, 'Dave, it's nice being here - it's such a lovely environment.'

"That comes from humility, respect, honesty and good manners – conducting yourself every minute of every day in the right way.

"It sounds simple, but it's not easy because kids are kids and you've got to understand that. All journeys, all paths are different."

Those talented enough to win places in the academy were given responsibility to shape their own destinies.

"We equip young people with the knowledge of what it takes to be a professional footballer.

"We always used to ask, 'What is being professional about?' The answer is that it's doing the right thing, at the right time, all the time.

"That starts with getting out of bed in the morning and making the right decisions.

'What am I going to have for breakfast?'

'What time am I going to set off to get into work to make sure I'm there on time and that I won't let anyone down?'

"We equip them with enough knowledge to make good, informed decisions. Unfortunately, some of them don't make the right decisions.

"It sounds all idyllic and everything, but it wasn't perfect. It was a challenge. It was hard work.

"Constant reminders, putting people back on track and making the right decisions is where you hope they will go in terms of lifestyle.

"And lifestyle is the key. Those who make the right decisions will thrive, but some make the wrong choices and wrong decisions in their lives.

"But we know we have done everything in our power to provide them with the knowledge about what the right decision looks like."

Under Parnaby, the academy has become an important part of the club's business model.

"We're up to near the £70-million mark in terms of funds coming back into the club through the sale of players.

"That in itself is not the sole reason, but one of the reasons we exist. The academy is not an entity in itself; it's a support mechanism – to support the club and the first team managers, which comes down to good recruitment, good players and opportunity, which came in many forms.

"Sometimes opportunities were forced by the players such as Lee Cattermole and James Morrison who leapfrogged the reserves and just went from juniors to first team.

"Stewie Downing had to go on loan to Sunderland, who were then in the Championship, and they unveiled his true potential and then Steve McClaren brought him back and he shone.

"And sometimes players get the opportunity when there is no one else. That is a fact of football - the manager had no choice but to put him in.

"There was also the League Cup and FA Cup that always opened doors and then the UEFA Cup.

"It's either down to good luck or good fortune, but we had a good programme. It was sink-or-swim, but I don't think any of them sank. Everybody that was given that opportunity had a good go at swimming."

Parnaby has a lot to shout about, but insists that the academy's success has been a team effort.

"The whole job was all-encompassing, but the moments of self-satisfaction, of knowing you've done a good job, is obviously the outcome – when you produce a first-team player.

"But that's not down to me. I've never produced a template, it's a team effort, so we – and I always use the word 'we' – always took our greatest pleasure from someone working out on the pitch in a first-team environment.

"Within all that there are the little cameos of the FA Youth Cup win in 2004, finishing runner-up the year before, semi-finals, reaching national finals with the Under-18s.

It really peaks when individual and team success come along, but then again it takes some beating when you are seeing a boy coming along from nines up to 16s and then being offered a scholarship.

"Key to that were Mum and Dad having full trust in the organisation and the set-up. I don't think we ever lost a player to another club in the 20 years I was there. That speak volumes for the staff and environment we created."

There is also the downside of having to tell young people their football dreams are over.

"Probably the hardest bit of the job is seeing boys who are talented, but having to face them and tell them the journey has come to an end.

"I always told parents, 'You'll think I'm wonderful, but the day will come when your son is nine years old or twenty-two years old and someday you'll be sat in my office saying, 'Bye, bye.'

"You'll have moved on to a new club and we've sold you for x-million pounds or we just think we have maximised your potential and it's time for you to move on.

"We always asked for support from parents and in nine cases out of ten we did get that support, but those are challenging situations.

"Is there a right way to do it? I don't know. But I thought we got better and had more empathy and sympathy, and support networks were put in place for those occasions."

Parnaby saw dozens of academy players go on to make the grade as professional footballers, including his own son, Stuart, who played 140 times across two spells for Boro.

An attacking right-back, he had the distinction of scoring in a 3-0 win at Sunderland and netting the winner in a topsy-turvy 4-3 win over Bolton at the Riverside.

"He did give us great pride as a family and I'm very proud of his career and what he achieved, but I would never say he was my favourite player.

"For that you need to look at who epitomises what you stand for and that would have to be Jason Kennedy who went on to play for Darlington, Rochdale and Carlisle.

"Jason was two-footed, he could hit the ball - he just didn't have any explosive speed which stopped him reaching the top of the game.

"But in terms of epitomising what you are about - working hard, enjoying what you do, being a really good lad as well, Jason comes to mind.

"And there's Nathan Mulligan, and wow, what a great story that is. To come through the challenges Nathan faced (following a leukaemia diagnosis) with mam and dad was inspiring. We're just so pleased he's come through the other end.

"Then there are the high-level performers - the Morrisons, the Cattermoles and, dare I say it, the Johnsons. There was also Chris Brunt who moved on, but he really appreciated what Middlesbrough had done for him."

Parnaby stepped down from his role as academy boss in March 2017 and handed over the academy reins to former Boro player Craig Liddle.

"When you go into football you have to be prepared for a 24/7 existence. If you don't give that and don't have a back-up like I had with my family and Jean, then I don't think you'll get the rewards you are seeking.

"I had 20 years of 24/7 – first one in, last one out. If you look at the really great leaders, that's what they do. Sir Alex Ferguson was always in at 6.30am and then was there through till nine o'clock at night.

"Obsessiveness has something to do with it, but at some point you've got to think it's payback time. For me the time arrived to give Jean something back and my sons and grandchildren, which is a wonderful experience.

"Also, I thought the academy needed something fresh and new direction and a new voice. Our record over the years has been a good one. And let's hope it continues in the new era. I'm sure Craig will be a great success."

• Boro owner Steve Gibson paid a glowing tribute to Parnaby when he stepped down from his role at the age of 61: "Dave has shown incredible commitment, dedication and hard work. It's not without personal sacrifice. He treats the lads like his own children. He is going to be very, very difficult to replace."

Bone's Golden Boys

It was a now-or-never scenario for ace talent-spotter Ron Bone.

The man who shepherded scores of up-and-coming young players to Boro had his eye on one of English football's most coveted trophies – the FA Youth Cup.

A fine crop of players came through the ranks in the 1980s under Bruce Rioch, but, two decades later, Bone was more bullish than ever.

And he was certain the stage was set for the club to win the FA Youth Cup for the first time.

What gave him so much optimism was the presence of so many young Teessiders following Stewart Downing on the path from academy to first-team football.

"It was many years ago, but I still remember chatting to Stan Nixon, who was the assistant academy director, about that crop of players," Bone said.

"It was over a cup of tea and I said to him, 'If we don't win the FA Youth Cup with one of these two age groups, then we'll never win it.' We had not one but two special age groups coming through the system."

Ross Turnbull, Andrew Davies and Chris Brunt would feature in a team that lost the 2003 final to Manchester United before Aston Villa were crushed on aggregate in the following year's final.

The Villa side boasted Gary Cahill, Gabby Agbonlahor and Craig Gardner, but they were no match for Boro. In a squad coached by former Boro star Mark Proctor, under the auspices of academy manager Dave Parnaby, there was an embarrassment of riches.

"I thought they were a really special bunch of lads on and off the field, who were highly motivated," Bone said.

"We got to the final in 2003 against Manchester United and we lost, but we had seven players who were eligible to play the following season.

"I really fancied our chances that year and going to Villa, who were the favourites, and beating them 3-0 at Villa Park was an unbelievable feeling.

"And that night when we finished the job off in front of 20,000 fans at the Riverside was just magic."

Captained by Tony McMahon, the squad included: David Knight, Matthew Bates, David Wheater, Peter Masters, Seb Hines, Andrew Taylor, Gary Liddle, Anthony Peacock, James Morrison, Jason Kennedy, Tom Craddock, Chris Pennock, Lee Cattermole, Josh Walker and Danny Reed.

"Danny was probably the most talented of the lot. He played for England against Brazil and was voted the most skilful player on the pitch.

"He was a terrific talent, but he had cartilage problems and had to quit when he was a teenager which was a real shame."

The prolific striker, Danny Graham also gets an honourable mention.

"Danny was building conservatories when I spotted him playing for Chester-le-Street Town juniors in the Youth Cup against Hartlepool.

"We got him and he became a goal machine with 49 goals in season, but was restricted to league games because of the date his birthday fell on."

Bone had harboured his own dreams of making it as a professional footballer as a youngster when he was on the books at Sunderland, "which didn't last long," before a trial period at Northampton.

But then illness intervened. Bone was "hit for six" by rheumatic fever and didn't play football for five years.

He would go on to scout for Newcastle and ran the successful Hilda Park juniors side, where the sons of Boro managers, Bruce Rioch and Colin Todd, and Nottingham Forest legend Ian Bowyer, were on the books.

Bone would become one of the most significant Boro signings of the 1980s, thanks to Rioch.

"They were on my back at the time and in June 1987, Bruce asked me for lunch. I knew what he was going to say and he persuaded me join Middlesbrough.

"It was part time until I got a call in March or April 1990 from Colin Todd saying that Bruce had gone, he was the new manager and would I come in as youth development officer and take over the youth set-up?

"I had loads of players who went on to good things – Graham Kavanagh, Alan Moore and Ben Roberts and then there was Mark Summerbell who was my favourite one.

"That's because he was so small. I had him at Hilda Park and when he was 16 he was tiny. I wasn't going to give him a YTS (Youth Training Scheme) or apprenticeship and I thought we'll wait till we see if he grows.

"But I remember John Pickering saying, 'Where is he going to develop best - with us or at school?' And I said, 'Well obviously with us,' and John said, 'Well it's a no-brainer, we take him.'

"He made his debut at the age of 19 when I was away in France and I'd heard he'd played alongside Juninho in a 1-1 draw at Spurs and I really was absolutely delighted.

"They used to put him in against the Roy Keanes of this world because he was a tough little so-and-so, but a good footballer, too."

Bone changed roles when Boro's centre of excellence became an academy in 1998 and he recommended Parnaby for the manager's job

"You needed to be a full UEFA A-Licensed coach and I was made head of recruitment, which was my forte in the first place.

"It was funny recommending someone to be your boss, but Dave and me had a fantastic relationship.

"Dave was great with the coaching and the discipline because he was an ex-school teacher. He did what he was good at and I did what I was good at and it proved to be a good mixture."

It is estimated that Bone's eye for talent has been worth £100 million to Boro.

"You're looking for kids with technical ability, intelligence and preferably speed, but sometimes speed of thought counteracts speed of legs, as it were.

"And there is also the ability to compete – mental toughness is a huge factor and a lack of it is one of the reasons why so many people fail."

Every player who has joined Boro's academy will have their own tale to tell of how they came to join the club, but for Bone, people like Cattermole, Morrison, Davies and Downing stand out.

"I remember being in Stockton one morning and I was told there was this little kid who just loved a tackle and I thought for one so young that's unusual and it turned out to be Lee Cattermole.

"I spent four years trying to persuade him to come into the academy and then, out of the blue, I got a phone call from his dad (Barry).

"It went along the lines of, 'Ron, I think it's about time our Lee comes in now because I'm sick to death of seeing people kick lumps off him.'

"It made me smile. I thought I can't believe that's the case, but we'll gladly take him.

"I still don't know why he was so resistant to Lee coming into the fold, but he thought it was too early and he just wanted him to play local football and you've got to respect their wishes."

It was the same with Downing and the waiting game Boro had to play with the winger.

"In fairness, Stewart Downing senior always said, 'Look, Ron, don't worry – Stewart will sign for Middlesbrough when he is 14,' and he did.

"He went to Man United, Chelsea and Newcastle, but his dad said ultimately he won't be going anywhere apart from Middlesbrough and he was true to his word.

"I remember when Stewart signed for us, we went to the Northern Ireland Milk Cup and he'd broken his arm.

"So he couldn't play, but he asked if he could come with us and he collected the balls and did all he could to help.

"He was absolutely brilliant, a really good kid. He's a super personality and I've got so much respect and time for him."

While Boro were made to sweat on Downing, some players are more forthcoming – like McMahon.

"I remember getting a letter from Tony's mum and it's still the only time we've signed someone following a letter.

"Tony had this self-belief that has carried him a long way. He wasn't the most talented of individuals, but he had this extraordinary belief in himself – he thought he was the best player in the world.

"He made his debut against Man United which meant he'd be coming face-to-face with his childhood hero Ryan Giggs and he couldn't wait to take him on.

"That's not always the case. I remember Keith O'Halloran was so nervous he couldn't sleep the night before he made his debut against Derby and he had an absolute nightmare. Tony couldn't wait and that summed up his mentality."

According to Bone, the same self-confidence applies to centre-back Ben Gibson.

"Ben was of a similar ilk. I remember spotting him in a tournament in Trimdon.

"He wasn't the most talented of players. We had a really good team that won the Nike Cup and he wasn't the best player in that group.

"But he had this real mentality of wanting to be the leader and the talker. When he went to Tranmere as a kid, their manager Ronnie Moore couldn't believe how he became the leader in the dressing room among all these old pros."

Sometimes finding the right player can be about being in the right place at the right time, as was the case with Davies.

"One day I was going to a game, which was called off and so I went to watch Stockton Schools Under-13s play and that was where I spotted Andrew Davies.

"Whenever he sees me he'll say, 'You, you – I owe everything to you'. I cringe in embarrassment, which is why I think he does it. He's a very funny lad."

And then there are recommendations from parents.

"James Morrison was 10 or 11 years old when we got a tip-off from someone whose son played for Darlington All-Stars and was in the centre of excellence.

"He came in one day and said we've got this boy in our club called James Morrison who you want to go and have a look at because he's something special.

"So I said to Keith Noble who was working with me, go and have a look at him on Sunday and Keith said, 'Wow, we've got to get him.'"

Morrison served Boro with distinction so Bone was saddened when he left for West Bromwich Albion.

"I'd travelled up to Carlisle with the first team and we were having a pre-match meal in Alston when Gareth pulled me to one side. 'Ron,' he said, 'would you sell James Morrison?' And I said, 'No, no way'.

"There was a feeling that he used to get really nervous before games, but I thought everyone does and anyway, he's only a boy, but a few days later he'd gone which I felt really upset about."

Morrison only left reluctantly, but most players are left with no choice when they are told they're being let go.

"It is always a difficult job when you are releasing kids, but I always say, 'Remember you came in as a good player and you go out as a better player and the fact you are a good player is the reason you were invited in here, so don't think you've become a bad player.'"

In 2015, Bone was honoured by the Football Association with a special award for Outstanding Contribution to Talent Identification and Recruitment.

But all good things eventually have to come to an end and that was the case for Bone who retired in May 2017

"It was terrible having to retire. It was a year ago, but I'm just starting to come to terms with it now. Middlesbrough Football Club was my life for 30 years and will always be part of my life.

"I miss the camaraderie and banter with the coaches and seeing people develop from little kids to England players and first-teamers. It's a feeling you can't beat."

No Gamble For Proctor With Young Stars

I count myself privileged to have been coaching at Boro in a golden period for the club and individual players, writes Mark Proctor.

I was fortunate to have been involved in the academy when the golden crop, as they were always known from the ages of eight or nine, came through the ranks.

They were identified early on as a special group of players in terms of numbers and quality.

They were special because they were a very talented group, but also talented in numerous positions.

They had seven or eight outstanding players and they had a belief and togetherness that was special. They knew they could be a force.

I was the head coach under academy director Dave Parnaby and the FA Youth Cup was the yardstick for the Under-18s.

They lost to Manchester United, in which Kieran Richardson starred, in the 2003 final and then we faced Aston Villa in the final the following season.

They fancied themselves and we beat a very strong Villa side – featuring Gary Cahill, Stefan Moore and Gabriel Agbonlahor.

The second leg was played out in front of 30,000 at the Riverside, so it was a great experience.

The scenes afterwards were great; we were thrown in the bath. There was such a buzz, it was like winning the World Cup.

I'm grateful to (head of recruitment) Ron Bone who was instrumental in bringing me in.

I wasn't sure what I was going to do once my playing days came to an end. So to get a call and start working at the academy was great – it's really exciting to stay in a profession you love.

One of the reasons we were so successful is because there was stability about the place. I was there for ten years, Ron and Dave 20-plus and there were no massive changes. Continuity was the message and the ethos; it was in our DNA.

There was a definitive message we put across and we were all on the same page because of longevity.

I bumped into one of the lads, James Morrison, at Stuart Parnaby's wedding. I was introduced to his other half as mentor after not seeing each other for four or five years which was such a nice show of appreciation.

McMahon Sets Tone

As debuts go, Tony McMahon's first senior assignment for Boro could not have been much tougher.

It might not have been Mission: Impossible but it was not far from it as he faced future FIFA World Footballer of the Year Cristiano Ronaldo.

And when the then Manchester United winger was not heading his way,

McMahon had Old Trafford legend Ryan Giggs to contend with before an expectant audience at the Theatre of Dreams.

But the rookie 18-year-old right-back coped so well that he was named man-of-the-match and Steve McClaren's Boro earned a creditable 1-1 draw in October 2004.

"I've still got the big bottle of man-of-the-match champagne with a Man U badge on - it's never been touched and probably never will be," McMahon said.

"The manager was waiting at the dressing room door with Gary Neville's shirt because he'd asked him to tell me I'd done really well, which showed I hadn't done too badly against two of the best players the Premier League has seen.

"It was on the bus afterwards that our skipper, Gareth Southgate, said, 'Here, the champagne's for you.' That was typical of Gareth; pure class.

"I could not speak highly enough of him, he was a massive help to us young lads, so it was nice that he did the honours and gave it to me."

It was some start to his senior career for McMahon who had skippered Dave Parnaby's Under-18 side to FA Youth Cup glory in 2004 and then entered the school of hard knocks.

"We used to kick the first team players as lads trying to get a game.

"Steve told us not to, but Gareth just said keep doing it because that's how you'll get a game.

"A few of us from the Youth Cup side stepped up to the first team for training, but then Steve McClaren pulled aside me and my best mate, James Morrison, and told us we were starting at Old Trafford.

"That just seems like yesterday. I remember him saying, 'Go out and enjoy

it, you've played together for years so just go enjoy yourselves,' which we did and James set up Stewie Downing's equaliser."

The former Staindrop Comprehensive pupil says he "owes everything" to his parents for helping launch his career and you can see why.

"My mum and dad, Tracey and Tony, wrote to (Boro chief scout) Ron Bone saying that people kept telling them I was a good player so he should check me out.

"But it turned out Ron was already aware of me and he ended up inviting me for a six-week trial and that worked out really well.

"I kept bumping into Ron when I watched my nephew play and he says I'm still the only one that came through from a letter and he got hundreds every week."

McMahon and his peers excelled as they came through the ranks and they finished FA Youth Cup runners-up to United in 2003 before winning the coveted trophy by beating Aston Villa.

"After reaching the final as a young team we knew right from the word 'go' that we would go on and win it.

"We really kicked on and when Dave Parnaby and Mark Proctor asked me to be captain it was a great personal honour.

"We were just a big group of mates who wanted to do well for each other and that's why we were so successful.

"It was great being at the club when we won the Carling Cup and FA Youth Cup. The European games were brilliant as well. The one that stands out is Lazio at home. It was extraordinary.

"One thing that always gives me a lot of pride is a photo up on the walls at the Rockliffe training ground that the club had taken of me and Gareth with the Carling Cup and Youth Cup.

"It just shows what a special year 2004 was for everyone at the club and all the fans."

McMahon, who was voted Teesdale's Junior Sports Personality of the Year when he signed his first full-time Boro contract in 2002, would find himself singled out for praise by Match of the Day pundit Alan Hansen as his career got off to a flying start.

"I was lying in bed one Saturday night and my mum and dad dashed up the stairs telling me he'd been raving about me. It didn't sink in because I was just a normal lad growing up in Evenwood doing a job I loved.

"I enjoyed every minute of my time at Boro and it's still the first result I look for. I actually thought that I'd stay there for the rest of my career, but it didn't work out like that.

"It could have been different, but I broke my leg twice. It takes some getting over, but over the last few years I've been injury-free."

McMahon, who still keeps in touch with the likes of Morrison, Lee Cattermole, Andrew Taylor and Andrew Davies, is now living in Bishop Auckland with his wife Lynsey and their two young children.

"It's as if my debut and the FA Youth Cup win happened just two minutes ago.

"It was funny because Ronaldo was on the telly and my son, Luca, said, 'Ah, Dad used to kick him!' He's football-daft. With a bit of luck, I'll write Ron Bone a letter about him when he's a bit older."

Taylor-made For Success

Andrew Taylor has revealed he "fell out of love with football at the club I love," during Gordon Strachan's reign as Boro manager.

In a candid interview, the full-back admitted to becoming disillusioned with the game while working under the Scot.

"My move to Cardiff stemmed from my time under Gordon Strachan," said Taylor.

"I did not enjoy working under him. I lost my love for the club and for football. It was one of the real low points of my career.

"I had to take a big pay-cut to go out on loan to Watford and a lot of people are not aware of that, but it just showed how badly I wanted out.

"I could have sat on my wages for the season and not played. But I needed to play. I wasn't enjoying myself at the club I loved. I hated working under him and had to get out.

"That's what I did and I had such a good time down at Watford with Malky Mackay that he made me love football again."

Taylor's career was certainly put back on track while on loan at Watford and even though he returned to Boro after Strachan quit, he eventually decided to follow Mackay to Cardiff.

"I came back to Boro and I have to say, Tony Mowbray was fantastic - he's a great man and manager and all the staff with him were really good.

"I had a really good back end of the season with Middlesbrough, but just felt that for me personally it was time to move on and face a fresh challenge.

"But it was hard for me to leave. It was a tough decision. I'd been close to signing a new contract at Middlesbrough because what Tony Mowbray was doing there really changed my perspective on things.

"I was enjoying life at Boro again. I was enjoying the way he played, but when it came down to it I just felt it was time for me to move on and hopefully kick on again."

Now Taylor is back to his old self again playing with a smile on his face like he has done ever since being spotted while turning out for Cleveland Juniors at the age of nine.

The left-footed tyro caught the attention of scouts Keith Noble and Ron Bone and Boro trials provided the platform for him and his teammates to make history with their FA Youth Cup success in 2004.

"The youth days are ones I'm still very fond of - we had a very good team and all the lads were very good mates.

"We had such a hunger to succeed and a competitive edge to always fight for each other.

"We never used to rest on our laurels and think we've made it already. We were always striving to be better.

"If one of us got into the first team, yes you were pleased for them, but it would spur you on to join them as well.

"The FA Youth Cup final win was one of the highlights of my career and will stay with me forever. We had a tight bond that you could not get anywhere else.

"We had been together for years, we were hungry and so to win the FA Youth Cup was unbelievable."

Taylor – a left-sided midfielder in that side - puts the success down to academy manager Dave Parnaby and his coaching staff.

"It's no surprise to me that so many of the lads are doing so well in their careers.

"A lot of the credit should go to the academy set-up. It's not just Dave Parnaby, even though he is brilliant in terms of taking players to the next level, but there is top-quality coaching throughout Rockliffe Park.

"There has been such an incredible amount of people coming off the conveyor belt. It's fantastic for Boro.

"If they can continue doing it then it will keep the club stable for many years to come because players coming through the ranks mean you don't have to go out and buy.

"If they're good enough they can play in the first team and then you can sell them for a big profit like they did with Stewart Downing and that money can be re-invested into the youth system and it keeps everything ticking over."

By his own admission, Taylor had a "baptism of fire" in his Premier League debut in the 7-0 defeat at Arsenal, but held his nerve and went on to become a first-team regular under Gareth Southgate.

"The FA Youth Cup final was great, but there are other landmarks that still mean a lot like my first-team debut, playing in the FA Cup and big UEFA Cup games."

Taylor also played in the dramatic European ties against Basel and Steaua Bucharest at the Riverside.

"I have a lot of good memories as well as a few bad ones - obviously the main bad one was being relegated.

"You don't want to be relegated at any level and to do it at the club where you grew up in an area that you have so much respect for means it was definitely the lowest point of my career.

"I've had a lot of positives in my career, but you have ups and downs and losses of form and injuries, but along the way I have been involved in some massive games and I've played with world-class players. That will stand me in good stead for the rest of my career."

• *Andrew Taylor suffered Wembley heartbreak when Cardiff lost the Carling Cup final to Liverpool on penalties and the occasion brought memories of his Boro days flooding back.*

"I remember the build-up and atmosphere around the area when Boro got to the Carling Cup final and it replicated that in the way our fans got so excited.

"I went to the Millennium Stadium with the rest of the lads from the academy and I remember being in the crowd watching.

"It got me wondering what it must be like to play in a major final and luckily for me I have had the chance to do it.

"For the Cardiff lads, the full Wembley weekend was an absolute rollercoaster of emotions with all the nerves and excitement.

"The amount it took out of us was quite draining, but it was an experience I'll cherish. It's just a shame we could not win it for ourselves and the fans.

"Everyone thought Liverpool just needed to turn up to beat us, but we did ourselves proud and made the final quite a spectacle.

"It was the first time I'd played against Stewart Downing since he left Boro. Although I was gutted to lose I was pleased for him that he played well and got the man-of-the-match award."

Bates Toeing The Line

Matthew Bates relishes the memories of learning the defensive ropes under Gareth Southgate and Ugo Ehiogu

The future Boro skipper enjoyed football master classes at Rockliffe Park after being fast-tracked towards the first team by academy manager Dave Parnaby.

It was a reflection of the promise the centre-half showed on joining Boro after leaving Manchester United's Centre of Excellence as a schoolboy.

"It was a fairly slow start, but when it got to Under-16s, Dave Parnaby asked me to play with the Under-18s, so I jumped up two years," Bates said.

"I went full-time when I left school and there was steady progress which was thanks to Dave.

"He was very good at what he wanted to get from us – he always kept people's feet on the ground but he was fair with every one.

"I ended up training with the first-team when I was a first-year scholar and then went on loan to Darlington and was then invited into the first team scene."

That was when his learning curve suddenly steepened.

"It helped being alongside the first team because in those days Boro had top players like Ugo Ehiogu - God bless him - and Gareth Southgate.

"They were great to us because they were absolutely perfect role models on and off the field for defenders like me and we were lucky because they took young players under their wing a little.

"They were really good players, but the way they looked after themselves and conducted themselves around the club really had a big impact on us lads.

"I'd attend the first-team meetings and the defensive meetings that were led by Steve Harrison, who was brilliant.

"We'd go through clips with the back four – we really analysed everything that was important. There was amazing attention to detail.

"It was amazing to be learning so much every day and I was lucky to be in that environment. I'm still very grateful for everything because it massively helped me."

Bates was a prominent member of the Under-18 teams that finished runners-up in the FA Youth Cup in 2003 before winning the competition the following year.

"The first time around we were battered by Manchester United when I was still at school.

"It was a step too far on the big occasion – I was a bit in awe playing at Old Trafford so it was doubly hard because they were a good side.

"But it set us up for the following season where we trounced it - we never looked like getting beat in any round before saving our best till last and beating Aston Villa in the final."

Bates, who was brought up in Eaglescliffe, moved through the ranks and made his debut as a stoppage-time substitute in a 3-2 win over Manchester City in December 2004.

"We had a great crop of players which was down to superb scouts, but we were successful because of the way the coaches developed us as players and people.

"There probably haven't been any better academy coaches in Britain than Dave Parnaby and he had some brilliant staff with him like Mark Proctor.

"But Steve McClaren was really important in all this because he really believed in youth.

"He put his money where his mouth was for the long-term future of the club.

He got us involved and that filtered down to the Youth Cup team because we saw a path to the first team."

Bates played more than 100 times for Boro despite a series of serious injuries – but his career could have been very different.

"As a kid, I was fairly high up the pecking order at Man United, I used to go down there in the school holidays and train with what they called their elite bunch.

"But I developed in-growing toenails on both my big toes, and I didn't really get it diagnosed because all I wanted to do was carry on playing.

"It affected me and for whatever reason Man U called me in one day and said we don't feel your gait – or in other words the way I ran - is correct and you won't make it as a footballer (a similar accusation was leveled at Jordan Henderson by ex-United boss Sir Alex Ferguson).

"That was that and I went to Boro at the age of about 14 and got it all sorted and it's why I'm stood here now with no big toe nails."

The Catt's Whiskers

Lee Cattermole can sum up his time in a Boro first-team shirt with one word - "madness".

The Boro academy product was 17 years old when he made his full first-team debut against Newcastle.

It was a baptism of fire at a jam-packed St James' Park on New Year's Day in 2006 when the combative midfielder produced a man-of-the-match display.

"When we needed people to stand up and be counted it took a 17-year-old kid to bring everyone together," said manager Steve McClaren.

The full-blooded Tyne-Tees derby, which ended in a 2-2 draw, propelled him into the thick of the action and a rollercoaster of a journey.

He broke down in tears as everything proved to be a bit too much for him as Boro were hammered 4-0 by Aston Villa at the Riverside.

Cattermole – and McClaren - recovered to play a key role in Boro's successful fight against relegation that saw his team beat Chelsea 3-0 the following week.

He netted the winner in a 1-0 victory at Manchester City and became Boro's youngest-ever captain at the age of 18 years and 47 days in the famous 1–0 defeat at Fulham in May 2006.

It was a reward for helping Boro reach the FA Cup semi-finals and pitting his wits against Serie A's finest in Daniele De Rossi for the mighty Roma.

And just a few days after the Fulham game, he played in the UEFA Cup final against Sevilla.

"It was all a bit mad and it was certainly madness for a couple of years for me, but they were great times," said Cattermole.

"I was so young when I was at Boro and I crammed loads in, but in all honesty I was too young to really realise what was happening.

"Looking back now I wish I had taken more of it in, such as the away game against Roma and the UEFA Cup final."

They say there is no room for sentiment in football, but Cattermole still cares deeply about the club he joined as a schoolboy despite spending so long up the A19 at Sunderland.

"I have unbelievable memories and I would hate to say that one stands out because in my first season so much happened within the space of a few months.

"If I could spread that out over my career I would be delighted. I suppose the highlight would have to be my debut up at St James' Park, which was everything I hoped it would be, even though we should have won.

"I thought I was going to get a game two weeks prior to that midweek at Bolton when I was expecting to play because I had been training really well and there were a few injuries at the time.

"I got a knock on the door at about 5pm and I thought it would be the manager telling me I was going to be playing and to get my head right.

"But it turned out it was someone saying the game had been called off and we were leaving for home, so I was really disappointed which made the Newcastle game even more special. It was well worth waiting for."

It was also a special evening for dad Barry, who played alongside Graeme Souness as a winger for Boro reserves before becoming a regular at Billingham Synthonia.

Cattermole, who left Boro for Wigan in a £3.5-million deal in July 2008, is still in contact with his former colleagues and reckons they all owe a huge debt to academy manager Dave Parnaby.

"I stay in touch with all the lads I played with at Boro, but they are all playing for different clubs now which is a bit of a shame really, but that's football.

"We all tried to make the most of our education at Boro and a massive part of that is down to Dave.

"The set-up he developed there and the people around him was class and to have so many players that he nurtured playing in the Premier League is unbelievable.

"It's a shame we couldn't still all have Boro shirts on, but things move on in football and people move on for different reasons."

Cattermole's will to win came to the fore at Boro's academy.

"I'd get in trouble when I was younger," he told reporters. "There was a rule for the under-13s at Middlesbrough that you were never allowed to swear. If you did, the manager had to take you off as punishment.

"But I couldn't stop myself. I'd just get frustrated, I guess. Dave would be standing on the touchline shouting, 'Last time, Lee. One more time and you're off.' I'd be like, 'Whatever!' I just couldn't bear it if we weren't winning."

Cattermole would leave after falling out of favour once Gareth Southgate succeeded Steve McClaren as manager.

"Once McClaren had gone it was like I'd hit a standstill," Cattermole told The Guardian. "The new gaffer took over and suddenly I was in and out of the team.

"But I haven't got a bad word to say about him. He was the best player I've ever played with, a great leader and a model professional and he sent me a nice letter when I left. But he preferred other players to me, which can happen, and I wanted to play more regularly."

Cattermole followed Steve Bruce by swapping Wigan for Sunderland and then from strength to strength under new Black Cats boss Martin O'Neill.

There was even talk of full England recognition for the former Under-21 international – once compared to Liverpool hero Steven Gerrard - which never materialised.

"I hope it is not too far away, but all I have to do is keep playing well for Sunderland and we will see what happens," he said during the O'Neill rein which represented a false dawn for the Wearsiders.

"People say that I have looked better under him and I'm not sure whether that is down to just having a new voice or wanting to prove myself to a new manager.

"Whatever it is, it has worked because I feel as though my form has been brilliant since he took over. I felt that I have set my standards so high with him and I have to maintain them."

Had it not been for injury problems, Cattermole would surely have England caps to his name as he has excelled for Sunderland while fit.

Indeed, he was named North East Player of the Year by members of the Football Writers' Association in 2014 while with Sunderland.

His loyalties were tested to the limit when Sunderland were paired with Boro in the FA Cup at the Stadium of Light and Cattermole had to watch from the sidelines.

"It was awful having to sit and watch if I'm being honest. I found it really difficult and I would have rather not watched it because it was so hard sitting there.

"In football you try to keep looking to improve and look to go forward and put things behind you, but Middlesbrough is always a club I have cared about and the club will always have an important place in my family and in my heart."

Morrison's Bitter-Sweet Boro Journey

He played in the UEFA Cup final against Sevilla, but the game that will always stand out for James Morrison will be that end-of-season match at Fulham.

It was, of course, the day that Morrison and his Boro colleagues headed to Craven Cottage in May 2006 and helped create a niche in club history.

He impressed out on the right wing that day in London as Boro ended the game with a team comprised entirely of homegrown players.

"We lost 1-0, which was a shame, but that still has to be one of the most special days of my career," Morrison said.

"That just said it all about what a great club Boro is because young players were developed properly at the Academy and given their chance by the first-team manager.

"It was a very proud day for me, the club, for all the players, their families and the whole area and it's something that might never happen again in the Premier League."

Morrison, who is now plying his trade with West Bromwich Albion, has had to deal with his own fair share of ups and downs since making his Boro debut in January 2004.

He had helped Boro win the FA Youth Cup for the first time before flirting with relegation under McClaren.

And then he came roaring back to gain a place in the UEFA Cup final which, of course, ended in disappointment just days after the Fulham game.

"You've got to deal with setbacks in your career and that's what I've always been determined to do.

"That's a philosophy that comes from my family, but also from the Boro academy manager Dave Parnaby.

"I'm sure everyone who came through the ranks with Boro will say the same. He was the perfect mentor."

The former Hummersknott School pupil, who lived in Darlington, was brought to chief scout Ron Bone's attention while playing for 21st All Stars in the Teesside League and was on the club's books from the age of nine alongside the likes of Andrew Taylor and David Wheater.

He was one of the stars of Parnaby's Under-18 side that won the FA Youth Cup in 2004 and he netted in the two-legged final against Aston Villa.

"Right through from when we were all together at nine years old, Dave equipped us with what we needed on and off the field to do well.

"So it was nice to have something to show for our efforts in the end and leave a bit of a legacy."

Morrison has been around the block many times but insists "the spirit and camaraderie" among the academy players "was the best I've been involved with".

"Dave is an incredible coach and incredible person. A lot of us were ready for the Premier League because of Dave and his coaches, Mark Proctor and Stephen Pears.

"But it was Dave who got the best out of us. He was a father-figure to all of us, even when we moved up to the first team. He was always there to chat.

"He always drummed into us the need to give everything you had on the pitch and off it he always emphasised the importance of being respectful.

"He was all about working hard and doing your very best for yourself and your team.

"That's what is instilled into you at Middlesbrough as a young player and it is something that has to come from within as well otherwise you'll get nowhere fast. That's why we made a bit of history at Fulham."

It helped that Morrison had a family who were right behind him as well with dad, Charlie, having been an apprentice with Chelsea before playing for local clubs.

"We've a very sporting family and they all put in a lot of hard work to help me get along.

"People on the outside looking in often don't realise what it means to become a footballer - it's a team effort.

"If you have a really solid base - as I did with my family who were supportive but not too pushy with me - then you are on your way.

"They'd take me to training twice a week which doesn't seem like a big deal now, but it involved a lot of personal sacrifice for my family, so I'll always owe them.

"No one's perfect, though. I still remember the odd occasion when my dad did pipe up on the sidelines. I'd go ballistic and tell him to shut up. Parents should let kids and coaches get on with the game."

Morrison, who went on to become an established Scotland international after leaving Boro, certainly did get on with the game.

"I was lucky in that there were many highlights for me at Boro.

"It started with the FA Youth Cup teams, getting to two finals and losing one before winning the other.

"Then there was me making my debut (a 2-0 FA Cup win over Notts County) and then playing in Europe and scoring on my European debut (a 1-1 draw at Banik Ostrava) and then getting to the UEFA Cup final.

"We also had an FA Cup semi-final and we finished seventh in the Premier League which was good going. But at the time you don't fully understand the magnitude of what you've achieved.

"I remember a fan running onto the pitch and throwing his season ticket at Steve McClaren when we lost 4-0 at home to Villa.

"People say it's a funny old game and that incident with the fan shows it is because you've got to look at Boro now fighting to get back out of the Championship."

Boro can take inspiration from Morrison because he has come fighting back after leaving the Riverside for West Brom during Gareth Southgate's reign in a £2.2-million deal.

"I was a bit gutted to leave Boro with it being my local club and I felt it could have gone differently considering I was only 20.

"I could have been sent out on loan, but I dropped down a league with West Brom to link up with Tony Mowbray who was great with me. I really kicked on and we've had some great times at the Hawthorns."

There will, though, clearly always be a place in Morrison's heart for Boro and his former teammates.

"I still look for the results and still feel a real warmth towards the club and I'm proud to have played for Boro.

"I've got some great friends from my days at Boro like Tony McMahon and Andrew Taylor who I'm still in touch with and we still go on holidays together.

"Plus, there's Ross Turnbull, Stuart Parnaby and Lee Cattermole and Andrew Davies.

"We're all close friends and even the older players like Chris Riggott and Ugo Ehiogu I regarded as friends.

"There were real good people around the club. We were really close-knit which is down to playing together from a young age. We had days together I will treasure forever."

Morrison has no regrets about opting to play for Scotland – despite representing England at youth level.

"I heard Garth Crooks saying on the telly that he wanted Roy to pick me for England even though I'd played for Scotland.

"I could see the funny side of it, but it was nice of him to say what he did because I'm sure he meant it as a compliment.

"I made my decision and it was one I gave a lot of consideration to, but I think I've made the right one.

"My family enjoy coming to watch me play. They have been smashing towards me and if it wasn't for them I wouldn't be playing international football or Premier League football now.

"It was my parents who put me first by taking me to training with Boro when I was a kid two nights a week, standing in the cold and rain, sitting waiting for me.

"My grandparents on my dad's side are Scottish. The whole family goes up for the internationals and our relatives that still live in Scotland.

"It's great to meet up with them. The whole family is really proud, but I think my grandparents would have been even prouder."

Mulligan Recovers In Style

"Some people believe football is a matter of life and death. I am very disappointed with that attitude. I can assure you it is much, much more important than that."

Many of us would question the former Liverpool manager Bill Shankly's famous assertion, but not Nathan Mulligan, and that is down to personal experience as he overcame leukaemia as a teenager dreaming of becoming a first-teamer at the Riverside.

He was part of Boro's FA Youth Cup-winning golden generation, but though his career suffered a major blow with a leukaemia diagnosis he was determined not to be beaten.

"It's easy to remember my reaction to being told I had leukaemia - I just wanted to know when I would be back playing football," Mulligan said.

"My doctor said I don't think you should be worrying about football – I don't think you'll be able to do that.

"She put it as bluntly as possible so I could get my head around it as quickly as possible.

"That was when I signed my scholarship contract at 16. I had a year out through treatment and a year of regaining fitness and then I managed to play again when I was 19, 20.

"No one imagined I could play professional football again, but I managed to with Darlington. I worked hard. I always had that goal of getting back playing."

Mulligan joined the Boro set-up at the age of seven after being spotted playing for Stockton West End.

He practised under the auspices of ex-Boro winger Terry Cochrane in the Ayresome Park days before moving through the ranks and making the transition to Rockliffe Park.

"It was a great upbringing to play alongside the best players in the area with the best coaches and the best possible mentor in academy manager Dave Parnaby.

"I couldn't have asked for anything better. Playing with people like Matthew Bates, Tom Craddock, Lee Cattermole, Adam Johnson and in the year above James Morrison, Andy Taylor and Tony McMahon was only going to make me improve. It was fantastic."

Originally a striker, he moved to right back and vividly remembers pitting his wits against future England winger Aaron Lennon who was on Leeds' books: "He was just rapid. No matter how much of a head start you had he'd always catch you up."

Still, his career was heading in the right direction - until leukaemia reared its head.

"I went for a run and felt unfit and I just put that down to not doing as much running as I should have during the off-season.

"But obviously there was something wrong inside me I didn't know about.

"On the second day of training we all went for medicals. There was a bit of fluid around my heart that was picked up on scans and then tests showed what it was."

He spent a year in and out of James Cook Hospital, sometimes undergoing chemotherapy for two to three months on end as specialists fought back the cancer.

And yet, against the odds, he eased his way back into the Boro fold.

The FA Youth Cup final came too soon for Mulligan who was unable to force his way into first-team contention and eventually moved on without realising his Boro ambitions at the age of 18.

"I couldn't knock the club, but I just wish I'd had another year to try to prove myself.

"I needed another year to get back to where I was before I became ill, but I was getting to that age where I needed to be challenging for a first-team place.

"There were no hard feelings about being released because they'd done everything they could.

"I wasn't playing for two years, but they stood by me. I was still getting paid and made to feel part of things to keep my spirits up."

Yet he still maintained a boyish enthusiasm for football, which enabled him to become a full-time professional with Darlington.

"I went back training once a week and playing at the weekend in the Northern League for Norton when I was spotted by Darlo manager Steve Staunton.

"I made my senior professional debut and that felt like a bit of a fairy-tale after everything I'd gone through.

"I wish it had lasted, but a new manager, Simon Davey, who was only there for a month or so, came in and released 17 players and killed everyone's careers."

There was no stopping Mulligan who played in the Northern League with Whitby Town, Marske United, Norton & Stockton Ancients and Billingham Synthonia.

And then he starred in Stockton Town's run to the 2018 FA Vase final at Wembley.

"In football terms, I was brought up in the right environment and there was no way I'd allow that to go to waste.

"Some lads think that's it and I'll sack it off when they get released, whereas I want to play at as high a level as possible and make the most of my ability."

Mulligan is in good shape mentally and physically.

"People have asked me what I thought about having a career-threatening illness, but it wasn't career-threatening – it was life-threatening.

"I should not even have been thinking about football. I should have been thinking about just getting through it all and making sure I was alive at the end of it.

"I just classed it as a setback, albeit a massive setback. That was down to mental strength, something I've always prided myself on."

BACKROOM BOYS
– Boro's Unsung Heroes

Shepherdson – The Global Ambassador

My dad was very much from a very working-class background - his father worked in what used to be called the coke ovens, writes Harold Shepherdson's daughter Linda Spraggon.

Him and his brother had to share shoes at one point, but his father worked every hour that God sent to try to make sure Dad always had a pair of football boots because he knew he had that talent for the game.

He went to the famous Huw Bell School – which used to be on the corner of Albert Road and Grange Road. He had a brother and sister and he was the one who did well at school and acquired school certificates.

While he was quite intelligent and did well academically, he really excelled at sports and captained the school football and cricket team and Yorkshire Boys at football and cricket as well.

He played for a club called South Bank East End and then turned professional for Middlesbrough but sadly war intervened and he had to go off and do National Service.

It was during his National Service that he worked as a rehabilitation physiotherapist, trying to rehabilitate servicemen who had been injured. He was a PE instructor, but took a particular interest in anatomy and physiology.

When he finished his Army career he came back to Middlesbrough, but his playing days were cut very short by a knee injury (after a senior debut at West Bromwich in May 1937).

He went to Southend because he didn't want to give up, but then the Middlesbrough trainer, Charlie Cole, contacted Dad and said he was going to retire and needed an assistant to train up so he came back to Teesside.

He was the assistant trainer and he'd be at Middlesbrough for 50 years in all, which is a long time by anyone's reckoning.

From what I can gather, he fulfilled probably every role there was to fulfil at the club, but his main responsibility was really looking for young talent and bringing young lads into the club and helping them come through the ranks.

He persuaded the club to purchase a hostel so lads could be together and didn't have to go into digs alone. He appointed a housemother so the lads were in a safe environment and living together, which was so much better for them.

Dad was very affable - the kind of person who could get on with anybody, whatever class, which was probably down to him being Middlesbrough born-and-bred.

From the family's point of view, he seemed to be so highly regarded by everybody and a lot of players that he had quite an influence on their careers at Middlesbrough and beyond.

They had nothing but nice things to say about Dad, but he wasn't that nice when I started my romance with my now husband, Frank, who was a Boro player under dad.

It was, 'Over-my-dead-body is a daughter of mine going out with a professional footballer'. He said, 'They're all drunkards, gamblers and womanisers.' It was a bit of a struggle to persuade him otherwise.

He had caught the eye of England manager Walter Winterbottom when he used to go on Football Association coaching courses at Lilleshall and Walter invited him on a temporary basis to be the England trainer in 1957.

That was the start of his international career that comprised four World Cup campaigns and 171 international matches.

He did that alongside his job with Middlesbrough where he worked as a player, assistant manager and, when Stan Anderson resigned in 1973, he took over as caretaker manager.

He was in charge for the rest of the season and guided them on a brilliant run; they lost just three times and finished fourth in the Second Division on 47 points.

He then became influential in the appointment of Jack Charlton as Middlesbrough manager, which is quite a legacy to leave.

Having been with England for all that time, he knew Jack well. He'd seen his qualities first-hand so he recommended Jack to the directors and he came to Teesside.

The other person involved was Neil Phillips who was on the board of directors and was also the England doctor from about 1968. They had this discussion that if they were looking for a new manager that Jack was worth considering.

My dad was Jack's assistant. Jack relied on him a lot because he had a network of scouts across the country and produced all the reports on their opponents.

Like Jack, my father was best known for his role in England's World Cup win in 1966 when he was the team trainer under Sir Alf Ramsey.

His first World Cup was in Sweden in 1958 and he always seemed to be away on tour with England so we didn't see an awful lot of him.

He always kept in touch with my mother and me and my two sisters and sent us postcards from wherever he was. We got used to it, but in 1966 he was gone for six weeks prior to the actual tournament itself.

We just recall the national fervour and how suddenly our dad, who was just that to us, was part of something that was just so tremendous for the whole country.

Still, it's only been after the event that we've realised what a significant moment that was and what a privilege it was for him and us as well that he was centrally involved.

But I know it meant an enormous amount for him because he worked with Sir Alf throughout his term as manager and although Alf got a lot of bad press they got on like a house on fire.

They were very different in lots of ways but were very close up until the time that my father died and my father could not speak highly enough of him.

It was nice that my mother, who'd had to stay at home and bring up three girls while dad dedicated himself to the England team, got the opportunity to go to the final to spend time with other wives and enjoy the whole spectacle.

It was a very special time in our lives and great for my dad who was so thrilled with it all.

He kept a diary almost every day of his life and all the phone numbers and names talk about celebrities. He was on a par with all these people, and well known throughout the football world.

The notes on the World Cup win are a reflection of what a moment in time it was. I remember him saying what a fantastic achievement it was and how it was the most amazing thing to be involved in.

How a set of lads who were so ordinary - no divas - worked as a team and worked for Alf and deserved their success.

The day after the final Dad and my mother went out for lunch with the Ramseys. Then they got the train home and he said it was the most wonderful down-to-earth journey because there was a pre-season friendly with Hartlepool to look forward to.

In the later years, when he got a bit forgetful, there are everyday things in there like, 'Put the dustbins out,' but there are a few passages from his diaries that stand out for me like these from 1966:

'Third match - Nobby booked for horrendous tackle on Simeone. Told the ref he had mistimed the tackle and accidentally caught him in the balls.'

'Fourth match Argentina. Beat them. They kicked everything above grass, the captain Ratan sent off for continuously arguing with the German referee.'

'He tried to get into the England dressing room but Big Jack grabbed him by the scruff of the neck and threw him out.'

'England 2 Portugal 1. Semi-final. Nobby did great job on Eusebio. Frightened life out of hm. Eusebio went pale every time Nobby went near him.'

'Alf told Jack to mark the big 6ft 2in centre forward Torres very closely.'

'What exactly do you mean boss?'

'Do exactly what I say Jack – stick to him and don't give him any room.'

'Are you asking me to kick him up the arse?'

'Jack, you do whatever is necessary to do what I have asked of you.'

'And Jack says, 'Okay boss - I'll wallop him early on and see how it goes from there then. If that doesn't work I'll kick him where it hurts.'

'Final. Fantastic occasion, wonderful support from the whole country. 98,000 people at Wembley. Dream come true to win the World Cup final. A game that will never be forgotten and a £1,000 win bonus for each player, (physio) Les Cocker, and myself. Magnificent victory.'

"After Sir Alf stepped down, Dad, who was awarded the MBE in 1969, continued to work for Joe Mercer, but was finally ready to step down in 1974 after Don Revie took over.

"But he did local radio and after-dinner speaking because he had a lot of stories to tell which went down well and he worked at Boro until 1986 when he retired.

"I think now about when I was a kid and the phone would ring at home and I'd answer it and I'd shout to my father, 'Dad – Jimmy Greaves is on the phone or Bill Nicholson or Bob Paisley' – all these household names. But I didn't think anything about it then."

• Harold Shepherdson died at the age of 77 on September 13th 1995. He clearly never lost his sense of humour, judging by his obituary by football journalist Ivan Ponting in The Independent. When one national newspaper mistakenly announced that he was dead, in 1993, he laughed: 'Like Mark Twain before me, reports of my death have been exaggerated.'

• In June 2009, players and staff of England's World Cup-winning squad who did not get medals at Wembley were handed the mementoes in a ceremony at 10 Downing Street. That was after world governing body FIFA decreed that medals go to every non-playing squad and staff member from all World Cup-winning countries from 1930 to 1974. Prime Minister Gordon Brown presented 11 ex-players and staff medals, including Margaret Shepherdson on behalf of her husband.

Anderson - Boro's Golden Oldie

Anybody that saw Bryan Robson play for England, Manchester United and even Boro will know what an influential character he could be on the field.

But have a chat with Viv Anderson and it quickly becomes apparent the former Boro boss was a highly persuasive character off the field as well.

For Robson convinced his former England and Manchester United colleague to leave the player-manager's post at Barnsley to become his right-hand man on Teesside as the Riverside Revolution took off.

"When we played together, Bryan and myself had always agreed that if things were right then we'd get together again," said Anderson.

"And he promised me it would be a good experience for me if we finally did work together when the Boro job as his No2 loomed.

"I took the assistant's job, but I wouldn't have left Barnsley if it wasn't for the exciting vision for the future of the club spelled out by Steve Gibson, Keith Lamb and Bryan.

"They wanted to make Boro a top-half Premiership side and while we would have money at our disposal to strengthen the squad it was still a tall order.

"That was because it was always going to be difficult as a newly-promoted side because the main target for clubs that come up is survival.

"But our aim was not just to survive, but to kick on and move up the pecking order. We got relegated, but fortunately everyone held their nerve and we bounced back at the first attempt."

Anderson hailed the "charismatic" Juninho, "inspirational" Fabrizio Ravanelli and "talismanic" Paul Merson as Robson's best signings of an eventful period.

"It was a rollercoaster ride, but most of memories of my time at Boro are great. It came to a sad end (when he left along with Robson in 2001) but that's the way football goes.

"We had ups and downs and relegation, but we managed two promotions and three Cup finals in one year when the club had never been to a major final before, although beating Liverpool in the League Cup semi-final stands out."

Anderson had a distinguished playing career, helping Brian Clough's Nottingham Forest win a League Championship and the European Cup twice before heading off to Arsenal in 1984.

Manchester-based Anderson, who works in the football hospitality business, also wrote himself into the Boro history books by becoming the club's oldest ever debutant under Robson.

He was way past his 38th birthday when he was pressed into action as an emergency centre-back during the 1994-95 promotion campaign, but he was no stranger to landmark occasions.

Anderson, who received an MBE for services to football in 2000, had already become the first black player to represent England in a full international.

"It didn't really feel at the time that I was making a bit of history because I was just a footballer that wanted to do well."

McQueen Has Plenty In Reserve

The familiar Scottish voice might still be a little bit hoarse, but listening to Gordon McQueen speak should be music to the ears of every Boro fan.

The former Boro coach and club sounds croaky, but it quickly becomes clear when chatting to McQueen that he is very much in fine fettle following his throat cancer scare.

The former Sky Sports pundit is upbeat about the past, present and the future even though his world was turned upside down when he had to come to terms with a devastating bombshell when Teesside specialists diagnosed him as having cancer.

But now following treatment at the James Cook University Hospital, the 6ft 3in former Leeds, Manchester United and Scotland centre-half insists the doctors could not be happier with his progress.

"I lost a lot of weight, but I have put it all back on again and a bit more besides, but the doctors are very happy, though," McQueen said.

"It is something that means I will have to keep on going back for tests for a couple of years. Bryan Robson had the same thing and he keeps going back for tests to keep an eye on things.

"I was shocked by the initial reaction when the news came out about my situation. There were messages of support from people in Middlesbrough, Manchester, Leeds and Scotland, but also from America and the Far East and places like that. It was unbelievable.

"I just think people fear that cancer is a death sentence, but it isn't nowadays. It is a horrible word, but it does not mean what it did 10 or 15 years ago."

McQueen, who lives in the North Yorkshire village of Hutton Rudby, is full of praise for the medical team who wasted no time in getting to the bottom of his medical issues.

"I was on Sky and my voice was getting huskier and huskier and I was thinking it would get better any time, but I waited a few weeks and thought I'd better get this checked out," he added.

"I went into the James Cook Hospital and they said, 'We think you've got cancer, so you'd better come back in the morning.' I had an operation the next morning and once that settled down I had radiotherapy.

"Right from day one the prognosis has always been pretty good because modern-day treatment is so good and so advanced. The care that I got at the James Cook was spectacular. The doctors, nurses and all the staff there were brilliant.

"I was a wee bit uncomfortable with the treatment, but they got on top of it by Christmas. Unfortunately, for the time being, it seems to have damaged my vocal chords and my larynx because that is where I had the cancer.

"I was all set for going back to work and doing a few things for Sky, but I'm not quite ready for that yet.

"I'm doing next to nothing at the moment. I am doing a bit of corporate work with Manchester United and I've just been in the Far East – Tokyo, Vietnam and Jakarta - with them on what they call a 'trophy tour' with the Premier League and meet fans and sponsors."

It was former Boro manager Robson that McQueen had turned to for advice when cancer was diagnosed as his former Old Trafford colleague had also been treated for throat cancer.

They became firm friends at United and McQueen became part of Robson's 'Riverside Revolution' when he headed to Teesside along with another United old boy in Viv Anderson in 1994 when Ayresome Park was Boro's home.

"Robbo was and still is a great mate of mine as when he told me about his plans to move to Boro he told me it was a club that could really go places because Steve Gibson was so ambitious and he thought it was a good time to muck in with him because the club was going places and he was right," the former Boro reserves boss added.

"It was such an exciting time when Robbo was in charge. It was quite sad the way it all ended for Bryan because he did such a good job and it finished on a bit of a sour note with the results not being good and the fans being unhappy because they had become so used to exciting things under Bryan.

"I see Bryan all the time and I know he looks back fondly on his days there and

Middlesbrough fans do. It took a few years to realise just how good things were with Fabrizio Ravanelli (McQueen's former next-door neighbour) and Juninho, getting near enough 30,000 fans in the Riverside every game and then 35,000 the following year. It was brilliant.

"There's no doubt at all what my favourite memories are. They're special ones of Ravanelli's debut when he scored a hat-trick against Liverpool, the impact Juninho had on the club and the area when he arrived and the night we beat Liverpool in the League Cup semi-final at the Riverside."

McQueen left Boro when Steve McClaren took over as manager in 2001, but came back with a spell in a scouting capacity, and although that role came to an end he still finds a strong connection with Boro and the region as a whole.

"I have never wanted to move away because my wife (Yvonne) and I love the Middlesbrough area.

"All my kids (Hayley, Anna and Eddie) grew up here and went to school in this neck of the woods. It is just one of those places that I really love. I have always lived in the North of England since coming down here from Scotland.

"I chose Hutton Rudby when I first came here and that was a good choice because it is a village that I really enjoy being part of.

"I've also got a strong attachment to the football club. I know we had that spell under Bryan, but I've always had an association with the club and they've always been good to me and my son has always been a season-ticket holder. They are my team now."

All-Round Hero

Steve Round is one of Boro's ultimate unsung heroes.

As manager Steve McClaren's right-hand man, he played a vital role in Boro's dramatic UEFA Cup comeback against Steaua Bucharest.

But, until now, what Round did behind the scenes will have gone unrecognised by those lucky enough to witness arguably the greatest night in Boro's history.

Boro were on the brink of semi-final heartache against the Romanians, when Round retreated to the sanctuary of McClaren's office, adjoining the Riverside's home dressing room, well away from the madding crowd.

Most fans will have had their heads in their hands, but Round remembers it was just before the interval and Boro were trailing 3-1 on aggregate when McClaren told him to hatch a plan of action to salvage the club's European dreams.

"We were down and almost out, but Steve was cool, calm and collected and did something really smart," Round recalled.

"Massimo Maccarone gave us a lifeline and we grabbed it with both hands. He was on as a sub when we were 2-0 down and scored just before half-time.

"We had renewed hope and with what happened against Basel we knew anything could happen.

"Steve just turned to me and sent me into the dressing room. He told me to get in our little office and get some tactics up on the board – some new ways of playing, some ideas - for when he'd finished coaching the rest of this half.

"So I ran into the office – and no one will have noticed - and starting sketching out three or four formations.

"When he came in at half-time he came straight into the office. He discarded three and said one might have possibilities and he added something extra.

"He said I'm going to do that, but not straight away. I'll bring Yakubu on after ten minutes to keep the momentum up."

It was all or nothing for McClaren who gave his own take on the drama in an interview with *Four Four Two* magazine:

'Steve said: "Move the wingers to full-backs, and put attackers on as wide players." I thought: 'That's committing suicide – we'll get thrashed by seven or eight'. But I followed his advice and we won 4-3. Unbelievable."

It worked as Maccarone showed lightning can strike twice with the late winner to book Boro's passage to the UEFA Cup final in Eindhoven.

"To send me in to think about things away from the hustle and bustle was a clever move.

"I'm not sure if anyone else has done that, but it gave him something clear to think about when he came back from the frontline.

"There was no ranting or raving - it was a now-or-never message. There was a quiet resolve. This was our chance to get to a final and he told the players to never pass up the opportunity without having given everything possible.

"We re-organised tactically and ended up playing a 2-4-4 formation. We thought 'go for it' and fortunately they also changed and went 4-5-1 plus they sat back.

"We were dead and buried but turned it around. The players did the business, but the atmosphere generated by the fans and the momentum that came with it meant the crowd sucked the ball into the net.

"Both UEFA ties against Basel and Steaua Bucharest showed that in football anything can happen, which is what makes it so exciting.

"But a lot of it was down to Steve. He got a bum rap with England because he didn't succeed, but if you look at his managerial track record, it shows he's a very talented manager."

Like McClaren, Round entered coaching at an early age after rupturing knee ligaments at the age of 22 just after breaking into Derby County's first team.

He spent two years on the comeback trail, but his rehabilitation work failed so he quit playing at the age of 24 and concentrated on coaching.

"Fortunately, I was already working within Derby's academy at the time and I'd done my coaching badges at 21 because I'd always enjoyed coaching.

"I was working with the juniors - the under-12 and 14s – since I was 18, so it was quite easy to move. Jim Smith was the manager at the time and I went through the ranks to become his assistant before joining Steve at Boro."

Round looks back on his days on Teesside – where his children were born - fondly.

"Steve Gibson was great to work for because he was upfront, fiercely ambitious and uncompromising.

"It was an incredible time because we won the club's first ever major trophy, spent two years in Europe, had the club's highest ever points tally in the Premier League and the highest finish in the Premier League.

"But one of the things that get overlooked is the amount of young players that came through the ranks. That was incredibly important.

"It was something that I regard as highly as any of the other achievements.

"They had a very, very good academy manager in Dave Parnaby, they got encouraged to push for the senior side, and to see so many of his graduates play for the first team was very special."

As well as the big games, Round still cherishes the thoughts of coaching top-class players at Boro – but believes Gareth Southgate remains the most significant signing.

"I'll always treasure the memories of working with tremendous talent, such as Jimmy Floyd Hasselbaink, Mark Viduka, Alen Boksic, Paul Ince and Juninho.

"They challenged people like me to raise my game so I could push them and get the best out of them.

"In terms of pure talent Gaizka Mendieta, Juninho, Boksic were top-quality players. Mark was an exceptional talent, a great guy as well and top professional.

"Jimmy was a major signing because he changed the mentality within the dressing room. He gave them a bit more toughness. He'd played at the highest level and his desire and commitment to succeed was vital.

"George Boateng and Bolo Zenden were great fun and great players and then as the young crop came through Stewart Downing was the pick of the bunch and he came right the way through from 16 to play for the England senior team.

"But probably the player that had the most influence during our five years was Gareth who was brought to Teesside from Aston Villa in our first window. He was our captain and he led by example not only on the field but off it too."

• *Steve Round experienced plenty of amazing occasions with Boro but a reserve game stands out.*

"Beating Jose Mourinho's Chelsea 3-0 was special because we worked on a specific game-plan, but the 4-1 over Manchester United was outstanding.

"I say that because we had been stripped to the bare bones with defenders. So we decided to play 3-5-2 against Man U with a young back three – Matthew Bates, Franck Queudrue and Chris Riggott.

"We had the 'let's-go-for-it' mindset. If we'd prepared not to lose we probably would have been beaten. But we set off like a house on fire and were 3-0 up at half-time.

"That was some occasion, but one of the craziest games was when I took charge of the reserves when Juninho returned to the club for the third time.

"It was supposed to be played at Billingham, but was changed because they expected a few thousand to turn up and in the end 20,000 came to watch.

"We beat Bradford 9-0 with Juninho getting a couple of goals. It just showed how passionate Boro fans are and what a hero Juninho will always be."

Agony and Ecstasy In Barron Times

Paul Barron brought a whole new meaning to anger management in his Boro days.

He hit the proverbial roof when Boro seemed set to pay the ultimate penalty for a dreadful mishap that threatened the club's celebrated European adventure.

The goalkeeping coach, a key member of Steve McClaren's Boro managerial team, was furious when the club seemed certain to miss out on their second and most famous UEFA Cup campaign.

Like most visiting fans who were at the City of Manchester Stadium, Barron could not bring himself to watch when Boro conceded a late penalty on the final day of the season at Manchester City.

But a sudden retreat into the sanctuary of the dressing room was more to do with saving himself from himself than anything else as he vented his spleen behind closed doors.

Thankfully for Boro, of course, Mark Schwarzer won the battle of wits with Robbie Fowler to pave the way for Europe in one of the defining moments of the McClaren era.

"I had murderous thoughts," Barron said. "When Mark was in the process of saving the pen I was in the dressing room volleying water bottles all over the place. It took me a day and a half to stop being angry.

"Franck Queudrue gave away the pen but someone else had done something silly at the other end and they broke away. We had lost our concentration right at the end and that was completely unnecessary.

"I was absolutely fuming because you think of all that hard work being undone with virtually the last kick of the season. Thankfully, Mark came to the rescue and we were on the road to the UEFA Cup final."

It was not the first time Barron's charge, Schwarzer, had been the centre of attention during a high-profile match.

Schwarzer dropped a clanger during Boro's 2004 Carling Cup final victory that allowed Kevin Davies to score in the 2-1 win.

But it was the manner of the Australian's response that won Barron's admiration as their behind-the-scenes work reaped handsome rewards in the shape of the club's first piece of major silverware.

"In the final, I didn't have to get Mark back on the right tracks – he did it himself.

"He started off the game well and made a decent save and a couple of interceptions and then let in one of the softest goals you could imagine.

"Then in the next ten minutes he made four of the best saves I would remember. He made a brilliant recovery.

"Fair enough he made a ridiculous schoolboy error, but to come back from that in the most important game of his career at that point and then have a blinder was a tremendous testament to him.

"I worked with Mark for six years. He was very professional, hard-working. They were all like that but he led by example. If you couldn't work as hard as him then you had a problem. He was an all-round spot-on individual."

Barron joined Boro in 2001 as part of manager Steve McClaren's new backroom staff that included Bill Beswick, Steve Harrison and Steve Round and stayed on Teesside for a total of six years.

"There was a big changeover because we lost the first four and the last four of our first season, but got 45 points from the middle 30 and we had an FA Cup run to the semi-finals.

"Memories of that year are that it was tough, but the fans were pretty patient because we went in and made things instantly worse.

"It was a question of first year, 'Can you consolidate a bit?' Second year, 'Can you try to push forward?' And in the third we won the Carling Cup and so qualified for Europe.

As well as looking after the goalkeepers, Barron was responsible for hotel and travel arrangements, but also had an input into many first-team issues as part of McClaren's brains trust.

"All us coaches were encouraged to make a decent contribution at our meetings. We were all involved in everything. Steve would always listen and then make a decision.

"I was involved in a lot of general work and 95 per cent of time he left me alone to get on with it, but sometimes he'd stick his oar in and then once he'd proved himself to be right – or wrong - he'd step back."

After Boro, Barron became goalkeeping coach at North East rivals Newcastle before heading off to America as head coach of Las Vegas Mobsters.

Barron certainly did his best to make up for a playing career that, by his own admission, left him feeling unfulfilled although it took him to Arsenal, Crystal Palace and West Bromwich Albion before he started coaching at Aston Villa.

"As a player, I enjoyed being at West Brom and some of my time at Palace, but Arsenal was my favourite.

"I was a Gunners fan, but I had a massive problem getting into the team because Pat Jennings was there.

"I loved being there and had I got a chance to be No1 that would have been perfect.

"My over-riding feeling on my playing career is that I would have done better.

"But that is a long time ago and I've tried to put as much into my coaching career as possible to get the frustrations over my playing days out of my system."

Harrison Makes Boro Smiles Better

They say it's good to play football with a smile on your face and that was certainly the case at Boro, thanks to coach Steve Harrison.

Harrison was part of the Riverside backroom staff for seven years and played a key role in helping Boro win the Carling Cup, reach the UEFA Cup final and twice finish seventh in the Premier League.

"I always saw my job at Middlesbrough as being to gel the dressing room into a unit," said Harrison, who worked under both Steve McClaren and Gareth Southgate.

"And I've always thought the best way to do this is when – and I've not been proved wrong - people are relaxed, smiling and having a giggle.

"Ranters and ravers and shouters used to frighten me to death when I was a kid, so I knew that approach wasn't for me.

"Thankfully the Middlesbrough players bought into it and we had a great time on and off the field.

"It helped that I was the son of a stand-up comedian. My dad earned a bit of money in working men's clubs, which he needed to because he spent plenty of it.

"He was a funny man. I was more slapstick than stand-up – WC Field my humour was more like."

The former Blackpool defender had just signed a new contract at Aston Villa where he was on John Gregory's coaching team when he was approached by McClaren to join his team when he headed to Teesside in 2001.

"I was on holiday in Italy with my wife when I got a call from Steve who had a great reputation from his days with Manchester United with the master that is Sir Alex Ferguson.

"I'd met Steve when he was running Derby reserves and I was taking the Crystal Palace side and I enjoyed chatting to him, but I still had to ask, 'Why did you think of me?'

"It turned out that when he was at Man United he spoke to the likes of Teddy Sheringham and Dwight Yorke and they both recommended me as a coach.

"Thing is I thought Villa was my Utopia, but Steve squared things with John Gregory and I went up to the Rockliffe Park training ground.

"It was a lovely sunny day and when I saw the facilities, my first thoughts were: 'I'll have a bit of this'."

The former England coach lightened the atmosphere after McClaren replaced Bryan Robson following a turbulent campaign that saw Terry Venables come to Boro's rescue.

"I've never experienced anything like it - there was an extraordinary transformation.

"When we first went there the mood was a bit fragmented. It was a disjointed team, low on confidence, who'd avoided relegation by the skin of their teeth thanks to Terry Venables' brilliance.

"Then there was this young manager taking over who was full of great ideas about attacking football who had to change his philosophy."

McClaren was forced into a re-think because the first four games of his reign ended in defeat with 11 goals conceded and just one scored.

"To say we failed to hit the ground running was a massive understatement.

"The players didn't want another struggle, but then those first four games unfolded and it was a case of déjà vu.

"What Steve wanted to do was play like Man United, but when Arsenal thrashed us 4-0 at home it became clear we needed a different strategy to get a foundation in place."

McClaren called a meeting to get things sorted out.

"We sat down around a table and he asked us coaches (Harrison, Bill Beswick, Steve Round and Paul Barron) 'What do we do?'

"I told him we had to go two banks of four, defend properly, stay deep and counter-attack. We all agreed and to cut a long story short that is exactly what we did.

"We'd asset-stripped Villa to get Gareth Southgate and Ugo Ehiogu, and George Boateng, who could destroy but thought he was Juninho, and they gave us strength right down the middle.

"We defended deeply because he knew we had a good defence that could soak up pressure and year by year he built that team up to be a fantastic attacking force."

The atmosphere in the dressing room might have been tense in those early days, but it did not stop Harrison from bonding with the players.

"I used to go into the dressing room every day whatever the result and shake hands with every player every morning.

"You can feel a dressing room, but you have to be in there from the start or players will be a bit wary of you, a bit cautious.

"I'd always first knock on the door and ask permission from the Governor, that being Paul Ince, because it was his manor.

"The lads liked that routine, they laughed at it, and I picked up the mood. You'd pick up the eyes. You'd know who'd not slept or who'd been up with the baby all night or had too many beers or who was nervous.

"You'd pick up the vibes. You'd have a few stories and tell a few tales and have a laugh as Steve prepared for training.

"Then he'd ask, 'How are they?' And I'd be able to tell him, 'They're a bit jaded, so go easy on them.' Or I'd say, 'They're in a good mood, so let's just keep them bubbly.' Steve listened which was magnificent."

Harrison had an input with tactics, but he was mainly charged with making sure the players were ready mentally for match days.

"When I arrived and we were establishing our roles I told him I'd get his players right for Saturday. He said that's what he wanted to hear because he knew what I was good at.

"Steve appreciated my role. If the Friday session went well, he'd wink at me as if to say I'd done my job well."

Harrison was also helpful to McClaren's players.

"One player said it was like I was the favourite uncle. Players could come to me if they had a grievance and we'd chat and iron things out before anyone went steaming into his office.

"I'd never tell tales unless there was something Steve needed to know or I'd go to (assistant manager) Bill Beswick. I was the middleman before players bashed the manager's office door down."

Harrison is no longer involved in football on a full-time basis, but still helps up-and-coming coaches develop their skills.

"It was great at Boro because some brilliant players were signed, but we also had a great academy that churned out excellent players like Stewart Downing and James Morrison.

"The academy lads were not only good players, but they knew how to win matches and that was down to Dave Parnaby.

"That game at Fulham, when every one of our players was home-grown, was a day that everyone at Boro could be proud of. It was one of many highlights for me of an amazing seven years."

Fitting The Bill In Mind Games

Bill Beswick insists it was a "tremendous leap of faith" by Steve McClaren that had everyone connected with Boro jumping for joy.

Beswick was installed as McClaren's right-hand man when he became manager in 2001, despite being regarded as a sports psychologist rather than conventional coach, but the move paid rich dividends.

"He even surprised me by asking me to become assistant manager because I was a non-football person," Beswick said.

"But by the time he had got the Boro job he knew enough about me to be sure I could have an impact.

"We talked about the Boro situation and at that time the issue was certainly a football one, but it was a state of mind issue as well.

"The job was to change attitudes towards taking responsibility, so as well as getting better players in and improving the existing players, the real challenge was changing attitudes.

"There were issues of lifestyle and lack of professionalism, commitment and attitude to training and Steve decided that was the major thrust of the turnaround and I would be useful in helping that."

The pair had worked alongside each other at Derby and Manchester United and McClaren turned to Beswick when asked to take the reins at the Riverside and they masterminded the most glorious five years of the club's history.

"When Steve was a youth coach he listened to me speaking about the importance of coaches not just coaching physically, but also mentally and the power of attitude and he was very keen to explore that.

"We worked together on that at Derby and built a blueprint for putting it into action, developed it at Man United, and Middlesbrough was the perfect opportunity to put it into place.

"That was a tremendous leap of faith by Steve, but we had some very good football people on the staff in Steve Round, Paul Barron and Steve Harrison.

"He felt there was a place for somebody who would develop a culture, an attitude, a mental strength and that was my role."

Beswick believes McClaren deserves credit for not appointing friends "which can be the downfall of some coaches" because they "don't get the backing of the right experience or expertise."

Eyebrows might have been raised externally by Beswick's appointment, but he found himself embraced by Boro players.

"When I went to Derby I remember players running the other way down the corridor when they saw me, but by the time I got to Boro I was reasonably well known and appreciated.

"I had been at Derby, Carlisle and Man United and I was coming in as part of a powerful team of staff and the players were becoming more attuned to the idea of having a sports psychologist on board.

"They felt less threatened. Some of the leaders, such as Robbie Mustoe, Paul Ince and Mark Schwarzer had experience of sports psychologists, so they weren't intimidated. They were relaxed, so I got real help from them."

The signing of Gareth Southgate was pivotal for Beswick – who had worked closely with Roy Keane and Gary Neville at United - and the club as a whole.

"Here was a team that was struggling, but we signed a great player and a great person in Gareth. Getting him was the key moment in turning the culture around.

"He immediately took over the captaincy and was very open about dealing with me on the state of the dressing room psychology and mentality of the team and what we could do about it.

"So, slowly but surely, I integrated into the fabric of the club and I honestly don't think people thought of me as a psychologist. They thought of me as a coach who from time-to-time got the team together and talked about mental strength."

The formula certainly worked and Boro went on to win the 2004 Carling Cup final and reached the 2006 UEFA Cup final, as well as chalking up a series of incredible wins along the way.

"That first year was a struggle because it takes time to turn a big ship around.

"Europe was the icing on the cake, but the Carling Cup win stands out because we proved with that win that we could achieve success with Boro. It bought us the time that took us to the European final.

"The Carling Cup was a great sign that what we were doing was working – we were producing mentally-strong winners.

"Until then the club had been in several major finals and lost them all. There was a bit of fear and anxiety around, but we prepared the team so well they scored two goals in the first seven minutes against Bolton in Cardiff.

"That was the moment I knew the team had taken on the mental strength to play a big game at a big moment and see it through.

"That set us up for Europe which is about having the mental strength to get results away from home.

"Sometimes we were fielding kids, but they were all strong-minded because they believed in us and what we were doing."

Beswick, a successful author who once coached the English basketball team to the gold medal in the Commonwealth Games, regards his time at Boro as the most enjoyable in his time in football.

"Boro has to be the highlight because, although Man U was great, it was Alex Ferguson's team and we were just there to support and work round the fringes," said Beswick, who lives in Cheshire.

"Being assistant manager at Boro for a non-football person and having a chance to influence the development of a team in terms of mental and emotional strength was quite something.

"We really turned it around and created an environment where kids came through and, thanks mostly to academy manager Dave Parnaby, there was a conveyor belt of top-quality young kids.

"For me, being handed a chance to shape the destiny of a great club by a manager who wanted to twin the physical and tactical alongside mental strength was an honour.

"I'm not sure if it was an unusual time or a great time, but I remember five very happy and successful years.

"The major job was to build a safe Premier League place, which was the most solid thing we did.

"We came when the club was low and finished in a European final. That was some achievement."

BOSSING THE GAME
– *Boro Managers*

Anderson Sets High Standards

Stan Anderson has the distinction of being the only person to have captained all three of the North East's top clubs in Boro, Sunderland and Newcastle.

But he will be best remembered from a Teesside point of view for his seven years as club manager following a spell as player-coach.

He laid the foundations for Charlton's Champions to surge into the old First Division by signing a host of players who would become club legends.

He brought in the likes of John Hickton, Frank Spraggon, Stuart Boam, Willie Maddren, David Armstrong, Jim Platt, John Craggs, David Mills, Alan Foggon and Graeme Souness.

Anderson joined Boro as a player-coach in November 1965 and played 21 times for the club before taking over after Harold Shepherdson had a spell as caretaker boss following the dismissal of Raich Carter.

A while back, Anderson wrote his memoirs in *Captain of the North* and he said that as he looked back he realised he deserved to be taking things easy after working beyond the call of duty at Boro.

"I have to say it was an honour to captain Boro, but I was lucky in that I also got involved in coaching under Raich Carter who was my manager," Anderson said from his home in Doncaster.

"But really I had little idea about what management entailed when Raich got the sack and Harold Shepherdson and I took over. It wasn't just working overtime – it was working all hours that God sent.

"Harold was coaching England and didn't want the job and the responsibility that came with it. He clearly had more sense than me. I was offered the position and thought, 'What the hell, I'll take it, I'll give it a go.'

"It was what people now describe as a steep learning curve because we had a very poor team and we had to get rid of a lot of players. It needed a radical overhaul.

"It was difficult being a player-coach and it didn't go down too well with the directors, who were tight so-and-sos, but I told them I honestly couldn't do both jobs.

"I'd work all day, training in the morning and then coaching youngsters in the afternoon before having a bite to eat at home and going out to watch a game in the evening.

"My private life was nil. I was really keen on the job, but regret that in certain ways I didn't see my daughter growing up and she was 18 when work finally settled down."

Despite his best efforts, there was nothing Anderson could do to stop Boro being relegated to the old Third Division.

And after letting go of 15 players, Anderson then had the task of re-building the club, which he did by signing the likes of Boam and Hickton.

"Things started badly, but we made good progress and eventually won promotion to the Second Division (behind League Cup winners Queens Park Rangers) which was fantastic for me and the club.

"In my opinion, we'd turned things around, we were on the up, but we just needed a couple more players to kick on again and get back to the top flight.

"But we just got to a point where you think, 'I've done five or six years and it needed a new face.' Jack Charlton came in, bought Bobby Murdoch, it took off again and the club was back in the big time."

By this time the former England midfielder was working in Greece where he was managing AEK Athens.

"I'd often talk to Jack and he said the problem is that I stayed around at Boro too long.

"If you look at his record he generally stayed for about four years in any job. He was a wise man.

"Jack reckoned that the longer you stick around, the more they get used to what you're doing, take you for granted, and then they start criticising. 'Do a job and move on,' was his motto.

"He might well have been right, but all in all I like to think that I left Boro in a good state because they got promotion the following year to the First Division under him."

Anderson certainly deserves credit for being responsible for one of the shrewdest bits of business that Boro has ever seen thanks to his days in charge at Ayresome Park.

That is because he managed to bring Souness from Tottenham to Teesside for next to nothing and then watched the midfielder go on to conquer English and European football with Liverpool.

"It all started when I got some good information from Bill Nicholson, who was the Spurs manager.

"Bill told me that they had a good player on their books who was desperate to get first-team football, but he couldn't get him in apart from when people were injured.

"He said, 'This lad wanted to move further North to be closer to his family and friends back home in Scotland.'

"We'd watched him and I thought let's get him signed up, but the directors said while he wasn't bad, he wasn't worth the £35,000 Tottenham were asking.

"So I was asked if Bill would take a bit less and we eventually got him for £27,500 which was a bit of a steal, but I think Bill agreed to it for my sake and Graeme's.

"Graeme played at inside forward for a spell before settling into midfield, and a director at the next board meeting after a defeat at Fulham told that me I had wasted club money on a reserve-team player.

"A few years later I saw that director at Queens Park Rangers just after Graeme moved to Liverpool for a club-record £350,000. I jokingly asked for my ten per cent of what was a great deal and that director stalked off."

• *Gordon Jones paid a heartfelt tribute to Stan Anderson after he died aged 85 in June 2018.*

"As a player, manager and all round person, Stan Anderson was the absolute tops," said Jones, who was Anderson's captain.

"I'm absolutely certain we won't see the likes of him again. I can't speak highly enough of him. He's a Newcastle legend, a Sunderland legend and, for me, a Boro legend too.

"He was my mentor. He taught me so much, not just about football but also about life. He knew how to treat people on and off the field.

"He was unlucky not to win promotion, but I know why he didn't win it. At the time, we were winning most of our games at home and just the odd game away.

"I said to him that maybe we should put defensive system up when we go away. But he told me, 'The day we have to go away to put a defensive show is the day that I'll pack the game in.'

"He wanted entertaining football all the time, to entertain the supporters. Jack Charlton came along and they walked promotion with virtually the same players, but not playing such attacking football."

Big Jack's Giant Jump

The move between the dressing room and manager's office can be a daunting one.

But for Jack Charlton there was not a single hint of trepidation when he arrived at his career crossroads at Ayresome Park.

Charlton insisted that he relished the prospect of changing direction following 20 years as a player that saw him reach the pinnacle of world football and the summit of English football.

The former England international centre-back, speaking from his home in rural Northumberland, might not have scaled the heights he did for club and country with Leeds and England as a manager.

But he can look back on a managerial career that ensures he will always have a special place in the hearts of anyone who supported Middlesbrough in the 1970s.

Charlton was 38 years old when he headed to Boro in 1973 following an approach by then Boro chairman George Winney after 20 trophy-laden years at Elland Road with Leeds.

"It wasn't difficult at all to make the jump from playing to managing so I don't know what all the fuss is about," Charlton said in an interview for Backpass magazine.

"I'd been learning the ropes with the Football Association so I felt ready. I spent a long time with the FA, most of my summers, learning about coaching and how to get at players.

"I knew I was going to be a manager or something like that because I had spent so much time trying to learn everything about that side of things.

"I had made my mind up that I was going to pack playing in after my testimonial at Leeds (against Celtic) but then the Middlesbrough job came up which worked out pretty well."

Charlton's appointment as Boro manager was confirmed in May 1973 on the same day of his testimonial that attracted almost 35,000 supporters and saw the star of the show limp off with the recurrence of a hamstring injury before Jock Stein's side won 4-3.

"It was time to do something different away from Leeds. It was my first job, but I didn't find it particularly daunting or anything like that.

"It helped me that Harold Shepherdson, who I knew from England, had been caretaker manager before I arrived and they were going well under him. Anyway, I was lucky because we had a good bunch of lads at Middlesbrough.

"I can't remember everything about Middlesbrough, but what I do know is that Stan Anderson (who resigned in January 1973) had put together a good team. It just needed tweaking so I brought in Bobby Murdoch from Celtic.

"Bobby brought everything together. He was a wonderful player and one of the best passers of a ball I saw. Then I just had to get things organised."

The move for Murdoch – who played in Charlton's testimonial alongside Kenny Dalglish - proved to be a masterstroke.

The Scot was head and shoulders above everyone else in the old Second Division that Boro took by storm and 'Charlton's Champions' went into Ayresome Park folklore.

Thanks to the European Cup winner, callow talent like Graeme Souness and David Armstrong who played alongside him in Charlton's three-man midfield, excelled.

That meant Boro romped to the Second Division title, winning promotion back to the top flight of English football for the first time since 1954 with eight games to spare.

Off the field, Charlton made sure future Liverpool skipper Souness – brought to Teesside by Anderson from Tottenham - fulfilled his potential despite questionable re-fuelling habits after initially leaving him out of his 1st XI.

That he did get Souness on the path to glory was thanks to the man-management skills he had learned under England manager Sir Alf Ramsey and Leeds counterpart Don Revie.

"I told Graeme, 'That is what you should be doing, not that,' and to his credit he listened and took everything in because he is a smart lad.

"Graeme could support the forwards and he was a good striker of the ball and good ball-player. He was in a position where he could get backwards and forwards well which he did well.

"I'm told he said if it wasn't for me then he wouldn't have had such a good career and I'm sure he's right because he was at a crossroads when he was at Middlesbrough."

Murdoch and Souness were at the heart of things for Charlton, but it was deploying Alan Foggon just behind his two strikers that proved to be a tactical masterstroke.

"Foggy was a winger and I moved him back into the middle of the park because he was such a strong runner.

"He was very quick, a good part and a big part of what we did because he could burst from midfield.

"I brought Graeme Souness into the centre of midfield and David Armstrong on one side and on the other there was Foggon and it worked a treat.

"John Hickton led the line for me. He could do everything that you would want from a centre forward.

"John was a good header of the ball, he was decent on the ball and he always got himself involved. He was a good player and one that I enjoyed watching."

Boro became a side with a reputation as being hard to beat and his central defenders got the ultimate seal of approval from a World Cup-winning boss.

"I had Stuart Boam and Willie Maddren as my centre-halves and they were a good partnership.

"It's sad that Willie is no longer with us. He was a lovely man and a very, very good player. Willie didn't argue with anyone. He quietly went about his business, but he was very stylish.

"And I liked Stuart Boam because he made sure everyone did what I told them to do when we were defending. At corner kicks and free-kicks he would always push players into position. It was a bit like the way I used to play at Leeds."

Charlton's efforts were recognised as he was named as the Bell's Manager of the Year in what were happy times for the Boro players on and off the field and for Charlton as his club thrived in the old First Division.

"I didn't spend much money as a manager. I preferred developing my own players with my coaches (Harold Shepherdson, Ian McFarlane and Jimmy Greenhalgh).

"I didn't ask for much money, but when I did feel as though I'd need something I did have to go the directors to see if they would make it available. I was generally happy working with the lads I had.

"They were a good lot. It is helpful when you can have a go at the players and they can take it. I did that in different ways. I didn't get annoyed with them - well, not really annoyed.

"But sometimes I'd have a go when I looked on to the pitch and I thought, 'That bugger there, he's day-dreaming on me,' and I'd put him right, make no mistake."

"I've heard people say that I set my dog on them, but that wasn't true. I had a Labrador and when the wife was away I didn't want to leave it in the house, so I used to bring it with me. She was a smashing little dog that we picked up.

"I took them shooting and I'd take the lads that wanted to come with me. There would be four or five of them. It was because of them that I was very happy in

Middlesbrough and it was home for us for four years."

Boro won the Anglo-Scottish Cup in a two-legged final with Fulham.

After resigning his position at Boro at the end of the 1976-77 season, to take what he said would be a six-month break from football, he took over as Sheffield Wednesday manager in October 1977.

He went back on Teesside as caretaker manager when he helped Boro avert relegation after Malcolm Allison was fired before heading to Newcastle where the fans turned against him.

"I did all okay at Middlesbrough and at Sheffield Wednesday. The only problem was at Newcastle where the fans in one corner started having a go at me, shouting, 'Charlton out, Charlton out,' so I said okay.

"I wasn't having that so I just went in to see the board and told them, 'That's it, I'm finished,' and I left. It was a pre-season friendly against Sheffield United and I played a few of the young lads, like Paul Gascoigne.

"I ended up being out of a job, but I thought, 'Never mind, something will turn up,' and it did. It worked out well for me."

That episode at the start of the 1985-86 season also vindicated his decision to join Leeds United as a youngster, despite being a miner's son from Ashington, Northumberland, where most youngsters dreamed of playing for Newcastle.

That's where his mother's cousin Jackie Milburn was a hero, but Jack and younger brother thought differently as they headed off to Leeds and Manchester United respectively.

"I ended up at Leeds instead of Newcastle because we had family down there in Yorkshire.

"It was Jimmy Milburn and my uncle George and my uncle Jack, who were my mother's brothers and lived and played in Leeds. It was a good decision to go there.

"We were very successful. We had a good manager and good trainers and we used to just do what we were told."

Middlesbrough-born Revie was the inspiration behind Leeds and Charlton picked up plenty of tricks of the managerial trade.

"Don Revie was a great person to learn from. He was the sort of person who would happily come and talk to you.

"He would always seem to agree with you, and not many managers would agree with you, but Don always seemed to do that.

"Don would always get you to agree with what he wanted you to be doing as well. He was a very intelligent manager who was good enough to manage England.

"I was lucky that I played with some very good players like Norman Hunter, Johnny Giles, Mick Jones and Alan Clarke and Peter Lorimer and Eddie Gray and Paul Reaney. Gary Sprake was the goalkeeper, but I never trusted him."

Charlton helped Leeds to the old Second Division title before going on to win the League Championship, the League Cup, Fairs Cup (twice) and the FA Cup and was also named Footballer of the Year by the Football Writers' Association in 1967.

He played in 629 games for Leeds between 1953 and 1973 and also scored 70 goals, mainly at set-pieces. It was at the ripe old age of 29 that Charlton forced his way into the England team that won the World Cup in 1966.

"I was lucky I got into the squad a couple of years before the World Cup and I was put in alongside Bobby Moore, who was a great player, and our Bobby.

"Sir Alf knew what his team would be and stuck to the same set of lads apart from when there was an injury or something like that. We did well together."

Charlton followed in Sir Alf's footsteps by guiding the Republic of Ireland into unchartered territory in the shape of the 1998 European Championship and two World Cups.

He did so by travelling far and wide to make the most of FIFA's 'Granny Rule' that allowed players to represent the country of the birth of parents or grandparents.

"The main thing is that at international level you've got to hunt around for players to represent your country.

"Me and Maurice Setters, when we realised there was some Irish link, we went and had a look at them at all sorts of different football clubs," said Charlton, who took over the job in February 1986 on a part-time basis.

"There was Andy Townsend, who was very good, and there were a few others we discovered like (Kevin) Sheedy, (John) Aldridge and (Jason) McAteer.

"We didn't have the best players, but I'll tell you what, we had some really good players and the best one of all in my eyes was Paul McGrath.

"Paul had to be the best player I ever managed. He was brilliant. You didn't have to tell him what to do. It normally just came naturally to him.

"It was because of people like Paul that we were difficult to beat and we did lots of good things on set-pieces. I did okay with Ireland."

That is another understatement as Ireland rose to sixth place in the FIFA world rankings under Charlton's watch.

Charlton went on to "thoroughly enjoy retirement" with wife Pat in the heart of the Northumberland National Park where he is still able to indulge in his favourite pastimes.

"I go to watch the odd game of football when I get invited along. I couldn't be happier. I still love the countryside and I like my shooting days and my fishing days. It's one of the most beautiful parts of the world up here."

• *"Jack Charlton was a really first-class defender who did his job really well as a centre-half," former England goalkeeper Gordon Banks told Backpass magazine.*

"On the one hand, Bobby Moore was the man that covered around him, picking everything up and anticipating and stopped the attacks.

"On the other, Jack was the man who would mark the centre-forward and he'd do a really good job of that, always getting really tight on to his man and getting tackles in.

"One of the main things is that because he was very tall he won a considerable amount of stuff in the air, whereas although Bobby was a great player that was probably Bobby's weakness because he couldn't climb like Big Jack. Jack was always the favourite to win the crosses that came into the dangerous areas just outside my six-yard box.

"Jack always did what he was told by me because he knew that I was helping him to do his job and the other defenders as well by shouting orders to cover or to get tight or to win it, or if I shouted 'away' he knew I wasn't coming or if I shouted 'keeper's' then he would block the forward from jumping at me although he didn't make it obvious enough for a penalty to be awarded, but it just mean the guy couldn't jump with me.

"Sometimes if Jack thought it was a 50-50 situation then he would still be there to head it just in case I didn't get there, but when I knew that was the case I'd punch right through and whack him on the side of his head and it still makes me laugh remembering the way he'd be rubbing his head as he ran back up the field, but he was a big, strong lad, so he could take it.

"Off the field Jack was great, but then again all the England lads were. We always had a good laugh and made fun out of different things and took the mickey out of each other. It was just a great atmosphere in that dressing room and Jack was one of the lads who made it that way.

"Jack will have learnt from Sir Alf Ramsey, who got to know the players, and whatever he asked them to do he did it for them. He would keep those players together and results came for him.

"He made sure that those players played together in the lead-up to the World Cup finals so they would get to know each other's games and play as a team and that is exactly what we did. Alf always knew exactly what to say before a game and at half-time and he did the job really well."

Maddren Between Rock And Hard Place

It speaks volumes that tributes poured in following the death at the age of 49 of former Boro manager and defender Willie Maddren following his five-year fight with Motor Neurone Disease in August 2000.

The father-of-four Maddren served Boro with distinction, playing more than 350 times for Boro between 1969 and 1978, before retiring at the age of 26 due to a serious knee injury.

Maddren was brought up in Haverton Hill and went on to become a local hero after joining Boro from amateur side Port Clarence in 1968 as a highly-rated centre-back who played for the England Under-23s.

After helping Jack Charlton's team win the old Second Division title in style in 1974, he became Boro coach and physiotherapist after hanging up his boots before being appointed manager in June 1984.

Elsewhere in this book, Gary Pallister could not have spoken more highly of Maddren who he held responsible for launching a career that propelled him to the top of the English game and international honours.

Maddren was sacked in February 1986 as relegation to the old Third Division and bankruptcy loomed, but still left an important legacy, according to former Boro striker David Mills, who worked under him as player-coach.

"It was tough because we had no money, the club was struggling and we didn't have a good enough group of players," Mills said.

"But what Willie did do was bring in or develop some really good young players because he had a real eye for talent.

"He signed Stephen Pears, who became a top keeper, Gary Pallister from Billingham, Brian Laws from Huddersfield, Tony Mowbray was coming through along with Stuart Ripley and Colin Cooper and we got Bernie Slaven for next to nothing.

"If you look at the players he brought in for relatively little money and the players he nurtured through the youth team I think people forget that in the short term he was there what sort of a legacy he left.

"We knew we had a good crop of young players such as Lee Turnbull and Gary Parkinson, but Willie didn't want to risk those players' careers by playing them too early in a struggling team.

"Willie was between a rock and a hard place. He protected them, but circumstances sometimes dictate situations.

"When Bruce Rioch came in, the club went into liquidation so they couldn't buy anyone and Bruce was left with very little choice but to throw some of the young players in and they handled it well. A lot of that was down to Willie."

The Willie Maddren MND Fund has raised hundreds of thousands of pounds for research into the degenerative disease.

Bruce's Boro Bonus

It was a close shave in more ways than one for Bruce Rioch's Boro 'Band of Brothers'.

For starters, they came within a whisker of swapping professional football for the dole queue amid the financial meltdown of the mid-80s.

But, when Steve Gibson came to the club's rescue and Rioch got a grip of things, they ended up facing a bright future again.

That was thanks to his highly disciplined regime, which saw players fined for turning up for work unkempt.

"It's no secret that I was a disciplinarian, but I didn't do that just to be a rotter - that was only because I firmly believed it was required for us to be successful," said Rioch from his Cornwall home.

"The circumstances required discipline because they were young lads and they responded well to the strict regime and discipline I set out – which I just felt was necessary to keep them focused.

"I said that because there was so much speculation on a daily basis that the club was going to fold and they'd be on the scrapheap.

"There were these young men, at the start of their careers, who would have been forgiven for not knowing whether they were coming or going.

"One of the criteria was to come in clean-shaven because I wanted the players to present themselves as smart and tidy. It was a case of 'Look smart, think smart, look the part, be the part'.

"They were really committed to Boro, but there was so much uncertainty about the club's future and their own careers that I felt it needed a very firm hand on the rudder so to speak.

"They needed firm guidance from myself and (assistant boss) Colin Todd because the club was in turmoil."

As Rioch's dad, Jim, was a regimental sergeant-major with the Scots Guards, it should be no surprise that there was a militaristic element to the Boro regime.

"My father used to say to us if you can't play the part you can still look it.

"They accepted it - they might not have liked it but they got on with it. It kept us focused and united them as a group.

"I didn't take that approach because I thought they were a bunch of good-for-nothing rascals, far from it.

"Every time we left a hotel on away trips the staff would always comment on what an impeccable group of players they were.

"Not only did they behave magnificently, but they would dress with the club blazer and tie for evening meal.

"Nowadays, players would probably come down and have dinner in tracksuits which is fine, but we just had it different.

"I wanted to create a good impression everywhere we went and it paid off. It was like a band of brothers because they were always there for each other and still are.

"They were a fine bunch of lads who were a credit to their profession and to themselves, their families and the club.

"Ask anyone if the players made headlines for the wrong reasons and the answer will be no. That says it all."

Rioch was promoted from Willie Maddren's coaching staff to manager in February 1986 as relegation to the old Third Division loomed.

Things went from bad to worse when the official receiver locked the gates of Ayresome Park with Boro on the verge of bankruptcy.

Money was so tight that Boro borrowed £30,000 from the Professional Footballers' Association to pay the players' wages.

That summer, Rioch was just two days into his family holiday in Spain when he was summoned to the hotel reception.

He went from splashing around in the hotel pool with his children to being told to make the biggest decision of his life.

"It was when I was on holiday with Mallorca with my lovely wife and our two young children that I was told to come to reception.

"It was a phone call from the provisional liquidator which I had to take on reception because they didn't have mobiles in those days.

"There was no messing about, no niceties, he just said that I had two options.

"The first was that 'Your contract with the club is finished,' and the second was that 'You can work for the club without pay'.

"My wife and I had discussed both scenarios, so I said that the second option was no problem and I worked for the club without salary. We knew it would work out well. We had faith."

After being told by new owner Steve Gibson that the club was going into provisional liquidation, Rioch had already started revamping the playing staff as the club adapted to the hard times.

"We had to release about 20 players. We'd looked at our personnel very carefully to work out who we wanted to keep.

"And they ended up mainly being really young players – with the exception of Archie Stephens, who was a seasoned striker.

"In the end, we got by with just 14 players that season because of the cutbacks and we relied upon mainly home-grown players in our ranks.

"That summer all the players were uncertain about their careers and when they came back for pre-season training we were literally all over the place.

"We had great support from local clubs and we played in Billingham, Stockton, parks with jumpers and jackets down for goalposts.

"But because they were a young group, tremendous camaraderie emerged because of the adversity that they were going through.

"Most of them hadn't even played a proper league match and yet here they were right on the brink.

"There was a lot of worry about what might happen to them due to liquidation and the fact we all stayed together as a group and didn't jump ship made me think they were a 'Band of Brothers.'

"Even now, if there was a call for them all to get together for an important cause, they would all be there like a shot. They are incredible people who achieved incredible things.

"It helped that there was a tremendous show of support from the fans who were desperate not to see their club go out of business.

"We went from average crowds of about 3,000 to attendances of over 10,000 at the end of the next one.

"They could see with their own eyes that the players on the pitch were giving it their all for the club and the town as a whole."

Under Rioch, Boro achieved back-to-back promotions to the old First Division and were on the brink of a first ever Wembley final in the Zenith Data Systems Cup when he was sacked.

"My time at Boro really stands out because of the circumstances and the very special people who were involved with the club.

"My best Middlesbrough memory is the day we came out of provisional liquidation - the club being stabilised, being a member of the Football League and being able to progress from the Third to First Division.

"On a more light-hearted note, it's funny to think of my son, Gregor, sitting in the dressing room talking to Mogga (Tony Mowbray) who was his hero – and still is."

"I came back with Millwall and the fans gave me a really warm welcome. A manager at another club said he'd never heard anything like it. It blew me away.

"There has always been an affinity and it will never change to the club, the fans and the players.

"The players were competitive footballers, but they were real gentlemen. A very close friend said to me great ambassadors never get into any trouble.

"The players I had at Middlesbrough will always have a special bond because we went through such adversity."

Red Robbo The Riverside Revolutionary

Bryan Robson was a talismanic figure on the field and he proved to be one off the field as well with Boro.

He was an inspirational presence for Manchester United and England in the midfield trenches and he was pretty much the same when he moved to the touchline on Ayresome Park.

Robson was an instant hit on Teesside after his arrival as player-manager in 1994 after embarking on a new chapter in his glittering career that saw him skipper United and England Boro.

He guided Boro to promotion twice and inspired the club to three Wembley finals in a seven-year stint as manager after being persuaded to spearhead chairman Steve Gibson's so-called Riverside Revolution.

But the self-effacing Robson put his success as a rookie manager down to dressing room camaraderie.

"Having a good atmosphere in the dressing room was a huge factor in getting us up both times," Robson said.

"The first time I came here when we were still playing at Ayresome Park, I inherited good solid professionals, such as John Hendrie and Paul Wilkinson, and Alan Moore and Craig Hignett could score goals from wide positions.

"And I was lucky in that I inherited John Pickering, who was a first-rate coach, to help him hit the ground running and he was invaluable.

"But then I brought a bit of experience from the Premiership with me and Viv Anderson coming in, and then Clayton Blackmore and Nigel Pearson, which gave the squad a nice balance and we clinched the only promotion spot with a game to spare in the last match at Ayresome Park."

The stakes could not have been higher that day when Luton visited, but Robson focused his players' minds with the shortest team-talk of his life.

"David Pleat did me a favour because he more or less did my team-talks for me.

"He said, 'I know what Middlesbrough need to do on the day, but I always spoil parties and I'm going to spoil this party.'

"If they'd beaten us we would still have had to go to the last game. For him to say that, I just said to the boys, 'There you go.'

"He said he's going to spoil our party. Well, what sort of party do we want? That was that for my team talk. Probably the shortest I've ever done."

Boro spent two seasons in the Premier League before slipping back into the Football League thanks to a three-point deduction for cancelling a fixture due to a debilitating injury crisis.

Despite the set-back, Gibson retained his faith in Robson and he was paid back in style as Boro bounced back at the first attempt.

"The second time round was difficult because we had a good team that was very unfortunate to get relegated, but that was due to the cup success that showed what a good team we were, but took its toll in the league.

"I changed things around the second time round because Juninho, Fabrizio Ravanelli and Emerson wanted to leave, but I got great professionals in, like Neil Maddison, Paul Merson and Andy Townsend and they did a great job for us.

"They were confident players and good lads and it meant that we had a really good dressing room which for me is always important if you want to achieve things. We had a good atmosphere in both successes that we had.

"If the lads are good characters that is what they encourage and that's especially what Nigel Pearson did as my captain because he's a good, strong personality.

"People like him generate an atmosphere within the club and a belief that they will achieve things. When I brought in Andy Townsend that's exactly what he did as well. That helped the boys who were already in the club."

Robson's signing of German striker Uwe Fuchs on loan from Kaiserslautern also proved to be a shrewd move.

"My old England teammate Tony Woodcock was over in Germany and told him that he had a striker over there who could come in on a free transfer and he'd do a great job.

"That is exactly what he did with nine goals in 13 games to push us over the line. Contacts are always important. That is why networking is always a really important part of the game. Without England we wouldn't have got him."

Fuchs may have had an incredible short-term impact, but Robson still hails Juninho's arrival as his biggest coup in the transfer market.

"Without doubt the most important signing was Juninho because it captured the public imagination and staggered the press because a Brazilian should never have been a success in England because of the weather.

"But his charisma and skill proved the doubters wrong and a lot of people couldn't get their heads round it."

Robson left Boro in 2001 and although he enjoyed plenty of good times there is still a tinge of regret.

"I'm disappointed that I didn't win Boro's first trophy because we got to three cup finals, but I've got fantastic memories. I got on really well with Steve Gibson and (chief executive) Keith Lamb and all the staff at the club.

"I really enjoyed my time there because of the finals and the type of football that we played because when we were on song the level of entertainment and excitement was really high.

"The day I left was really sad because I enjoyed my time there. There were a few fans who had a go at me, but nowadays it doesn't matter where I go in the world. When I meet Boro fans they say I did a great job."

El Tel's Houdini Act

Terry Venables managed the England national side and the world's most glamorous football club. But his time at Middlesbrough still evokes extraordinary memories.

Venables almost reached the twin peaks of European football with England and Barcelona - but the way he successfully negotiated Boro's passage out of the doldrums somehow stands out for the managerial maestro.

Towards the end of a glittering career, he was hired by Boro to give manager Bryan Robson a helping hand as head coach when the club was teetering on the brink of relegation from the Premier League in December 2000.

Just for those who don't remember, Venables sparked an incredible turn-around in fortunes that saw Boro beat the likes of Chelsea and Liverpool on Teesside before winning at Newcastle and Arsenal as mid-table security ensued.

"There were lots of people who thought I wouldn't enjoy living up in the North East, but to tell you the truth that couldn't have been further from the truth," Venables said.

"We lived in the lovely village of Croft and although my wife didn't join me up there for a while she'd have hardly missed me because I hardly had a second to spare early on.

"That was because there was so much work to be done at the club, but it was a challenge I relished and, from my point of view, everyone made me feel very much at home from the word go, which helped me on my way."

Venables - nicknamed El Tel thanks to his spell at the Nou Camp - used all the experience he had gleaned at the likes of Crystal Palace, QPR, Tottenham and Barcelona to inspire a Boro recovery at the Rockliffe Park training HQ.

"I really liked it at Boro. The players were so good and interested in what was going on every day they would come into training with a real spring in their step to see what I was going to do next.

"I enjoyed their company, but the same applied to Bryan Robson who I worked alongside with for England at Euro 96, Gordon McQueen, Viv Anderson and the three of them were excellent.

"Although it wasn't too easy for them at first, me coming in, we got on really well. Everyone pulled in the right direction. And with that there was a power of synergy that went on through the group. So Boro holds very special memories for me."

Once strategies were finalised on the practice ground, Venables set about the challenge of securing Boro's top-flight status with a simple plan when the action started in earnest.

"The first thing was not to give any goals away – or as few as possible. They had played with three-come-five at the back before I arrived.

"You could take a risk with that formation at home, but make life very difficult for the opposition away from home by playing five defenders and still attack.

"We could do that because we had people like Christian Karembeu and Keith O'Neill who could break forward and we had Alen Boksic who was a clinical finisher and a handful for any central defensive duo, even on his own.

"We tried to play to everyone's strengths and get the best out of everybody and that was a joint-effort from the four of us.

"We got stuck in and we were fortunate that when we played Liverpool and Chelsea and won those games it gave everyone a lift. If you start well you get a belief and develop momentum."

Venables did such a good job he could have stayed on at Boro, but decided to honour his media commitments which paved the way for Steve McClaren to take the reins when Robson left Teesside.

"I was working for ITV and they had just got the Match of the Day contract and they were kind enough to let me go in the first place because I was under contract and they could have blocked it.

"They were understandably more excited about the next season and they had let me go because I had given them my word that I would go back to the studio and that is what I did."

When McClaren left to take over the England job in 2006, Venables was also the shortlist of possible replacements, along with Martin O'Neill, but he decided not to go back.

"I was tempted. But it was just one of those things. I wasn't able to do it. These things rely on sometimes you not being able to do it and when you want it they are maybe not able to do it.

"It's a two-way thing. Like most things in life, the timing has to be right. It was right when we first went there because it just felt like natural progression.

"Now I feel terrific because when I was at Middlesbrough and Leeds I had a bad hip problem and it made me suffer, but that is fantastic now so I feel like a young boy again."

• *Former Boro skipper Gareth Southgate made no secret of the fact he regarded Terry Venables as his favourite ever coach.*

He gave an insight into why he thought so highly while managing the England side in the 2018 World Cup finals.

"As a player, you play for coaches who help you develop as a person and a player," said Southgate.

"Terry Venables challenged us tactically. With international players, you're dealing with top players so they want to keep learning.

"He created an environment that was fun to be in. One of his sayings was, 'This is not a rehearsal.'

"This isn't a rehearsal for us. You might only get one crack at a World Cup, so we

wanted to give it as good a go as we could, and generate memories.

"You learn from all your coaches, from watching their teams play, watching them, from discussions.

"Any coach wants to keep finding new ways to help players and teams. But you have to be your own person, marry things to your beliefs and values."

McClaren's Penalty Prize

It was the moment that everything changed for Steve McClaren.

European football was within touching distance for the second season running.

Boro's fortunes were on the up, as was McClaren's career trajectory, but then a Manchester City player was brought down and everything was up in the air.

"I have a defining moment, the biggest one of my career," McClaren said in a revealing interview with Colin Murray for BBC Radio 5 Live.

"It was in my fourth year at Middlesbrough and we were seventh. Man City were eighth and it was the last game of the season, we were playing them and Stuart Pearce was manager.

"They had to win and we had to draw to claim seventh to get back into Europe, which went on to give me the opportunity to reach the UEFA Cup final and become England manager.

"It's injury time and the score is 1-1, they get a penalty and Robbie Fowler steps up. I think this was the most defining moment of my career.

"Everyone was going crazy and saying it wasn't a penalty and I looked up to the heavens.

"After 38 games, 94 minutes and it all came down to this. My future - in terms of England, Europe, Boro - was all on this.

"If we hadn't gone into Europe again, all the money we'd spent would've gone and I could've been in oblivion the next season, sacked after this penalty.

"I know Robbie well. I'd never seen him miss a penalty in training. He stepped up, I've still got the photo and the memory is in my mind, Mark Schwarzer saves it and we finished seventh, getting into Europe.

"The rest is history, but that's the biggest moment in my career. I could've been in oblivion - either that, or go on to better things."

McClaren may have led Boro to the UEFA Cup final on the back of that game, but it was a bumpy road.

"It was a bizarre season. We'd come back from a training camp and I remember thinking that was a great camp, we're okay now, we're ready.

"We still had Europe but we're okay and we ended up getting beaten 4-0 by Aston Villa at home.

"There was the season ticket incident when a bloke came onto the pitch, threw his season ticket at me and yelled, 'Get lost, McClaren!' I just couldn't believe it.

"I remember having to get in a car to get to my car around the other side of the stadium because there was a protest at one end. I expected to be sacked.

"I was thinking, 'Oh, wow, this is a moment,' and then going up and seeing Steve Gibson.

"I always used to go into the boardroom after games and he was up there and I walked through the door and he was having a pint with David O'Leary, whose side had just thrashed us.

"Imagine my face! I am trying to be polite and said, 'Well done, David, good win,' and everything like that, and I'm thinking, 'Is that the next Middlesbrough manager?'

"David downs his pint and off he goes. I was thinking, 'Oh no, he's my replacement' and Steve says straight away: 'Don't you worry – don't you even think about it. He will not be the next one – you are it. Your job's safe.'

"And I went, 'All right,' and the next week we went and beat Jose Mourinho's Chelsea 3-0 and a couple of months later we were in an FA Cup semi-final, pulling off miracles in the UEFA Cup.

"After the Basel game I told the players: 'Enjoy the night, as this will only happen once in your career.' Then three weeks later against Steaua it happened again.

"People often say why do you keep coming back with all this stick and all the ups and downs, and its because you can have a season ticket thrown at you and two months later you're playing Seville in the UEFA Cup final. That's why we do it."

SEASON FROM HELL

The Year Boro Went Bonkers

They converged on Wembley Stadium in their thousands, hope in their hearts and anger, too.

The joy at Middlesbrough reaching their first – and only - FA Cup final was laced with pain, euphoria tempered by relegation from the Premier League.

No set of fans had ever gone to Wembley to protest until the 'Smoggies' arrived, at war with officialdom and the Football Association suits they were blaming for the club's demise.

Little did they know, however, that Boro players were at war amongst themselves - all too literally unwilling to go down without a fight.

That may have been the case off the field, but not on it as Roberto Di Matteo scored for Chelsea after 43 seconds to fire himself into FA Cup history and the game was over almost as soon as it started.

But what can be revealed for the first time is the full story behind Boro's calamitous season that ended in fisticuffs with Fabrizio Ravanelli and Neil Cox kicking off well before referee Stephen Lodge had got the 1997 final started.

It was at the team hotel where, according to Cox, Ravanelli took exception to a story he'd done with the *Daily Star,* suggesting that the Italian superstar be dropped by manager Bryan Robson in favour of Mikkel Beck.

"I did an interview as a favour for a mate on the pre-match Press day and left Rav out of the starting XI because, like me, he was struggling to be fit and we couldn't afford to gamble," Cox said.

"On the Saturday, it was all over the back page of the *Daily Star*: 'Cox – Rav should miss out.'"

"When we were having the pictures for the suits and the sunglasses, he decides to spit and throw a punch.

"I dived in, fists flying. I wasn't slagging him off. I was right. That's why it got nasty and we had a scuffle."

Tempers flared as players were about to board the team bus where comedian Stan Boardman was preparing for the toughest gig of his life.

"It turned into the most awful final preparation for the biggest game of most of our lives," said teammate Robbie Mustoe.

"In the team photograph, you basically had Ravanelli trying to reach across players in the team photograph to have a fight with Neil.

"There was just so much crap even on the way to the game when Rav was shouting at Neil at the back of the bus.

"There were players not involved in the game on there who's been drinking the night before and Bryan Robson thought it would be a good idea to have Stan Boardman telling jokes. It smacked of unprofessionalism."

According to midfielder Craig Hignett, Boro were their own worst enemies.

"Back-biting, bitching and people wanting to fight and then to go and play the biggest game of our lives, we didn't give ourselves a chance," Hignett said.

"As a boy I'd dreamed about playing in an FA Cup final, but behind-the-scenes chaos meant it was surreal and definitely contributed to that goal."

There was anger in the stands, too, 30,000 Boro fans raising three fingers and shouting three points as they vented their spleen in the direction of FA chief executive Graham Kelly as he led the Royal entourage to meet the players.

The Duchess of Kent found herself in the firing line amid a protest at the three-point penalty imposed for failing to fulfill a fixture, which had ultimately led to the relegation on the last game of the season, six days before at Elland Road.

"It was a difficult day at the end of a difficult season," said then club secretary Graham Fordy, "and so you can understand why the fans wanted to vent their anger at those in authority who they felt were to blame,"

The in-fighting contrasted sharply with the start of the season and the buzz created by the arrival of Ravanelli in a £7-million deal not long after 'The White Feather' scored in Juventus' Champions League final victory over Ajax.

Ravanelli, who signed a four-year deal initially worth £42,000-a-week, marked his debut with a Riverside hat-trick in a 3-3 draw with Liverpool – although it seems they could have done with more than one home dressing room.

"It was like getting a Messi or Ronaldo," Hignett said. "But he was like Marmite. Half the squad hated him, the other half loved him.

"He worked unbelievably hard and was one of the best finishers I'd seen, but as a man he rubbed people up the wrong way. He was selfish in everything he did."

Eric Paylor, who was then covering Boro's fortunes for the Evening Gazette, said Ravanelli "electrified" Teesside.

"All the fans wanted to read about was Rav, Emerson and Juninho. It was easy-peasy. Rav was larger than life. There'd never been anyone like him on Teesside.

"This was the big season for Steve Gibson. They'd just finished 12th with Juninho, they had money in the bank and they splashed out big-time on Ravanelli and Emerson and showed the rest of the Premier League: 'We're on the march.'

"It was Gibson's dream to resurrect the glory days which we hadn't seen since the Jack Charlton era in the 1970s.

"All they had to do was stay up because, if they had, the next season he'd have provided money to sign another Ravanelli, another Juninho and another Emerson and they would have had six top-class players in the team.

"It didn't really work for me that season because you had two Middlesbrough teams on the pitch at the same time. You had the three world-class stars and the other eight.

"Very rarely did they blend. Rav would pass it to Emerson, Emerson would pass it to Juninho and Juninho would pass to Rav.

"I can't ever remember Rav once passing the ball to Mikkel Beck. He had almost no respect for Beck, but would always insist he passed the ball to him when they were attacking.

"I always felt as if the others were making up the numbers. Their job at the back of their minds was just to give the ball to the big three, then sit back. That's why it didn't work.

"But the fact they were so successful in the cups, but a disaster in the league, is something no one will ever be able to explain.

"They lost home game after home game in the Premier League, which is overlooked, but they're still undone by the fact we hadn't turned up for the Blackburn game. We'd have stayed up even if we'd been beaten 15-0."

Ravanelli had quickly become disenchanted, judging by Jan Aage Fjortoft's recollections of a team meeting in a hotel ahead of the visit to Aston Villa in November when the striker was accompanied by Gianni Paladini who was translating proceedings.

"Rav turned into a rant, having a go, wanting to leave, loud and in Italian, right in the middle of the meeting. I couldn't stop laughing. At the end, Bryan said, 'Okay Rav?' and Paladini was, 'Yes, it's okay.' You could not make it up."

They lost 1-0 at Villa Park as a campaign that began brightly careered downhill; a 5-1 Anfield thumping in December stretched a winless league run to 12 games.

Morale was sinking, injuries took their toll and a virus swept through the camp, which meant that, combined with suspensions, Robson was without 23 players on the eve of a visit to Blackburn just before Christmas (December 21).

Paylor was the first person outside the club to find out all was not well. "I walked into Robbo's office at the Riverside and he said, 'Don't ask me what the team is - I haven't got one.'"

A meeting was convened by chief executive Keith Lamb in his office, with Robson, club doctor Laurie Dunn and physiotherapist Bob Ward to discuss the situation.

Lamb called the Premier League for guidance. He was warned unequivocally there were clear rules against arbitrary postponements and if they called off the game it was at their peril. The club gambled and lost the biggest bet in Boro history.

"I was responsible for cancelling the game," Lamb said. "I'm convinced we did everything properly. We were 'invited' to postpone that game, but there was a U-turn in the corridors of power that rebounded on us very badly."

Boro miscalculated, thinking they would escape with a financial penalty, but a month later ended up being clobbered - despite medical evidence to back their case - with a £50,000 fine and three-point deduction after an independent Premier League tribunal.

The punishment, which left Boro four points adrift at the foot of the table, was upheld despite Gibson hiring formidable barrister George Carman at an FA appeal to argue their case, but he suffered a rare defeat.

"The punishment was an absolute joke," Robson said. "Three more players had dropped out on the Friday, so we were absolutely decimated."

"But if I'd have known there was any chance of a points deduction, I'd have fielded the YTS lads and the laundry ladies.

"We just didn't have enough players. I was injured and I had to play at Arsenal at Arsenal the following week which made me bail out for good because I couldn't move for three days afterwards."

Lamb still insists the club was "harshly treated" but Gibson was apoplectic, saying at the time: "The problem lay with the people in the Premier League. Many of our questions were never answered. No one involved came out of it with any credit. We weren't treated fairly. It was easy for people to feel bitter and resentful."

Those emotions were not confined to the Riverside stands or those who thought the authorities were at fault.

"I don't mind saying it was a bad, regrettable decision from the club and manager," Mustoe added.

"I'm very bitter. It's a relegation I won't take. It had nothing to do with my team or me. We could have put a team out. It was just wrong. It was a very badly managed situation."

Afterwards, Boro bumped along at the foot of the Premier League, but raised their game for knockout competitions, reaching the League Cup final where Ravanelli's extra-time goal put the club on course for its first major honour before Emile Heskey equalised.

Robson was held responsible for the defeat by Ravanelli over his failure to deploy any of his substitutes as the clock ticked towards the final whistle at Wembley.

He might not have rated Robson's managerial acumen and nor did he rate fellow striker Mikkel Beck.

"He always said he didn't want to play with him," Fjortoft said. "Once in the dressing room, he said in broken English: 'Jan, I want you play … for me Mikkel Beck Serie B.' The problem was that Mikkel was also listening to our conversation."

Back home in Italy, Ravanelli also showed he had a neat turn of phrase in a damning indictment of the club's lack of training facilities.

"They have a Ferrari, but they don't have a garage," scoffed Ravanelli, fed up being shunted around Teesside in what Mustoe described as a "crappy old beat-up bus" to practise at public parks and Kirklevington Grange Prison.

"The prison was all right because the playing surfaces were good," Mustoe said.

"If there was lots of rain we practised on what was called 'The Avenue of Trees'.

"That wasn't even a public park, it was just a green strip of land between big trees which sucked up the water so it was a decent place to train."

Emerson was described by Paylor as, "The greatest player I'd ever seen in a Boro shirt," due to his midfield performance in the opening phase of the season before "having his head turned" by stories linking him to Barcelona, becoming restless and going AWOL.

"Emerson always seemed to have a ticket back to Brazil," said Fjortoft, who would leave mid-season along with Nicky Barmby and Brazilian World Cup-winner Branco, who he remembers being "six kilos overweight when he arrived and 10 kilos overweight when he left."

Games came thick and fast due to Boro's cup exploits, which included a topsy-turvy semi-final at Old Trafford against Chesterfield, described as, 'One of the finest FA Cup-ties in the competition's 125-year history,' by *The Daily Telegraph*.

"My abiding memory was looking to my left and (reserves coach) Gordon McQueen was shaking so much he couldn't put a cigarette in his mouth," said Ward. "I was killing myself laughing but it was frightening."

A grueling contest ended up 3-3 after extra-time, hardly ideal preparation for a League Cup final replay three days later which Steve Claridge settled in extra-time.

"It was a major disappointment losing the finals, especially the Leicester one, because we were the better team and deserved to win it, so I really felt for the boys," Robson said.

"They were devastated. We had a real good team, but I needed four or five more squad players because it wasn't strong enough when we had all the cup games."

Chesterfield were eventually overcome, but Boro faced a fixture pile-up ahead of the FA Cup final and played four league games in nine days – including the re-arranged Blackburn game which was drawn 0-0.

The league season culminated in a 1-1 draw at Leeds that condemned Robson's team to relegation by just two points, leaving Juninho crestfallen. "It was the worst day of my career," the Brazilian said.

Later, Juninho went into more detail with Four Four Two magazine: "Football has made me cry in moments of joy many times, but that was the only time I cried because of sadness.

"It was a big frustration for everyone – we had put so much faith and energy into that project, reaching two finals at Wembley and overcoming so many problems.

"We used to send out one team in the Premier League and another in the cups because we were confident we'd be able to recover our league position nearer the end of the season.

"When we finally got to the last few games, we realised we were in big trouble. We had to win the last game away against Leeds United and it didn't happen."

The cause was hindered by Ravanelli suffering a hamstring injury in a 3-3 draw at Manchester United, putting in doubt his chance of making the FA Cup final.

"He disappeared off to Italy for treatment," Ward said. "I was bemused. We should have been stricter.

"We treated him 12-15 hours a day trying to get him ready for the final, but he wouldn't let us fitness-test him and he came off early. It was rubbish."

Ravanelli traipsed off after 24 minutes and Chelsea were unforgiving; Eddie Newton's late goal finally put Boro out of their misery.

"There'd been that horrendous realisation after the Leeds game that we should have played kids at Blackburn," said Boro defender Curtis Fleming.

"But there wasn't a hangover - FA Cup final day arrived and it was a dream of mine to play in such a big game.

"I remember waking up and going for a walk and there was a bit of edge in the air.

"But you have to look after yourself and I was nervous - I even had my mates and family there to watch, but I loved all that.

"In terms of the argy-bargy between Rav and Coxy, I was thinking, 'Just calm down, I've got an FA Cup final to play.'

"When it kicked off it was all crazy, but it summed up our season and I still thought we'd dust ourselves down and give them a good run for their money. We'd had to pick ourselves up, but then got hit with a sucker-punch.

"I don't know what it's like to fight 15 rounds in a boxing match, but I think that's how we all felt afterwards.

"But the lasting memory for me was Nigel Pearson saying, just before kick-off, 'Right lads, we haven't had loads of luck this season, I think this could be our day,' and then 53 seconds later we realised maybe it wasn't."

All Played Out

"It was the season from Hell," is Robbie Mustoe's verdict on Middlesbrough's tumultuous 1996-97 campaign. "There were amazing highs and awful lows. We got so close to glory and ended up so, so far away."

Mustoe was the midfield mainstay in the star-studded Boro side that reached two Wembley cup finals and ended up being relegated from the Premier League, thanks to a monumental miscalculation by the club's administrators.

"I went around the block quite a few times with Boro, but that 96/97 season was truly extraordinary by anyone's standards," said Mustoe, who is now a TV pundit in the United States with NBC.

"I know footballers talking about rollercoaster rides is a blooming cliché, but in our case it was absolutely spot-on. It was an unbelievable time.

"Bryan Robson taking over as manager (in 1994) was the catalyst for Boro's upward mobility and (Fabrizio) Ravanelli coming in just seemed like the next stage in a remarkable rise of what the club owner Steve Gibson was trying to do.

"Steve wanted to give the area a team who could not only bloody the noses of the big boys, but also compete with them as well on a regular basis.

"We were on the up, but that squad wasn't all about the Juninhos, the Ravanellis and Emersons, although they were the ones who captured the public imagination.

"There was an underlying good squad there with the likes of Nick Barmby, Craig Hignett and Jan Aage Fjortoft that had got the club promoted and had a bloody good season in the Premier League before Rav rocked up.

"It was Bryan Robson who attracted the likes of Rav. He really put the club on the map and I loved playing for him. He was a hero of mine. I lost my place to him when he first arrived as player-manager, but I'd have run through that proverbial brick wall for him."

Mustoe had been brought to Boro by then manager Colin Todd in a £375,000 deal with Oxford when the club was attracting crowds of just 6,000 to the old Ayresome Park ground.

He went on to play 367 times for the club and saw crowds rise to 30,000+ at its plush new Riverside home.

"It was a remarkable journey. But for someone like Rav to come from winning the Champions League with Juventus to join our club just seemed plain crazy.

"We were excited about getting him to the club, but there was a thought of 'my goodness' as well.

"He was on something like £42,000 a week and there was shock that someone could come in and earn that sort of money when your Mustoes, (Curtis) Flemings and (Steve) Vickers were on incredible multiples lower than Rav's money.

"But it didn't bother me. I knew Rav would elevate us as a team and that would help us. You have to get your head round that. We'd all signed contracts and were happy with what we got. What the club decided to pay other players was their thing.

"Others might have been resentful because we were all in the same team doing the same job, but not me. Anyhow, Rav was headline news and in the dressing room it was a case of 'wow' this is huge.

"Sometimes he'd get frustrated and throw his arms in the air when he looked back down the pitch, which I hate. That annoyed some of the squad, but for myself, overall, I admired his professionalism and his quality.

"I could put up with the miserable, moody bugger. It's my personality. Other parts of the squad were not as forgiving."

Ravanelli's 31 goals in Boro colours that season showed he was a handful on the pitch for opposition defenders but, according to Mustoe, he was a handful off it as well for teammates and management.

"My main memories of him are as an incredible, exemplary professional and we got that in Gianluca Festa as well," Mustoe said. "Problems arose with Rav when he went off on international duty with Italy.

"It's the same now. Players say things when they're away that they don't think will filter back, but they do and they're often critical and controversial.

"There was a bit of resentment about what he said because the British newspapers went big on Ravanelli blaming the back four for our woes. That provided a bit of angst and concern, but we used to laugh as well. It was just the way he was with his moody temperament."

Nowadays, Boro have an impressive, state-of-the-art training ground, but back in the mid-90s, Mustoe and his colleagues made do with practising at the local prison, local council-owned parks and even open countryside.

"Our training facilities were a joke. There was no swish Hurworth training ground.

"It was no wonder Rav came out with one of his quotes which went along the lines of, 'They buy Ferraris – referring to himself – and they don't have a garage to park them in.'

"But on the back of him saying all that we did get a brand new training ground which was fantastic."

Boro's season took a turn for the worse when the decision was made not to send a team to Blackburn in mid-December.

"I do remember the absolute bollocks that the club put out, but the whole thing was probably never reported accurately, but what I do know for sure is that it still rankles.

"I vividly remember that day when we were in the dressing room and there were injuries and suspensions.

"People were saying, 'You're crocked,' and, 'You're looking ill,' but I looked around and thought we could put a team out. It was just wrong. It was a regrettable decision from the club and the manager."

Boro's hopes of escaping with a financial penalty were dashed as the club was fined and docked three points by the Premier League, a sanction that ultimately proved decisive.

"We could have gone to Blackburn and lost something like 10-0 and still stayed up. It's still very painful for me and very annoying because I've got another relegation on my record when it's got nothing to do with me or my team."

The cup competitions and what Mustoe described as a "stupid run of fixtures" took their toll and weary players went into their final game of the season at Leeds on the precipice of relegation with an FA Cup final to look forward to the following weekend. A 1-1 draw was not enough and Boro went down by two points.

"I remember walking across the field. That was probably the worst I felt all season.

"There was a realisation we were done, we were all played out. All our hard work had counted for nothing, and it would take a monumental effort to get us up for the final.

"The cameras went straight on to Juninho and all our star players, but they were the ones who would get moves to top-flight teams so they'd be fine whatever the outcome. They'd be all right. For me and for others like me, it was a big blow.

"It was embarrassing to go down, but you worry about your future. Missing out on being a Premier League player is huge because of the contracts and so you worry about security for your family. In those days, it wasn't just a sporting disappointment; it was a lifestyle concern."

Things went from bad to worse as Boro's preparations for the FA Cup final were beset by a pre-match skirmish between Ravanelli and Neil Cox on the morning of the showpiece event.

"From what I remember, Neil had done a piece for one of the big tabloid papers and said those who say they don't want to stay here, like Ravanelli, shouldn't play in the final.

"Then in the team photo at the club hotel you had Ravanelli basically reaching across other players trying to grab and have a fight because of the story. It was an awful final preparation for what should have been the biggest game of our careers."

Mustoe had other things on his mind having been "touch and go" before being passed fit for the game due to knee problems, which arose again soon after Chelsea went ahead on 43 seconds thanks to Roberto Di Matteo's long-range goal.

"I had a bad touch in that build-up, Emerson was out of position, Hignett didn't get across and Ben Roberts probably should have saved the shot.

"That was a bummer and then ten minutes later I reached around for someone after a throw-in and felt something go in my knee and hobbled around to get it going until I knew I was done. I blew out the cartilage in my knee. It was incredibly disappointing."

Mustoe sat on the sidelines with Ravanelli, who also went off early on with the recurrence of a hamstring injury, and the pair watched their teammates labour as Chelsea eased to a 2-0 win.

"There are pictures of us both looking dejected on the bench which shouldn't be a surprise because it must have been like having surgery without an anaesthetic for everyone watching who wanted Boro to win,"

"I'd love to blot the whole thing out of my memory but, unfortunately, human nature means you often forget the highs but remember the lowest lows most vividly.

"You tend to remember how you feel at the worst moments, and those after not contributing to the game, and family and friends and the whole world are watching and you're sat there and your team is losing, were really horrible.

"There was a real stillness in the dressing room afterwards, quietness and just desolation and exhaustion.

"Then we had a reception at the Grosvenor Hotel in London that night with families and friends and club staff and supporters. It was very low-key but I just remember being in pain all night. It was torture in more ways than one."

Fab's Dolce Vita

Exclusive Fabrizio Ravanelli interview

By Steve Brenner

You moved to Juventus in 1992 having never played in the top flight before - how amazing a feeling was that? Who were the best players in the Juve squad at that time? What was it like to suddenly be rubbing shoulders with those kinds of superstars? Any favourite anecdotes about Roberto Baggio or any of the others?

It was an amazing Juventus team. When I went there we had Roberto Baggio, Paolo Di Canio, Gianluca Vialli, Pierluigi Casiraghi in attack. Antonio Conte and Andreas Moller in midfield. I found out right away that the competition for places was on the training pitch. Baggio was a huge name at the time but for me, it was easy to become his friend and get settled in the changing room. All these top players were very humble guys. There was so much humility

I remember one time when we played in the Coppa Italia. We were winning 4-0 and got a free-kick. I really wanted to take it but Baggio wasn't so sure. 'It's impossible, Fabrizio. The only person who takes free-kicks at Juventus is me,'

he said. I looked at him and said, 'Ok Roberto, no problem. You are the best.'
I didn't try again for another year.

Your time with Juventus was particularly successful - you won the Scudetto, Coppa Italia, UEFA Cup and Champions League in just four years. How does that team compare to the best teams of the modern day? Better than the current Juve side? As good as Real Madrid/Barcelona?

For me, the team which won the Champions League in 1995 is the best ever team in the history of the club because Marcello Lippi came in and changed everything - the attitude, the mentality, the training. Before we worked mainly with the ball but Lippi had us in the gym. They would match up to teams like Real Madrid or Barcelona today. We were as good as them. It was a line-up with so much character and personality. We weren't scared of anyone.

You had just scored in the Champions League final. What are your memories of that night? How surprised were you that Juve were happy to let you go after playing a big part in winning the European Cup?

When you win that competition everything changes for you. When I scored I immediately thought about my family because I knew my dad was in the stands going crazy with the rest of my family. After the game it was like I was King of the world. You work hard every day for feelings like that. The party when we returned to Turin was crazy. Disco, dancing and champagne.

How did your move to Middlesbrough come about? Did you know anything about the club or the town before you signed? Did you have any offers from other clubs? What do you think would be the equivalent transfer now (a big-name international striker moving from the European champions to an unfashionable Premier League club)?

To be sold to Middlesbrough later that summer was, of course, a massive surprise for me. Gianluca Vialli had already gone but I spoke with the owners when that had happened and they told me I would be captain so I never thought for a second that I would be playing for Middlesbrough.

Glasgow Rangers came in for me earlier that summer but I said no and went on holiday. But Juventus wanted to make a deal and soon enough I was meeting with Bryan Robson in Milan. The Juve fans couldn't believe it. I was upset but it wasn't my decision. Crazy! It was like Karim Benzema going to Watford.

What were your first impressions of the town when you arrived? What were the people like? What did you make of the local nightlife? Did you ever eat a parmo?

I believed in how they wanted to build the club but when I arrived there things weren't good. We were training in the park or at the nearby prison. When I wanted to do extra gym work I went to the local David Lloyd fitness club. I did get some funny looks when I was on the treadmill but it was fine. When I met with Steve Gibson he assured me that a fantastic training ground was being built. But I am a professional so I got on with it. I had a nice house in Hutton Rudby and lived down the street from Gordon McQueen. Discos? No way. I had a young baby and a wife. Family and football was my life. And yes, I had a parmo.

How different were Serie A and the Premier League at that time? What were the differences? Which league was better?

In 1996, Italy specialized in a very tactical style of football. In England it was far more physical. The Italian teams would work so hard on the tactical side, but in England that was only a small part. I think it's important to mix it up and not go too heavy on one or the other.

But I preferred playing in England. It was fast paced and the atmosphere was amazing. After the game sometimes we went into the pubs and had a beer with the fans. I loved it.

You went from being managed by Marcello Lippi, to Bryan Robson. How do the tactics compare of those two? Describe how the preparations for a game differed?

Lippi was far more experienced than Bryan Robson who was just starting out. At Juventus the setup was amazing with all those brilliant players. Middlesbrough only had normal players, maybe four or five in a squad of 20 who were world class. At Juventus, all the players were of the highest quality.

The build up to the matches was totally different too. When I arrived in England they were building the club while Juventus were already an established club in Europe. You didn't want for anything - everything was provided for you. In Middlesbrough it wasn't like that at first but it was ok. I knew what they were trying to do.

You famously scored a hat-trick against Liverpool on your Boro debut - was that your best performance during your time with the club? Did it help you settle in straight away?

Three goals in the first game and I was already being compared with Robbie Fowler and Alan Shearer. I was on a good streak early on and it really helped me settle in really fast. The English style really complemented my style so it was a great fit.

There have been reports there were a few disagreements between players during the season - what was the atmosphere like in the squad? Who were your mates at the club? Are there any players you're still in touch with? Didn't you end up in a fight with Neil Cox before the FA Cup final?

Ha ha. Cox thought that he must play every match but he couldn't play in the Premiership. The technical and tactical levels were too high for him. He didn't have the quality. What happened between us wasn't important though - winning the final was the aim.

If there are sometimes problems with players that's OK as long as you put your body on the line on the pitch. There was a great atmosphere in the squad despite our struggles. I was mates with Gianluca Festa, Nick Barmby, Mark Schwarzer, Juninho, Emerson, Steve Vickers - I was friends with them all and still speak to them. The only problem I had was that my English wasn't very good. On the pitch though it didn't matter.

What are your memories of the Blackburn game in the December when the team didn't turn up because so many were ill? Describe the scene. Were you one of the players who fell ill? Did you think it was a strange situation? Did you think the points deduction was fair? Was it always an uphill struggle from there?

There was a lot of people ill at the training ground but to not play the game was crazy. I couldn't believe it. I had never seen anything like it. It was so strange. I knew it was a very bad idea. In fact, everyone thought it was crazy and so when we were penalized THREE points, we were proved right. There may have been a few arguments in the squad but the incompetence of the club was worse.

You scored 31 goals in 1996-97, with 15 of them coming in the two domestic cups - how exciting were those cup runs? Do you think playing so many matches ultimately cost the team at the end of the season?

We had a large squad and yes, we did play a lot of games but we had enough players to cope with every competition. The cup games were fantastic and to take the club to their first finals in 120 was special. I just wish we could have won one of them.

Surely a team with the quality of players Middlesbrough had shouldn't have been relegated? What went wrong? Was there a particular moment you realised the team was doomed, or did you think you could get out of it right till the end?

I knew in January we were in trouble. If we would have strengthened like I told them to, we'd have survived. Our midfield was fine - Barmby, Hignett, Mustoe, Juninho, Emerson. That was good enough to have finished in the top 10 but not getting the defender in was crucial. We kept conceding early goals. It was very difficult.

Would you rather have scored the winning goal in one of the two cup finals, or scored the goal that kept the club in the Premier League?

For me it's the same. I just wanted to score.

Was there ever any chance of you staying at Middlesbrough in the second tier (longer than the first two games of the season)?

I wanted to leave Boro after the relegation because I was so desperate to play at the World Cup. If it wasn't for that I would have stayed 100% because I loved my time there so much.

Do you consider your time at the club a success overall?

No matter what happened it was a success. My experiences there were unforgettable.

What was your favourite thing about England? Is there anything you miss about it?

The passion of the fans and you can live a good quality life. Very nice people. Back in 1996, when you tried to buy olive oil, you had to go to the pharmacy. It's not like that now - the selection and choice is fantastic. I always like going back to England.

If you could do anything differently (during your time with Boro), what would it be?

To make sure they would have signed some defenders when we needed them.

Did you enjoy your spell at Derby as much? Did you hesitate when you got the chance to move back to England? Had English football changed in that short time?

It was a difficult time. Jim Smith signed me but left and then Colin Todd came in but the fans kept me going. I loved playing in the Premier League and was keen for the move. It was more professional this time. Serie A was the best in 1996 but by the time I returned with Derby, England was the greatest.

What memories do you have from your short spell at Dundee? Were you aware of the financial problems the club was in at the time?

Dundee was a bad experience for me. The Italian chairman had a lot of problems. It was two months and it was fun but I regret what happened there. I wanted to stay in Scotland for longer but the club had no money so I went back to Perugia. I had no idea of the problem. When I spoke to the Chairman at the start he told me everything was ok!

He didn't pay me and a lot of the other players. It was a catastrophe for everyone. I liked Scottish football. I played at Rangers when at Juve. The atmosphere was amazing even if it was very cold and difficult to understand people but it was okay. You cannot compare it to England or Italy though.

What are you up to now? What have you been doing since you retired?

I worked with the youth team at Juventus, went to France to coach for a short time at Ajaccio but it didn't work out. Now I am determined to get a job in England and become a top manager - just like my good friend Antonio Conte.

SUPPORTING ACT
– Fans' Stories

Graeme Bailey: I was named after Graeme Souness, my mum fancied him at the time - my parents are huge Boro fans as they met at Ayresome Park in the 1960s - but then two months after I was born he left for Liverpool.

My friend Lee Hall and me both nicked off college to head down the Riverside when Emerson was paraded as our new samba star. We tried to deny we had bunked off until the tutor saw our faces on the back pages of every newspaper the day after.

The day we went up last day in 1992, we travelled down not knowing if game would be on due to people breaking into Molineux the night before and planting things in the pitch ... anyway we went down, game was on and won, afterwards, hung around - like most 15-year-olds do - the team came out, and Paul Wilkinson wasn't going to stop to sign, but his Mrs (nice looking blonde) shouted 'Paul, sign that' at him, and he stopped laughed, gave me his can of lager and walked off with a wink!

I actually got to interview George Hardwick after Wilf Mannion died, and I was going on about how great he was, and he said: "Mmm, yes he was good - but he was a bit lazy, not a team player – wasn't my first choice." Just because players play together, and both are legends - they don't have to like each other.

Tony Clish: I've been a Boro fan since 1970 when my father took eight-year-old me to see Boro play West Ham in the FA Cup. Their team was full of England's World Cup winners and up against Boro's mix of English, Irish and Scottish grafters of the old Second Division, finely tuned by the great servant of North East football, Stan Anderson.

They say your memories are best when they flow across all the senses. I remember the sight of the greenest grass I could imagine - in the days of black and white TV and grime-covered buildings. Seeing more people than an eight-year-old thought lived on the planet - Ayresome Park was packed to the rafters with 32,585 fans. The smell of John Player fags and half-time Bovril. The sound of the crowd - the roof came off when Hugh McIlmoyle and Derrick Downing scored.

I was hooked and my dad was hooked too - he was a converted Sunderland fan with the family having moved from Durham a few years before. We bought season tickets for the following season.

In September 1970 my dad couldn't make the QPR game so my mum took me. Not used to town centre parking we had a longer walk than usual by the time we found a big enough space. We arrived 10 minutes or so late, my mum wearing a very 1970s style red dress that looked a bit out of place in Ayresome Park- but an eager son didn't want to say anything.

We had cracking seats close to the half way in the south stand, in front of a bloke we'd already named 'Happy Harry'. We were never sure if he was called Harry - but even a few games into the season with our new season tickets, what we were sure about is he wasn't very happy!

So, eager to find out what we had missed having arrived at our seats late, I asked Harry what the score was. "They're already two-up' he said in a gruff unhappy kind of way. My mum, having heard our tales of Happy Harry, said, "Oh that's good," thinking it must be Boro 2 up. Harry replied, "They're 2 up. THEM - Queens Park f***ing Rangers!!"

So we sat down 10 minutes in. 2 goals down. To Queens Park f***ing Rangers.

But we weren't sat down for long! This was the McIlmoyle match - a match that will forever live on as one of the most amazing turnarounds in the pre-Basel and Steaua era.

If Ali Brownlee had been commentating it would have been legendary! A Hickon hat-trick, two from McIlmoyle, one from Downing. What a match. 6-2. My mum was hooked. The following season our two season tickets became three - and the build-up to the Charlton era started to ramp up.

Paul Smith Billingham: Going to Reading away in 97/98 and getting drenched on open terracing still stands out. We saw Gianluca Festa score what looked to be a last-minute winner then throw his shirt into the crowd to celebrate only for the goal to be ruled out and him frantically trying to find his shirt again while Reading attacked.

Jim Paul: Reading about Graeme Souness reminds me of the 8-0 win against Sheffield Wednesday. Souness got a hat-trick - and before the last goal - a tap in - he stood on the ball - allowing the converging defenders almost enough time to stop him! One of the best games (before the UEFA adventures) was the 6-2 win against QPR. 2-0 down after 5 minutes it then became the Hugh McIlmoyle show. He scored twice but set up Big John (Hickton) for a hat-trick - including the usual long run-up penalty! Definitely one of the best individual performances.

John McPartland: My first match at Ayresome Park was on October 10 1953. I was 10 and my dad and I went to our first game together. Boro beat Sheffield United 2-0 with Wilf Mannion scoring both goals. Sadly, I never saw Wilf at his best.

In all my years supporting the Boro, I remember with great emotion and excitement sitting on a concrete stand in the Bob End in 1958 to see Boro thrash Brighton 9-0. Brian Clough was already my hero but to see him put five past Dave Hollins, the Brighton keeper, raised him to Godlike status. At the end, Cloughie ran to Hollins both to congratulate and commiserate. Hollins had stopped the score being nearer 20. I'll never forget that wonderful gesture.

When Brian died I put together a fund-raising committee, which I chaired, to raise funds for a statue of Brian, which now stands majestically in Albert Park, a site chosen by Gazette readers. For me, Brian was my great hero until he died when I had the privilege of meeting his widow Barbara and their three children.

Bari Chohan: I've supported the Boro since my first game in the 1958/59 season. Therefore I have a huge library of experiences and memories ranging from the zenith of happiness to dire depths of the nadir.

As probably the first British Asian supporting the team this gave me a unique perspective from another viewpoint also. I've gone from the Boys' End at Ayresome Park over these many decades to having a box at the Riverside.

One very poignant memory was when my son Harroon passed away just before his 18th birthday and the club kindly dedicated a half-page in the next home programme in his memory.

We had a box at the Riverside during those wonderful years when we won the Carling Cup and had those unforgettable European nights. One week Alan Peacock popped in towards the end of a match, wanting me to meet the guest of honour in the restaurant. As we approached the table by the windows looking out at the Middlesbrough town centre skyline, I saw the guest was the one and only legendary Brian Clough and two others sat with him.

As I sat down and was introduced, he said, "This is Mr Fenton," and as he went on to say "This is...." I butted in. I said, "I know this is Mick McNeil" and gave out his list of achievements. Well Mick was shocked and said, "how the *#$+ do you know that?" I told him he was my hero playing as a full back, before went to Ipswich.

We then had a delightful chat with an as ever ebullient Cloughie in full form. About to leave, I requested his autograph on my programme. However, I also said "can I have your old strike partner Alan Peacock as well?" Cloughie laughed and said, "Why do you want his? You're the first to want the both of us together." I said, "Two Boro legends and England centre forwards from a Division Two team that is more than unique..." A few weeks later sadly Brian passed away but what a legend I was privileged to have spent a few glorious moments with.

My only regret was that I had forgot to mention and thank him for giving me three five to ten-minute sessions as a 16-year-old playing for the very first time against adults in my first professional football trial at Hartlepool when he was in his first managerial position. That was long before there were any black players, never mind a young British Asian boy.

Neil Caygill: People often ask you to name your most memorable or favourite game. As a man for me it has to be that night at the Riverside against Steaua Bucharest but as a teenager back in 1977 it has to be the 4-1 win against Arsenal in the FA Cup 5th round at Ayresome Park. Arsenal were riding high at the top of the old first Division and the week leading up to the game the national Press wrote us off. They were more or less saying that Arsenal just needed to turn up.

I took up my usual position in the Holgate just behind the goal. Within the first 15 minutes David Mills scored a brace. The 42,000 crammed into the ground couldn't believe what they were seeing. Malcolm Macdonald made it 2-1 but then David Armstrong scored and Mills sealed his hat-trick late. It was the most amazing game; everyone was on such a high. We couldn't wait to see what the papers had to say the next day.

Ian Douglas: Back in the late 60s as a teenager, I used to go to the matches with a couple of my mates from Billingham, and we would always stand in The Holgate End. The match I remember most was not because of the score, but of a certain incident against Millwall between Johnny Crossan, and their Eamon Dunphy. There was a bit of niggle through the game between the two. Johnny was my favourite player. He always played with a swagger, and he had his shirt sleeves over his hands, Denis Law-style. Anyway Boro were kicking towards the Holgate. They both chased the ball towards the goal line, but even though Johnny was a stride in front, he failed to keep the ball in which went out for a goal kick. Most of the players, and all the officials had turned to get in place for the goal kick. Anyway as Johnny came back onto the pitch, he ran past Dunphy and, out of the blue, punched him. Well the Holgate erupted, and the bonus was that none of the officials saw anything. Good players have come and gone, but Johnny Crossan still remains my favourite Boro player of all time.

Janet Hatfield: In the mid-70s, I went with my mam and friends to watch Tony Christie at the Fiesta Club when I was a teenager. The Boro team and Jacky Charlton were there and were being quite noisy while Tony was singing. During the interval my friend said that she wanted some autographs and with pen and paper told me who to ask. The team were just walking around. She said to ask someone called David I think and at that I turned round and walked straight into Graeme Souness' chest and got a big smell of aftershave, probably Brut. He smiled and said, 'Would you like my autograph?' 'What's your name?' I asked him. When he told me and because it wasn't this David, I turned and said 'No, I don't want yours, thanks very much!' My mam over heard and couldn't believe what I had just said to the top Boro player at that time. Now I think of that night and when I tell people their mouths drop which makes me feel even worse. Sorry Graeme Souness. It was my loss.

Stuart Whittingham: One of the stand-out memories of following Boro is the remarkable European adventure. The player of that moment was Massimo Maccarone, for his huge contribution to our team reaching the UEFA Cup final. The thought in my head of a small town in Europe reaching a major European final was what dreams are made of. Sitting on the plane kitted out in Boro colours bound for Eindhoven, I was excited and nervous and curious of how it might pan out. Flying on my own and meeting family members in Holland to experience the wonderful atmosphere in the main square with thousands of Boro fans soaking the atmosphere up and loving the Boro songs reverberating around Eindhoven. Then there was the walk to the stadium, the songs still being sung about our team, but louder every step, then lung-busting pride and excitement in the stadium, trying to take every minute of this once-in-a-lifetime occasion, not wanting the day to end. The result wasn't what we wanted but that didn't matter because I could say proudly I was there.

Gavin McCallum: I don't know whether to laugh or cry when I think back to my favourite memories. I bumped into the players at Athens airport after winning our first away game in Europe against Egaleo. There was no film left in my camera so I reverted to the new 'camera phone'. I got photos of me with Gareth, Jimmy,

Schwarzer etc but they were all later deleted by my nephew. Bloody phones. Also, after promotion in 1988, I bought a top in the club shop on the day of the civic reception. Gary Hamilton was in and he signed it then walked out with it, said he'd be five minutes. He took it on the team bus and got it signed by the whole squad. As a 12 year old I wore it and washed it!

Richard Brine: I once looked after Mikel Beck's girlfriend after meeting them both when he was very late turning up for a Sat 3pm friendly at Hartlepool. Never met her before or since but took her to the game with my mate and our sons. Went to Graz AK on the train from Vienna and my mate Mark slept off a hangover under the chair and another Boro fan from Swindon we did not know nicked his shoes and we found them 2 hours later in the Irish bar tied by the laces to a rafter 25-feet up in the air.

Once had lunch in the Purple Onion with 10 Swedish customers and literally within 10 minutes in there talking footie, especially Boro, in walked Juninho, Rav, Hignett and Clayton Blackmore. I couldn't believe it and Swedes loved it – and it helped us win work!

Same Swedes were in the suite at home against Portsmouth (1-1 losing at HT) & God bless Alan Peacock who asked about them and we said they were Swedes. So his five-minute speak introduces 'our Swiss friends' and that 'we like them because of Jan Age Fjortoft'. Thought us Brits were funny as anything.

Geoffrey: Boxing Day 1973-74 under Jack Charlton. Playing Sunderland. Arrived at the ground 1.45 and the noise approaching the ground was immense. When I got in the stadium it was already full. Great game which we won 2-1. Will never forget that.

Alex Bloomfield: Meeting Juninho at the Riverside and walking to Leicester Square with Craig Hignett! Lining up in a Bobby Robson charity match alongside Colin Cooper. Great, great memories. Running alongside big Ugo Ehiogu from one end of the Riverside pitch to the other. And him telling me he was knackered. Banter with George Boateng on and off the pitch and then sitting down with him and Ugo after the game. Ugo was a really nice guy.

Joseph Moore: Saw the Carling Cup as it was brought into the Cardiff hotel me and my family were staying at the night before the final. It felt like a sign.

StanIsStan (via Twitter): I bumped into Juninho and Hamilton Ricard in Sharkey's in Redcar and they ended up buying me and mate a pint and chatted to us. Then wouldn't let us buy them a drink back. It was pound a pint night.

David Mohan: I once gatecrashed a Boro players Christmas party and Juninho was dressed as a vampire. I also remember trying to get a few words with Robbie Mustoe for a school paper and he asked where I got the Dictaphone from as he was looking to go into journalism. Who knew eh?

Hazel Clay: I saw Ugo Ehiogu at Flamingo land. He was about three rides in front of every ride I went on. We all remember Ugo – seemingly seven-feet tall and giving strikers nightmares? That's the fella. Came off Velocity almost wetting himself laughing with tears streaming down his face. Legend!

Jaycee (via Twitter): I loved David Currie. Whilst the rest of the sparse Holgate End hammered him for a six-yard box miss v Carlisle, my brother and me loved the way he rounded goalkeepers. He scored class goals against the promoted teams: Newcastle, Sheffield Wednesday and Chelsea and that goal in the 3-2 win against Newcastle in 83/84 stands out.

Ayresome Gates (via Twitter): My mum wrote to the club to try to get a signed Stewy Ripley shirt for my little brother's 8th birthday. Rippers phoned my mum, got our home address and turned up as a surprise - did photos, autographs & had a kick about with us in the back garden.

Graeme Bandeira: Spending a week in Mallorca with mate Bernie Slaven, being a mascot in 1983, sharing beers with Robbo, Gibbo, Souness, getting to know Gareth Southgate, Proc, Pally, Coops, getting Adama's shirt, met hundreds of Boro players over the years. I used to go round Heine Otto's house, too, as a kid.

James Keen: I once drank an entire bottle of Southern Comfort at Keith O'Neil's house while he cracked on to the lasses I worked with. Woke up on his sofa in the morning before throwing up on his doorstep. Also once gatecrashed a Boro team night out after Curtis Fleming recognised me from working in his restaurant. I spent the night explaining to Robbie Mustoe why he needed to believe me he was a legend while my mate insulted Andy Campbell in the toilets. Also I once had to be forcibly removed from bowing at John Hendrie's feet because I didn't think he believed me that he was my favourite player.

Roy Thompson: I travelled to Marske to watch us in a friendly. We left a friend's wedding to go. After the match Tommy Johnson the kit man invited us into the clubhouse for drinks and gave us a tray of sandwiches. On returning to Stockton our one-eyed driver almost lost control of the car. We had to go down towards Norton and Stockton Ancients and wait for help to fix the car. Great memories.

Ian Smith: My family and I got to know John Hendrie quite well during his Boro days, and I once gave him a ball as an 11-yr-old outside the Riverside and asked if he could get it signed for me. He couldn't guarantee anything but took it in the ground. After the game he came out looking for me and handed me this ball full of signatures, including Ravanelli, Juninho, Emerson etc. What an absolute legend. I saw him about 10 years ago at a local school in Doncaster where he was managing a Bradford youth team then. He remembered me and my family. Top bloke - one of the best there is, such a genuinely lovely guy. I still long for that era, the early 90s Ayresome Park days were special.

Ross Mawhinney: I met my hero Paul Wilkinson in our promotion season, home against Notts County. I was in the changing room before the game. When I got his autograph, he put his arm around me and said 'You're a tall fucker aren't you!'

Daniel Sturdy: I was mascot for Middlesbrough when we played Leicester at Wembley in the 1996 Coca-Cola Cup final. I played on the pitch at Wembley with Juninho and Craig Hignett as they warmed up but sadly a potentially dream day ended in disappointment.

Lee Huskinson: My dad was selling Cleaneze products and he knocked on Juninho's door (not knowing it was his house) his dad answered. My dad knew who it was so asked to speak to Juninho. He invited him in and got autographed photos. My dad was buzzing. Pity there were no smartphones in those days. Lovely family.

Mark Cooper: My first ever match was us losing 5-1 to a John Hartson-inspired Luton at Kenilworth Road. After I cried! We went 5-0 down including two Paul Wilkinson own goals, scoring a consolation goal through Whyte - "1-5 to the Middlesbrough" screamed the fans!

Maly James: I always remember Barnsley away in 93, we won 4-1. John Hendrie and Alan Moore scored two each and I lost a trainer after we scored a goal but somehow me and my trainer were re-united thanks to a steward at full-time.

Louis Dixon: I spoke to Emanuel Pogatetz in Teesside Airport after he got elbowed by Bolton's Kevin Davies where he was cut badly. I ask him, 'how did you remain so calm (for him)?" He replied: "If I wasn't on a yellow card I would've chinned the fat bastard."

Keith Lilley, Marton Manor: Back in the early 70s, my mates and me were regulars at Ayresome Park and every other Saturday would take up our positions in the East End lower and an area known affectionately as the 'Chicken run', so named because of the abuse that opposition full-backs and wingers would receive as they ran up and down the flank.

I remember one guy who had a comical quip to make about everything and anything. This particular game there was a woman in the crowd who fainted and the fans were gesticulating to gain the attention of the St John's ambulance men. One of the crew arrived and soon acknowledged the situation and indicated that they were going off to commandeer a stretcher for her. Five minutes passed and then ten but still no sign of their return. Finally, after what must have been half an hour they returned with the stretcher to which this wag in the crowd shouted, "Good job she wasn't having a baby, it'd be starting school by know." I remember laughing out loud as did many others that day. To be fair he was like this most weeks. I often wonder what became of him and even if he still follows us today.

Stuart Patterson: I was the 13 year old Secretary of the Junior Literary and Debating Society in Grangefield Grammar School, Stockton and in 1958/9 I wrote to Brian Clough (my then hero) via the club inviting him to give a talk at one of our meetings. To my huge surprise and delight he accepted and sure enough turned up on the day and spoke for an hour about the Boro, his team mates and football in general. He was extremely charismatic and stayed for another hour signing autographs and chatting.

Looking back, when asked why the Boro kept losing matches against inferior opposition they clearly should have won, in the FA Cup for example, he alluded to a few bad apples among his team mates which in hindsight could have been Esmond Million, Ken Thomson and Brian Phillips who were all subsequently convicted of throwing matches at other clubs but played with him at the club. Brian was the subject of a round robin vote of no confidence at the time. By the way, I am now living in Cardiff, still a season ticket holder and one of the 5 members of the Boro Supporters club, S Wales!!

Doug Embleton: We were on holiday in Torquay and after pondering for not too long my Dad drove us all home right through the Friday night, in atrocious weather, to just make it in time to see Boro's opening game v Brighton. I think Clough scored 5 and Peacock 4 in a resounding 9-0 win! I vivdly recall walking back to our car and first seeing then sympathising with a young, morose-looking lad of about my age in his own Dad's car. His Dad had driven him a long way too – all the way from Brighton to see their first game of the season.

GLORY BOYS
– Cup of Joy

McClaren's Rude Awakening

Steve McClaren reckons he can pinpoint the exact moment that Boro's road to Carling Cup glory began.

It was at Ipswich Town's Portman Road ground when his Boro team had just been knocked out of the same competition.

With Premier League stability his priority, the Boro manager had gambled on fielding a weakened side in Suffolk.

But his risky strategy backfired and the visitors ended up heading home with tails between legs after a comfortable 3-1 win for George Burley's side.

McClaren would have seen Sir Alex Ferguson get away with such an approach in their days together at Manchester United when he routinely fielded sides full of fringe players and youngsters in the League Cup.

But this time he was in for a rude awakening as he incurred the wrath of Boro owner Steve Gibson for the first time – and the hair dryer treatment made such a lasting impression, the blast carried them all the way to Cardiff.

"I have to admit that Cup win goes right back to the time when we were beaten at Ipswich - I made a fatal error in putting a weaker side out," McClaren said at a reunion of his Carling Cup winners at the Riverside.

"It was probably the first time that I really saw Steve Gibson get angry which I realised was because the cup competitions are very important to him.

"When we first met, he told me his ambition. His five-year plan was to get all the kids through the academy and to win a trophy.

"It was quite simple - we wanted to win a cup and what he gave me then was tremendous support all the way through."

That Ipswich humbling took place in November 2002 when Boro rested their frontline players with the tie coming just two nights after a 2-0 defeat at Newcastle.

Stand-in goalie Mark Crossley had picked the ball out of the back of the net three times by half-time and debutant Andrew Davies would have been wondering what had hit him.

Gibson would have been cheered up when McClaren masterminded a 1-0 defeat of Liverpool at the Riverside the following weekend when Gareth Southgate scored a late winner.

But McClaren knew in no uncertain terms what the club's priorities were.

"When we got knocked out by Ipswich we really had a ding-dong and then in the next season I took every cup competition seriously.

"After Ipswich it was no more kids, it was only occasionally that we brought them on to bring them through.

"It was our plan to build an experienced team that could win a trophy and we became a cup team over the five years, culminating in the UEFA Cup final.

"When I look back at the Cup final it really is incredible because of all the experience we had packed into that side.

"They were all men. That back four, the goalkeeper, George Boateng just in front of them, Doriva and Juninho. They had all been around the block a few times and that's what we had to create to achieve our goals."

It was a plan that worked to perfection as Boro shrugged off their own cup final jinx to finally bring major silverware back to Teesside for the first time in the club's history.

A team whose predecessors had fallen at the final hurdle in three major finals under Bryan Robson got off to a perfect start as Joseph-Desire Job gave Boro an early lead – a moment McClaren actually missed.

"I was changing out of my suit and my very nice pink tie – why the hell we had pink ties, I don't know, and a pink rose – and I was getting my tracksuit on.

"I remember coming down the tunnel and my heart just skipped a beat because there was an almighty roar. That's it, I thought, somebody has scored, and so I had actually been dreading going out.

"I was actually stood half-way up the players' tunnel and instead of going out and finding who had scored straight away I was wondering if that was our fans singing.

"Then all I saw was one of the staff, I think it was the kit man, with his fist pumping, saying, 'We've scored, we've scored,' and I very nearly turned back.

"I'd never been superstitious, but I was wondering if that was a sign, but then I went out and had barely sat down and we got another goal."

Bolo Zenden scored from the penalty spot as Boro again caught Sam Allardyce's team cold before McClaren's defenders stood firm late on to withstand late pressure and secure a famous 2-1 win."

It ended 128 years of hurt and, looking back, McClaren feels he should have allowed his players to celebrate in style with fans back home so they could continue to savour victory together.

"My only regret was that we had to play Birmingham on the following Wednesday.

"I would like to have, in hindsight, got on the open top bus and just enjoyed the occasion because that was the problem with the five years – it wasn't appreciated at the time.

"But I think it is now. I get lots of people coming up to me now because I still live in this area saying what a great day it was.

"We were living in it and we were so consumed that they weren't really great days. They were working days and we didn't enjoy it.

"So I wish I would have said, 'To hell with Birmingham,' or whatever, 'Let's enjoy this occasion,' because looking back it was one hell of a tremendous day."

The Millennium Stadium triumph set Boro on the road to Europe and adventures in uncharted territory.

"Europe was fantastic. We'd fly in the afternoon the day before our games with a planeload of fans from Teesside Airport and we'd wonder what we'd do all day.

"So we said as a staff that we'd get out and about and see the local sights like the Coliseum when we played Roma.

"It was funny because there were so many Boro fans who said they had never ventured outside of Middlesbrough before - they said they didn't even know what a cappuccino was.

"We'd have people coming up to us saying, 'Wow! We've never been to Europe before,' and there they were making the most of it.

"That, for me, was great. Now I'm older and more experienced I appreciate things more, but I didn't enjoy it enough at the time.

"What I do remember is going round seeing old men crying and people now in the streets saying you gave us the best day of our lives. That's what I will always remember."

McClaren has had plenty of ups and downs for club and country since leaving Boro for the England job in 2006.

Many people outside Teesside will remember him as the 'Wally with the Brolly', but Boro fans will always cherish the memories of that day in Cardiff when he helped make history.

And, despite a checkered CV post-Riverside, he remains one of the only Englishmen to win a major honour in the Premier League era.

"I can say that I've won things," he told Four Four Two magazine. "But the two people that I wanted to win a trophy for at Middlesbrough were Steve Gibson and Juninho.

"At the end of that League Cup final, I just wanted to get Steve out on the pitch. He didn't want to at first, but eventually he was persuaded.

"Then I remember being doused with champagne by the players – funnily enough, wishing that I had an umbrella with me to keep my hair dry..."

Juninho's Unfinished Business

In the build-up to the Carling Cup final, Juninho insisted success in Cardiff could be equated with the day he helped Brazil to win the World Cup.

Superficially that might have sounded questionable, but an examination of the record books might persuade even the most sceptical to re-think.

When Brazil won the World Cup in 2002, thus enabling Juninho to realise a dream of anyone who has ever kicked a football, they were winning the ultimate football prize for the fifth time – and Juninho only had a cameo role.

In Cardiff, Teesside's diminutive talisman was facing an arguably more difficult task - helping Middlesbrough to a first major trophy after 128 years of trying.

"I've won a World Cup winner's medal but, in a different way, earning a winner's medal on Sunday will probably mean as much to me," Juninho said. "The game will be like the World Cup final for me.

"It was excellent to be in the World Cup, but it isn't right to say I've played in the tournament and so that is enough.

"It isn't enough. For example, I've always said that I would like to win titles with Middlesbrough.

"That is one of the main objectives of my career. Just because you've won the World Cup you can't think that's it.

"You need to win as many titles as you can and be as successful as possible right throughout your career.

"The only reason I came back to Middlesbrough for a third time was to win a title for the club.

"We have another opportunity and I personally don't want to waste it again. Reaching the final stage is a very important achievement, but once we get there we have to complete the job."

Juninho, who turned 31 a week before the Cardiff showdown, suffered defeat in the 1997 Coca-Cola Cup and FA Cup finals - at the hands of Leicester and Chelsea, respectively - and then a harrowing season went from bad to worse when Middlesbrough were relegated, prompting his £12 million sale to Atletico Madrid.

He was adamant Steve McClaren's Middlesbrough side was better equipped to achieve success than Bryan Robson's predecessors.

"In the first final in 1997 we were just two minutes away from victory and therefore a place in Europe for the first time but we shouldn't think about those defeats.

"We should only be looking forward. We should be proud we've got to another final, but must concentrate for the full 90 or 95 minutes and make sure we bring the trophy back to Teesside.

"Compared to the 1997 team, we are a much more prepared and more solid side. We have more experienced players and most of them have played in big games and finals before, which will be an advantage once we're in Cardiff.

"Players, such as [Gaizka] Mendieta and [Bolo] Zenden, who have won things before, have come to Middlesbrough with the objective of winning titles or getting into Europe."

Ahead of Cardiff, Juninho prospered in a roaming role just behind a central striker, but his season got off to an uncertain start when he was in and out of manager McClaren's starting XI.

He even voiced dissatisfaction at McClaren's overly cautious tactics, but then promptly scored the winning goal against Arsenal in the first leg of their Carling Cup semi-final to emphasise his point.

"I've been happy with the way the team have played recently, when we hold the ball and start to pass it around from the back up to the forwards.

"All our players are comfortable in possession and know how to pass the ball.

"When we pull the ball down and play football we can beat big clubs like Man United and Arsenal.

"But when we try to compete physically, like we did at Newcastle, we can lose games like that."

Having lost the 1998 League Cup final against Chelsea, Middlesbrough were under further pressure to shake off their perennial losers' tag, but that suited Juninho.

"I suppose playing with people like Mendieta and Zenden makes it slightly easier for me, but I like playing with pressure all the time in big matches because that would show we're playing important matches all the time.

"I've adapted to that because in Brazil when you wear the national shirt you're under constant pressure because you're expected to win every game. If you want to be a winner you have to play under pressure."

In his most recent interview, with Portuguese journalist Marcus Alves for Four Four Two magazine, Juninho made it clear that his Carling Cup winners' medal still means as much as his piece of World Cup gold.

Asked if winning the League Cup with Boro was still a better feeling than winning the World Cup with Brazil, he answered: "Maybe not better, but the same feeling.

"Of course, winning the World Cup is seen as a much bigger thing, but winning the League Cup meant a lot to me because we were reaching the goal we had dreamed about when the project started nine years before.

"It was special to me – really special. I had that feeling back then and I still have it with me."

Just The Job For Joseph

Carling Cup hero Joseph-Desire Job believes it was his destiny to play a key role in helping Boro end their long wait for a major honour.

His goal and then an assist guarantee him a place in everyone's affections on Teeeside, but it could have all been so different.

Job was, in fact, nearing the exit at Boro when Steve McClaren took over as manager, but stayed put and sealed his place in local folklore.

When he came to Boro in 2000, Job scored on his debut against Coventry, but early promise faded and the prospect of him becoming a local hero was remote.

Had it not been for the arrival of McClaren in 2001 after the departure of Bryan Robson, who initially persuaded Job to head to Teesside, he would not have been in the right time at the right place in Cardiff.

"It looked good for me in the first game, but things did not work out very well after that," Job said from his home in the French city of Lyon.

"I did not have a very good start and I even went out on loan for six months at Metz.

"McClaren came in and he did not know anything about me, but we had a very good chat and I had a chance to prove myself again.

"He brought in a lot of players because he wanted to change everything, which is understandable, and I was still looking for another club.

"But I couldn't find anyone so I stayed and did well in the pre-season. One day he came to me and said he didn't know me before, but he was really satisfied with the way I played.

There followed a full and frank conversation.

"I told McClaren I didn't want the same experience as I had with Robson. I was happy he wanted me to stay, but I wanted guarantees that I would play.

"He told me he could not guarantee that I would play, but what he could guarantee is that he wanted me in the squad.

"I was offered a second chance and so I thought, 'Okay, why not take it?'

"So I said, 'All right, I will stay,' and it was a really good season. I played in most of the games and then my friend Geremi came.

"Geremi was good for me and I really enjoyed it. It was so much better for me under McClaren.

"I felt good again. I am so glad that happened. It is like it was my destiny."

No Boro fan will forget the moment Gareth Southgate lifted the Carling Cup and nor will Job.

"When I look back, the Carling Cup final was unforgettable for me, personally and for the club.

"It was the first big trophy the club had won and that made everyone at the club and all the supporters so very happy. It was a very special achievement.

"To score in the final was great, but I was also part of a very good team who worked so hard for each other.

"That is something I will remember for the rest of my life. It was one of the highlights of my career. It makes me so happy to think about it."

As a Cameroon international, his playing career took him to two World Cup finals, which for most footballers is the pinnacle of their careers.

But Job insists the Carling Cup final is right up there with his time on the biggest stage in football.

"I still remember very clearly the Cameroon-England game at the 1990 finals when we lost 3-2 in the quarter-finals because of two penalties.

"But that tournament and the way people like Roger Milla played was very good for the whole of Africa and people like me who wanted to make it in professional football in Europe.

"Playing in the World Cup was special because that is a dream for any footballer, but winning a big final is equally significant.

"When you are young you want to win trophies and you want to play in the World Cup.

"I had the opportunity to play in two tournaments, which was a fantastic honour, and win a cup, which was very satisfying, especially with it being in England which is such a big footballing country."

As well as Carling Cup glory, Job has the distinction of being one of a select number of visiting players who can say they scored a winner at Old Trafford in Boro's 3-2 victory over Manchester United.

He also scored an amazing overhead kick in the UEFA Cup win over Sporting Lisbon, but was outgrown by Boro and fell down the pecking order as the likes of Jimmy Floyd Hasselbaink and Mark Viduka were lured to the Riverside.

"After the Carling Cup final, all the big names came to Middlesbrough and there was a lot of competition for the attacking places.

"I wanted to go, not because I did not feel good at Middlesbrough, but because I was not sure I could play regularly. That was why I went out on loan. I wanted to play the game I love.

"I did not really appreciate the way things ended, but these things happen to professional footballers.

"I had been on loan in Saudi Arabia for the last year of my contract and I never came back to Middlesbrough, which was sad.

"It was all over so quickly and that felt a bit strange because there were lots of people I wanted to say goodbye to."

Following a spell in Belgium, Job concentrated on building a future away from professional football.

"I looked forward to doing something else now because I had 15 or 16 years of playing at the top level.

"It is not easy to play at the top level for so many years, but now it is the time for me to move on and give someone else a chance.

"I have a couple of things in Cameroon, but it will take me two or three years to establish what I have in mind with the property company that I have over there. Definitely now I have got time to get that moving forward.

"I really feel that playing football is behind me for now, although I will always love the game because it has been so good to me."

There could also be a trip down Memory Lane in the offing.

"I still have family and friends in England and even in Middlesbrough.

"And I would like to think I would have time to visit now my career is over and see how things have changed at the training ground and at the Riverside."

The Power Of Zen

It was all smiles for Bolo Zenden in his two years on Teesside.

The former Dutch international says that he could hardly stop grinning from ear-to-ear as he mixed business with pleasure with Boro.

Zenden will go down as the man whose blow was ultimately decisive in the 2-1 Carling Cup win over Bolton at the Millennium Stadium in February 2004.

It was the highlight of two joyful years for Zenden and everyone else associated with the club - on and off the field.

"My Middlesbrough years were really enjoyable on a personal level and we achieved quite a bit as well by winning the League Cup and finishing seventh in the Premier League.

"It was great to be part of making history at Middlesbrough by winning the first major trophy and that is something that should bring a smile to everyone's face when they think back to that day in Cardiff.

"It certainly does with me, but then again I always found myself smiling when I think of Boro.

"With Steve McClaren there I always went to training with a big smile on my face.

"And I went home with a big smile on my face and for a sportsman that is so important.

"We had a very good team quality-wise, but we also had a very good team spirit.

"It is something that I really enjoyed and it is something that I will never forget. It makes me feel good just thinking about it."

Zenden is regularly reminded of that momentous day in the Welsh capital whenever he bumps into Boro fans.

"I come across a lot of Boro fans and they still thank me and the rest of the team for what happened at the Millennium Stadium.

"It was a fantastic day and there was a fantastic atmosphere in the arena where there was a white half and a red half.

"It still means a lot to me. It is just as if it was yesterday, isn't it?"

Boro fans who saw their club falter at the final hurdle at Wembley may have faced the final with a sense of foreboding, but Zenden felt no trepidation.

"I had a feeling that it could not go wrong. We just had to step up to the plate and do what we needed to do to win the game.

"There is nothing worse than getting to a final and then losing and I know that from first-hand experience with Chelsea.

"I have been there and it is horrible and I was desperate to make sure that did not happen and I knew it wouldn't because we were ready."

McClaren ensured Boro were first out of the traps with Zenden leading the way.

"We got off to a flying start. I set up one for Joseph-Desire Job and then I took our penalty when he was fouled.

"I actually slipped so I was pleased and relieved the ball still went in.

"There was plenty of pressure from Bolton in the second half, but we kept cool and were very determined.

"And then to actually experience that win brought us closer together. Everyone was delirious.

"The only downside is that we had to play Birmingham a few days later and we didn't have time to really celebrate it properly back home for a while.

"But when we did and had that open-top bus tour down Linthorpe Road it was worth waiting for.

"It was a very cold and chilly day, but the fans warmed our hearts by cheering us as one and thanking us for a great day."

Zenden spent just two seasons at Boro before heading down the M62 to Liverpool.

"Sometimes the fans don't really get that, but I am certain I made the right decision.

"It was obvious that when Liverpool manager Rafa Benitez came in for me and I was at the end of my contract that it was very difficult to turn down the chance to move and play for a club that was in the Champions League.

"I ended up playing in a Champions League final which is something every footballer strives for because you want to prove yourself at the highest level.

"Sadly, we lost to AC Milan in Athens and that put into perspective how good it was to beat Bolton."

Zenden served some of Europe's most illustrious clubs in Barcelona, Chelsea and Liverpool, but it says a lot that he is so fond of his time on Teesside which began with a season-long loan with Chelsea followed by a one-year deal.

That Zenden was prepared to take the risky option of just signing a relatively short-term, one-year contract at Boro shows why no one should be surprised that he took a year out of football after leaving Sunderland in 2011.

"There were a couple of things that interested me (he came close to joining Blackburn and Celtic) but nothing worked out for one reason or another.

"And then we had a little baby boy (Boan) and I had offers to go to China, but I didn't want to move that way, especially with the little one arriving.

"It was nice that I was in a position where I could put my family first because I was coming towards the end of my career.

"When you are 25 then you might choose differently, but I had got to a certain age that I could make a choice without pressure.

"I got some offers to go and play in the UK, but it was too late for us to move again.

"I didn't want to miss the birth of our first child so we stayed put and I would not have changed that for anything in the world.

"I want to do everything for my career, but also to enjoy life a bit because it is a fantastic experience.

"I always wanted to be there for my kids. I know you can take kids anywhere, but I wanted to stay in Europe and that is why I turned down the offer to play in China for three months."

It looks as though Boan will be the recipient of the souvenirs that his father collected during his Riverside spell.

"I have not had chance to buy him a Middlesbrough shirt yet, but he has plenty of time to grow into my old Boro shirts.

"I am sure that when the time comes he will keep the shirts that I have kept from my time there as souvenirs.

"The ones from the European games are nicely locked away and when he is older I am sure he will wear them all."

With plenty of television work to keep him busy as well as family life, Zenden is certainly content.

"Life is great. My brother and sister also have two kids each so this is the fifth grandchild for my parents and so I have been shown enough examples of how to do things with babies.

"So I knew what sort of trouble I was getting myself into. It is nice having a baby although my girlfriend has been doing most of the work. But I help out where I can, here and there."

Schwarzer's Mark Of Success

He spent more than a decade at Boro, but Mark Schwarzer insists there was "never a dull moment" in his Teesside days.

The Australian goalkeeper saw it all while at the Riverside over the course of 11 eventful years when he played 446 times for Boro.

After heading to the North East from Yorkshire in a £1.25-million deal with Bradford City in February 1997, Schwarzer enjoyed a turbulent journey.

It was one that saw the club go from Premier League fall guys to two top-seven finishes and from Cup final heartache to Carling Cup joy.

And then there were not one, but two European campaigns in the UEFA Cup - not bad for a player from just a small town in Europe.

"For me, both the highs and the lows with Boro were huge," Schwarzer said.

"My time at Boro was an incredibly exciting phase of my career. There was never a dull moment. There was nothing in between."

The same can be said of his career as a whole.

Born in Sydney, the 6ft 5in Schwarzer began his career with local side Marconi Stallions.

He headed to Europe and learned his trade with Dynamo Dresden and Kaiserslautern before coming to England.

He was initially on trial with Manchester City before Bradford's Middlesbrough-born manager Chris Kamara persuaded him to go to Valley Parade.

He only played 13 times for the Bantams, but a string of sterling displays caught the eye of Boro boss Bryan Robson and his scouts.

"The Boro move was all about my very first meeting with Bryan Robson and (his assistant) Viv Anderson in Manchester.

"It was all about having a manager who showed me quickly how much he wanted me and so it was a very easy decision to join Boro."

Schwarzer made his Boro debut at Stockport in a League Cup semi-final and was in goal for both the 1997 and 1998 finals of the competition, but missed out on the 1997 replay due to injury.

He also had to sit out the 1997 FA Cup final when Boro lost to Chelsea because he was cup-tied and was unable to stop his new club being relegated at the end of an eventful campaign.

"There were a lot of problems on the pitch with regards to results, the pile-up of fixtures and injuries and it would have been remarkable for us to have stayed in the league.

"But Robbo made it clear what the vision was for the club. In the worst-case scenario if we did go down we'd bounce back quickly because of Steve Gibson's backing."

Robson was true to his word and Boro were promoted in style after one season outside the top flight.

"We had some world-class players in Ravanelli, Juninho and Emerson and we were really unfortunate in the end to go down due to that points deduction.

"But the response to relegation from the club and the community was amazing. You couldn't buy tickets for home games, the atmosphere was electric and the expectations were huge.

"We were all confident we would go back up. Big-name players were replaced with very talented and more experienced players such as Andy Townsend, Paul Merson and Paul Gascoigne. They all played a huge part in a quick revival."

Schwarzer played a key role in helping Boro consolidate Premier League status under Robson and Terry Venables before Steve McClaren arrived to make history by guiding Boro to Carling Cup glory.

"That day we beat Bolton 2-1 in Cardiff has to be the most memorable day for every Boro fan, player and member of staff.

"We'd been in a couple of finals beforehand that we lost, but it felt like this was our opportunity.

"We had a dream start with two goals. Then, unfortunately, I decided to make it more interesting with a bad mistake and Kevin Davies scored.

"Thankfully, I played my part to make amends as we held on and deserved to win the game.

"That was because our team spirit came to the fore and everything fell into place.

"The excitement, elation, satisfaction and emotions when that final whistle went were awe-inspiring.

"There was an amazing atmosphere and unity. It was great to lift the trophy and salute the fans. I will not forget it as long as I live."

Schwarzer was part of the pioneering squad that competed in the UEFA Cup thanks to the Carling Cup win and then played a key role in ensuring back-to-back European competitions in dramatic fashion.

It was his last-minute penalty save to deny Robbie Fowler in the last game of the 2004/05 season at Manchester City that secured the point Boro required to have another crack at the UEFA Cup.

"I just played my part. If it had not been for Jimmy Floyd Hasselbaink scoring our goal in the first half (cancelled out by Kiki Musampa) we would have been looking down the barrel of missing out.

"That would have been tough to take, but you're talking fine margins between success and failure.

"It was a huge team effort. It happened to be a penalty in the last minute of the game, but that was one small part of a huge effort throughout the season.

"To play in Europe that same season and then finish so high in the league was testament to all the players and coaching staff and the way the fans got behind us."

Having been around for so long, Schwarzer savoured Boro's journey to the UEFA Cup final against Sevilla in Eindhoven more than most – despite the 4-0 defeat.

"To have gone from being relegated when I first arrived to taking part in a European Cup final is good going by anyone's standards.

"The final was possibly the biggest night in the club's history even though it ended in tears and it's something we should all be proud of.

"But when you get over the disappointment of the loss - not matter how dramatic and difficult to take it was at the time - I still have very fond memories and a feeling of real accomplishment as a player."

All good things have to come to an end and Schwarzer eventually headed off to Fulham when it "reached the point where the club and I were ready for a change".

After his spell at Fulham, Schwarzer, who is now a media pundit, went on to claim Premier League winners' medals with Chelsea and Leicester.

He also played for Australia a record 109 times and represented his country at the 2006, 2010 and 2014 World Cup finals.

"It's been a very long journey since I left Australia for Europe in more ways than one, but it's been a very exciting journey as well.

"I'll always look back fondly on my time with Boro. My kids were born in Yorkshire so my son can play for them at cricket.

"I have very happy memories of living in North Yorkshire and playing for Boro. It was a huge part of my life and a huge part of my family's life."

Mills And Boom For Danny

Like a pantomime villain, Danny Mills recoils in mock horror when it is suggested that he is hardly the most popular footballer in the British Isles as he prepared for the Carling Cup final.

"Am I not?" the Middlesbrough right-back retorts, convincingly feigning indignation. "Are you sure, because I don't think I've even noticed that?"

That would be impossible because Mills receives a level of stick reserved for those in the vein of Vinnie Jones or Joey Barton.

The former England international insists he will be unaffected by any abuse that comes his way from the Bolton section at the Millennium Stadium, but he is not thick-skinned enough to avoid being hurt by misconceptions.

"I can't do anything about being a hate figure and people will look at me as they look at me.

"But one of my biggest grievances is that I'm judged as a person for what I do on the football pitch.

"That's the only time it gets to me, when people write things about me and things are said about me.

"They make assumptions and have preconceptions about what I'm like as a person because of what I do at work.

"That is unfair and unjust. I have always said that what happens on a football pitch stays on a football pitch. After the game it's done and dusted."

Mills was speaking to reporters at the Riverside Stadium in the run-up to the Carling Cup final in the club's press day.

"I get stick, but if you're going to play the game in the style I was taught to, unfortunately that is going to be the case.

"When I was brought up in the youth team, if you didn't boot the winger or centre forward from behind in the first minute you were dragged off. It was compulsory.

"It was always: 'First tackle let him know what you're about.' You can't go round doing that these days, but you must have an edge to your game. All successful players have an edge to their game.

"Off the field I'm fairly laid back, and really the only things that matter to me are my children and my immediate family.

"That's how I relax and spend all my spare time. I don't go charging round supermarkets ramming people with shopping trolleys just because someone has got in front of me in the aisle."

Mills insists he has no intention of changing the style of play that has won him many admirers among the supporters at Norwich, Charlton and Leeds and then on loan at Middlesbrough.

It has also earned him 19 England caps. There is, though, another down side.

"Sometimes there can be a slight prejudice against certain players and the crowd can influence certain decisions.

"I've picked up a couple of bookings this season for 'adopting an aggressive attitude,' but that's why the manager [Steve McClaren] brought me here and it's what he wants me to do every week.

"But it is a facet of my game I'm not going to change. I've been like that since I was six or seven - since day one.

"Winning is everything. I've always hated losing. It's never been part of my make-up to be a good loser, whether we deserve to lose or not.

"I've had critics throughout my career about the way I play. Before the World Cup, I wasn't good enough to go there and my discipline was outrageous.

"I shouldn't have been there - but did OK. I did not have to prove people wrong, but was just happy to please myself and prove to myself that I could play at the highest level.

"I get plenty of stick when I'm warming up or your team are losing, but you just turn and have a laugh.

"It's all tongue-in-cheek and adds to the enjoyment. The fans are there to air opinions, get things off their chest and vent a bit of frustration after a week at work."

Mills was seeking his first major honour in Cardiff, with his wife, Lisa, and their children in attendance.

Archie, the baby the couple lost due to spina bifida and hydrocephalus when Lisa was five months pregnant, will also be in his thoughts.

"A day never goes by without me thinking about Archie, but I'm not the only one to have suffered a sad loss in tragic circumstances.

"You learn to live with it and deal with it. The loss of Archie will be with us forever. That pain and sadness will never get any easier."

Indeed, Mills has put his name to a campaign to raise £300,000 for a national helpline for those affected by spina bifida and hydrocephalus.

"It is very important to me to have my family at the final. The kids have been to quite a few big games and who knows when I will get to another final. It might be next year, it might be in five years' time, but it might be never."

• Mills has received a prestigious 'Outstanding Ambassador' award from national charity Shine for his work with the charity, formerly known as the Association for Spina Bifida and Hydrocephalus.

He had to retire from football at the age of 32 in 2009 due to a knee injury, but has many achievements he can be proud of on and off the field of play.

But the Carling Cup remains the only major honour on his CV which is why he has insisted it remains so special in an interview with the Evening Gazette.

"It was a great time, one season, one trophy - that's not too bad is it? You can't fault that," Mills said. "It was a fabulous time, to win a trophy. We had a good side, we didn't score too many goals but defensively we were very, very solid. We were a good, experienced side at that time. You can't take that away, can you? It was a trophy, my only trophy really. I'm not sure you can count a play-off final."

Ugo's Any Given Sunday Best

Al Pacino is not one of the people you would immediately associate with Boro's famous Carling Cup victory.

The Hollywood A-lister is famous for starring roles in The Godfather and Scarface, but it turns out he also helped inspire Steve McClaren's team to glory in Cardiff.

In an exclusive interview, Ugo Ehiogu, one of Boro's biggest Millennium Stadium heroes, revealed that the tactic of deploying Pacino in the build-up in Wales proved to be a masterstroke.

"It was a massive day that will go down as the greatest in the club's history, but what struck me was how relaxed we were as a group of players," Ehiogu said.

"We all knew about Boro's near-misses, but we all felt very confident and it was that pre-match meeting and the Al Pacino speech before the game that got us focused.

"We were at the team hotel on the morning of the final and Bill Beswick, our assistant manager, put in an Al Pacino DVD – fittingly called *Any Given Sunday* – and that speech by Al Pacino had everyone pumped up and ready to go.

"It certainly roused everyone. But it also eased nerves. We knew we were in a great position and it reiterated that belief.

"You always fear someone might not turn up, but there was nothing like that at all. Everyone seemed to enjoy the occasion."

McClaren gave the nod to the experienced Ehiogu ahead of Chris Riggott and it was a decision that paid off as he kept Bolton at arm's length late on to secure a 2-1 win.

But he was also the nerve-jangling centre of attention when the Trotters made frantic penalty appeals in the closing stages.

"The roof was closed so the atmosphere was strange, but I remember us dominating, being comfortable and even when there was a slip by Mark Schwarzer we were still calm.

"But there was a penalty appeal when I threw myself in front of the ball to get in the way of a goal-bound shot. It was the longest five or ten seconds of my life.

"It hit me on the chest and then rolled along my arm, but it was completely accidental so it would have been a total injustice had a penalty been given.

"In the end, there was sheer joy and jubilation, but one memory that will always stick with me is spraying champagne on Steve Gibson and drenching him.

"There was so much pleasure for him and the fans, who had been brilliant. Not bad for a small town in the North East."

It vindicated Ehiogu's decision to head to the Riverside to become Boro's record signing when he moved from Aston Villa in an £8-million deal.

"I must admit I did hesitate because I was going from a big established club to an up-and-coming club.

"But I'd been at Villa for ten years and had doubts about the future direction. I felt I needed a change and when Middlesbrough was mentioned I was intrigued.

"It was no secret that I had my heart set on joining a Champions League club when I was at Villa, but their valuation put off a lot of clubs.

"I hadn't really thought about Boro, but then I met Bryan Robson and Steve Gibson and I was quickly convinced Boro was the club for me because they were so ambitious.

"They said they were prepared to build a club around me, which was flattering, and that I'd get back into the England squad. They didn't let me down. It's just a pity things didn't work out too well with Robbo because he's a fine manager."

"But more importantly they proved to me that they were mightily ambitious. It was a big decision, but it was the right one - they were true to their word.

"They put their money where their mouth was, so to speak, in that they got me into the England team and bought Gareth Southgate from Villa which was great because we got on very well together as teammates and friends."

The Villa connection proved to be an important one at Boro as Ehiogu and Southgate were followed North by George Boateng and Steve Harrison.

"There was certainly a big Villa contingent with the three of us on the field, but Steve, as our defensive coach, was brilliant.

"We had a good understanding and Gareth brought a lot of good things to the club in terms of the way he conducted himself on and off the field of play and the same applied to George.

"Gareth and George were both top players, but they brought a winning mentality and intensity to the club as well as experience.

"It was the perfect balance and that's got to be down to Steve Gibson and Steve McClaren.

"Management is a difficult job, but McClaren did the business. He steered us to Premier League security and then we won a trophy. All in all, I could not have chosen a better place to go than Middlesbrough.

"As well as the players and backroom team, a lot of the other staff, such as in the kit-room, were great, as were the kitchen staff because players always need refueling.

"It's a well-run, family club and we had a real purple patch and a couple of really good years where we won the League Cup and reached the UEFA Cup Final. Happy days."

He certainly enjoyed day-to-day life at Boro. "The coaches like Steve Harrison, Paul Barron and Bill Beswick and Steve Round were excellent.

"I've always felt that if you can get your message across and have a smile on your face then it works wonders, because it's a great way to teach and learn and that was Steve's trademark.

"I enjoyed coming in every day for coaching and training with some really good people, and mixed in with that were good young kids who were hungry to learn.

"I'm thinking of lads like Tony McMahon, David Wheater, Adam Johnson, James Morrison and Andrew Davies. You could tell they had a chance and it's been nice to see them doing so well."

Ehiogu still looks back fondly on his time with Boro and ranks the Cup final as his finest hour in club football.

"Playing for England is a different level because representing your country is something everyone would swap a lot of things for.

"It was not my first major honour, but winning the League Cup with Boro was a bit more special because at Villa you were expected to compete for the top honours and we were in Europe most seasons.

"There was more expectancy. At Boro we were trying to change history. The fact we did was that much more pleasing and made it my greatest achievement at club level.

"So when I think of Boro I think of really good times. The club was geared up to be a great working environment, but it was good fun as well."

On a personal note, England duty creates fond memories for Ehiogu, but Carling Cup success still matters most.

"I only won four caps for England so my international career was a little too brief, but I look back on the day I scored for my country in a 3-0 win over Spain at Villa Park and view it as a very special occasion.

"Winning the Carling Cup was brilliant because it not only made history but also because the homecoming we received showed just how much it meant to every single Boro fan."

• A lot has been said about Steve McClaren, but few have been better qualified to pass judgement on his five-year rein as Riverside manager than Ugo Ehiogu.

"When he first arrived McClaren really was like the proverbial breath of fresh air," said Ehiogu.

"His training sessions were always excellent and we were always well prepared when matches came around.

"Plus, he was prepared to take advice and listen to what us senior players had to say.

"Towards the end things creaked, mainly because pressures from outside the club and other areas started to affect him.

"He ended up having a bigger squad and that made the job more challenging because he had to keep more people happy.

"Things started to become a little more negative and sour towards the end, but nothing should be allowed to detract from his historic achievements."

McClaren once deemed Ehiogu surplus to requirements, but there were no grudges.

"Bryan Robson wanted me to re-join West Brom and the thought of regular football certainly appealed to me so I agreed to leave.

"I was at their training ground completing formalities on a move when word came through that Gareth was injured and they wanted me back.

"I had a few loose ends to tie up, but I backed off because it didn't seem right and I'm glad.

"I played a part in the UEFA Cup run when I captained the side at Steaua Bucharest and ended up joining Rangers so I can't complain.

"I scored the winner in an Old Firm game against Celtic at Parkhead with an overhead kick. It earned me the club's goal of the season award."

• Ugo Ehiogu died suddenly at the age of 44 in April 2017.

On The Mend

Gaizka Mendieta believes he enjoyed the best of times with Boro because he suffered the worst of times with Valencia.

The cultured Spaniard played a vital part in helping Boro shake off their Cup final hoodoo to land major silverware for the first time.

Cool, calm and collected, there was never any chance that the big occasion would unsettle the midfield schemer whose creative spark kept Boro on the front foot against Bolton.

Indeed, he was regarded by many observers as one of Boro's best performers in that showpiece event in Cardiff thanks to his ability to turn Champions League pain into League Cup gain.

He feels that ability to keep his head in the hurly-burly of midfield is down to the bitter disappointment of losing not one, but two Champions League finals while with Valencia.

"I guess Valencia was where I made my name - it was one of the best times of my life from a sporting point of view," said Mendieta.

"But we had our disappointments as well because we lost the Champions League final against Real Madrid and then in a penalty shoot-out against Bayern Munich.

"The Bayern game was awful. We let ourselves down. But I would like to think those experiences helped me at Boro in the big games we played on the way to winning the Carling Cup.

"Like the rest of the team, I was not over-awed by Cardiff and it showed because we played some really good, controlled football."

Mendieta would leave Valencia in a £28.9-million deal in 2001 with Italian giants Lazio and when he failed to settle in Rome, Boro boss Steve McClaren pounced.

It was quite a coup as Mendieta, who had a season on loan at Barcelona, was then the sixth most expensive footballer ever and the costliest Spanish footballer of all time.

The international was signed in August 2003 on an initial one-year loan, which automatically turned into a four-year contract.

"I was at Lazio, but I knew it was time for us to go our separate ways and I was attracted to Middlesbrough.

"That was because McClaren made it clear that it was an ambitious project he was involved in.

"He came to see me at our training ground in Rome with (Boro chief executive) Keith Lamb and he told me that they were planning to bring in big players to move the team forward and take it to another level in Europe.

"I asked for time to think about it, but soon I thought, 'Why not?' I would go for it. It was a gamble and an adventure."

"I had gained lots of experience in Spain and Italy and I would aim to share it with the other players at Middlesbrough.

"And, to be honest, I was not disappointed because we won a trophy and got into Europe. It was a great time for everyone associated with the club – the supporters and the players."

Boro fans would be inclined to agree, as Mendieta was crucial to Boro's journey to Carling Cup glory, scoring the decisive spot-kick in a shoot-out against an Everton side featuring a young Wayne Rooney.

Mendieta does, though, harbour mixed feelings when it comes to his five-year stint at Boro that came to an end after playing 83 games and scoring six times in a Boro shirt.

"I have both very happy and very sad memories of playing for Middlesbrough.

"Winning the Carling Cup final was the highlight of my time and getting to the UEFA Cup final was great as well.

"I would never forget the day we beat Man United 4-1. Everything clicked for us and I even scored two goals so it will never be difficult to remember.

"But I also had bad luck with injuries which was hard to take. Unfortunately, I missed most of the 2004-05 season with a knee injury and then was injured after the Basel game at the Riverside.

"I came back fully fit, but didn't get back into the team. I know people thought I was injured but my situation had nothing to do with injuries.

"It was quite a weird situation and unfortunately for everyone it never got sorted and that's one of the sad memories."

He also slipped down the pecking order at Boro.

"Everything went wrong once Steve McClaren left and Gareth Southgate replaced him as manager.

"We had played together and got on well, but suddenly he told me I was not part of his plans.

"The one thing I reproach him for is the fact that he was never honest with me. The club wanted to go in the direction of using youngsters, and getting rid of a handful of players.

"I had offers to join clubs in Spain and England on loan. But I did not want to go away for six months, only to find myself in the same situation once more."

Nowadays, Mendieta still keeps tabs on the fortunes of his local side, especially as he still has friends with Boro links, such as Tony McMahon.

"I still follow football although I don't play anymore which means it does not dictate your life and I keep informed about what's going on.

"It's been great to see so many Spanish players in the Premier League. It's good for English football because of the quality that people like Fernando Torres, David Villa and Xabi Alonso bring to the competition.

"But it's also good for Spanish football because the experience of English football has helped them develop as players and that was seen when we won the European Championship and World Cup."

After leaving Boro and launching a media career with Sky Sports, the father-of-two daughters continued to live in Yarm until work commitments forced him to move down south to St Albans.

"I came to Middlesbrough to help the club make history and we did that in Cardiff. That is also what happened at Valencia. We won something for the first time in 25 years.

"It meant so much to the Valencia fans, but not as much as winning in Cardiff meant to Middlesbrough people. Our win was special – in fact it was extra-special."

• *Boro manager Steve McClaren was beaming at the Rockliffe Park press conference where Gaizka Mendieta was paraded before reporters. "I think personal involvement in transfers is vital, and I felt I had to go out to Rome," he said. "I had half-an-hour to sell the club and myself to him at Lazio's training ground, and it was probably the best 30 minutes' business I've ever done."*

When The Boat Comes In

George Boateng is one of those bubbly characters who are hardly ever lost for words.

So it speaks volumes that Boateng struggles when it comes to trying to explain how much he enjoyed life on and off the pitch at Middlesbrough.

"Words could not describe how happy I was under Steve McClaren at Middlesbrough," Boateng said.

"Even now, I look back and think, 'Boy, that was such a good time,' because of the football we played and the laughter we had.

"Sometimes, honestly, I couldn't wait for my alarm to go off in the morning so I could go to training. Seriously it was that good.

"For me, Middlesbrough was the right club, the right manager and the right bunch of players.

"It was one big happy family. We cried together, we laughed together, we learned together. There was not one single bad apple in the squad."

Boateng's football career began with Dutch side Excelsior where his efforts earned him a move to Feyenoord before he got his first taste of English football with Coventry.

He left the Sky Blues for Aston Villa for £4.5 million before moving to Boro in a £5-million deal in August 2002.

"Signing for Coventry was the best decision I ever made, but when it comes to being in the right place at the right time it has to be joining Boro.

"When I came to Middlesbrough to look at the place they would normally send a car to pick you up.

"But McClaren came to pick me up and drove me to the Blackwell Grange hotel in Darlington and we sat down and talked and that made me feel so welcome.

"I remember him saying, 'Now you have signed we will be playing European football in two years.'

"Just imagine that. It sounded so far-fetched because when I was at Villa going to Boro meant three points guaranteed.

"So for a Boro manager to say that to me showed me how ambitious he was and I was right behind the idea because I wanted to play in European football.

"The incredible thing is that we achieved his goal because we won the Carling Cup and then reached the UEFA Cup final two years later."

The fact Boateng's services were appreciated off the field as well means a lot to him.

"What made me feel so welcome is that from the start the fans got behind me because they valued the work I did.

"I met many friends locally and I am still in touch with a lot of people there. It was a joy to work and play with them.

"A lot of people go to stadiums to see players score goals and perform tricks, but the fans appreciated the hard graft I put in for the team which made me feel special.

"It is so strange. With my eyes closed I knew every bit of grass at the Riverside Stadium."

It was future Boro boss Gordon Strachan who effectively put him on the road to Teesside when he was in charge of Coventry.

"My agent met Strachan, I spoke to him briefly and he said if you sign for us before the weekend you'll play in midfield against Liverpool at Anfield and that did it for me.

"I'd been playing everywhere expect goalkeeper and striker at Feyenoord, so I was fed up and wanted to play in midfield because I thought that was my strongest position.

"That was just what I needed to hear, so I said to my agent 'Let's go, let's do this,' although at the time I didn't realise what position Coventry were in the table when I met Gordon and did the medical.

"It was the best decision I have ever made in my whole life really, because I enjoyed my time at Coventry although it is really weird to think back because I was an offensive player there and had to create and score goals."

That Boateng went on to become a box-to-box midfielder is principally down to Strachan.

"Gordon was very strict. There was no room for failure and no room to rest.

"In Holland, I was one of the fittest players, but in the early stages when we trained in the morning with Gordon I struggled.

"I found it really hard. I was exhausted, so I came back in thinking I'll get changed, have a nice swim and then have a sleep.

"That was until I realised when I looked on the board that we had to train again at 2.30pm. I was like, 'No way, I can't do anymore, I'm so tired.'

"I went up to the gaffer and said, 'Sorry, I'm too tired to train,' and he squared up to me and went, 'I'll tell you when you're tired. Now get your boots on and get out there and train.'

"I was like, 'Oh My God!' That was the hairdryer treatment. Right in my face.

Looking back it was funny, but at the time I didn't enjoy it at all.

"I played with some great players who might not have been gifted in terms of technical ability, but we enjoyed playing for each other.

"On top of that, we enjoyed playing for Gordon. He got the best out of the team. It was my first taste of English football and it was brilliant."

Boateng was at the height of his powers in the midfield trenches with Boro and enjoyed the combative side of football even though his uncompromising ways would appear to be at odds with his deeply held religious beliefs.

"Religion is an important part of my life and when I enter the pitch people see me as a soft Christian, but I am not.

"When I get on the field, it is business time. I read the Bible, but God also preaches that you have got to take your job seriously.

"Just because I'm a Christian doesn't mean I can't tackle or can't get a booking. Even in Holland everyone thinks, 'He's a Christian, so how can he foul like that?' It's silly because it's about winning football matches and it's a tough job.

"The position and the style I am playing say I am a destroyer and have to stop everything, but a destroyer does not come with a water pistol. You have to wear a mask and protect yourself.

"I'm not a dirty player and my record speaks for itself. Compare it with players like Patrick Vieira or Roy Keane who play in the same position.

"When I first came into the league I had to learn what was allowed and what wasn't. I picked up lots of silly bookings, but I improved a lot.

"You can see clearly that certain players lose their heads because of the heat they're in. It happens at least once every game, but if you're not self-controlled you make a lot of mistakes."

Boateng was appointed Boro skipper when Gareth Southgate succeeded McClaren as manager in 2006, but lost his place in the team and the captaincy midway through the following seasons.

It was enough for him to look towards pastures new and a move to Hull ensued after almost 200 games in a Boro shirt.

"After six seasons at Middlesbrough I'd had enough," Boateng told The Sun.

"It felt as if I was lost, like in the film The Truman Show. Every day was the same, every season was the same and football was becoming routine.

"On top of that we had in Gareth Southgate a young manager who made a lot of mistakes.

"He didn't pick me for the FA Cup quarter-final against Cardiff - he wanted to experiment!

"What utter nonsense, especially experimenting with your 32-year-old captain ... that's something you just don't do. We lost 2-0 and missed the chance of winning the cup."

Ricketts Has Last Laugh

Michael Ricketts fulfilled a footballing fantasy by scoring the winner at Old Trafford.

But for the former Boro striker it was the Millennium Stadium that really proved to be his ultimate Theatre of Dreams.

Ricketts notched the decisive late goal for Bolton in a 2-1 win over Manchester United in October 2001 as he took the Premier League by storm.

But Boro's Carling Cup final victory 18 months later remains the high point of his career even though he only played a cameo role.

"When I think of my time at Middlesbrough what really springs to mind first is Cardiff – I can honestly say it's the highlight of my club career," he said.

"I only came on as a second-half sub and been a bit of a pantomime villain in the eyes of Bolton supporters because I left them for Boro.

"But I still think I played my part – especially with that late equaliser in the quarter-final at Tottenham.

"The final was a brilliant occasion. The incentive was to win a major cup. The fact that it was against Bolton didn't mean anything. I just wanted to win the competition and thankfully, that's what happened.

"I know I scored in a couple of the penalty shoot-outs on the way to the Millennium Stadium, so of course there are nerves, but you get over them."

Ricketts shot to prominence under Sam Allardyce at Bolton following a move from Walsall, helping the Trotters to promotion.

And then he scored 15 goals in his maiden Premier League campaign in 2001-02 to earn himself an England cap in a 1-1 draw against Holland in February 2002.

"I do have some great memories from my time at Bolton.

"I made some great friends at the Reebok, won promotion, went to places like Liverpool and Man United and won.

"In fact we beat Man U twice at Old Trafford when I was there. They were happy times.

"Plus, I made it into the England side. That was a massive honour but, to be honest, I've never watched a replay of the game, because I never sit down and watch myself play because I'd be over-critical of myself."

Ricketts and Allardyce fell out and the Birmingham-born forward was allowed to move to Teesside in a £3-million deal after Steve McClaren missed out on Liverpool's Emile Heskey.

"McClaren really sold the club to me as ambitious and forward-thinking and I wasn't disappointed.

"He was spot-on. Looking back, it was his vision that persuaded me to join Boro back in January 2003.

"McClaren was very good with me, but I struggled with injury a lot of the time, which was hard for me to take.

"But when I look back I don't have any regrets. None whatsoever. What's the point in having regrets? I just wish I'd had better luck with injuries.

"I've seen Frank Queudrue and George Boateng a couple of times and we've reminisced a bit.

"But the team has changed so much since I was there, so I don't really know any of the players at the Riverside anymore, but I like to see my old club doing well.

"Since I left Boro my life has been good. My personal life is very stable, and with that your professional career becomes the same.

"Plus, I never thought I'd say this, but I've just taken up golf. I'm very sporty, but never thought golf was going to be for me.

"I've watched it a lot on TV and I've really got into it. It's relaxing. My handicap? My swing - it's terrible!"

Southgate Leads By Example

Gareth Southgate understood exactly what it meant when he proudly hoisted the Carling Cup aloft for Boro.

The Boro captain knew the trophy won at the Millennium Stadium was not just another honour to add to his distinguished CV.

Southgate was aware of its significance to every single Boro fan who trekked to Cardiff to witness the club win its first major honour in its 128-year history.

"The fans cheered and there was this immense release of energy, pride and passion from the players, staff and all the fans," Southgate said.

"I was acutely aware of the emotion among the fans. We took so many down there and I knew how much it meant to them to finally get over the line, having had finals before where it hadn't worked out.

"It was an incredible feeling when I lifted the trophy, but I knew why there was so much emotion.

"I had been at Boro four years and had a really good idea of what it meant to the whole area, so it meant more because of that."

Southgate was aware of its importance because he made a concerted effort to get to know Boro fans during his time on Teesside.

"I was at three different clubs and I got to understand all my clubs and the way they worked and the area and the way the supporters felt," said Southgate, who also served Crystal Palace and Aston Villa with distinction.

"I wanted to contribute away from the field as much as on it. All three clubs were all important parts of my life. I was getting out to meet Boro fans and that meant I knew how important that Carling Cup win was.

"I did my best to get into the community and to meet fans, and everyone I met when I was at Boro was immensely proud of Teesside and immensely proud of their football club.

"They were desperate for us to end that hoodoo and finally win a top trophy after three near misses at Wembley.

"I hope those painful memories would have made our success in Cardiff all the more sweet. I'd like to think it was worth the wait. The outpouring of emotion and the celebrations suggested it was. Everyone there saw a bit of history being made."

Southgate proved a calming influence in central defence as Steve McClaren's side withstood a Bolton comeback and won the final 2-1.

"I was so very proud to lift the trophy on behalf of the club.

"That was the highlight of my time at Middlesbrough, even though there were super European nights and the emotion of the comebacks in the UEFA Cup.

"People talk about finishing wherever in the league, but the game is about winning things and the joy that brings and the memories that it creates can never, ever be taken away. That topped everything.

"As a player you get to that stage of your career when you wonder if you'll get the chance again to win something.

"Once we got to the final we knew that was our moment because opportunities like this do not come around very often. That's why it was so extra special for us as well."

Southgate also savoured the celebrations back on Teesside when the club staged a victory parade as a feel-good factor gripped the area.

"Seeing all the fans down in Cardiff as we headed to the Millennium Stadium reinforced the feeling that Sunday was going to be our day.

"There were so many people in Boro shirts down there and the backing they gave us was incredible.

"But it went up a notch when we had our victory parade on the bus back home in Middlesbrough.

"It was as if every single person on Teesside had come out to celebrate and that underlined just how much it meant because we were representing them. They really had something to seriously shout about after the near-misses."

Southgate would lead Boro into the UEFA Cup the following season as Boro went from strength to strength under Steve McClaren, who played a key role in attracting the England international to the Riverside.

"I'd been on the transfer list for a year at Villa and a proposed move to Chelsea fell through the summer before.

"I liked the work I'd done with Steve McClaren with England and how he wanted to go about things at Boro.

"I'd hoped to play Champions League football which wasn't possible, so I wanted to be in at the start of something special."

.... a reflection of Southgate's high standards that he does not feel his ambitions were totally fulfilled.

"Winning the Carling Cup and the emotion it brought to the town and being part of the team that made club history were very special and to get to a European final was amazing.

"There were some great nights and to go toe-to-toe with the likes of Lazio and Sporting Lisbon and Roma were great experiences.

"Did we quite get to where I'd hoped in terms of league performance? No. But as you get older you realise that whatever you achieve you will never be satisfied.

"I have to look back on it as being part of a very special era in the club's history and to bring so much joy to the area was great.

"When you look at our side, there were guys who'd played at the highest level. It's a horrible phrase but we were one of those 'on our day teams'. We were a threat in cup competitions, but not consistent enough for the league."

Southgate, who succeeded McClaren as Boro manager, went on to become England Under-21 manager before leading the senior team into the 2018 World Cup.

"After Boro, I spent a lot of time working out where I wanted to go and get the experiences I needed and improve the areas where I needed more knowledge.

"With my experience of managing and the qualities I have for dealing with young people I felt the England Under-21 job was a great challenge and something I thought I'd do well.

"Only time will tell whether I can do that, but I feel it is a bright time for England. That's also the case with Boro."

• *Gareth Southgate's reign as Boro manager might have ended badly, but the memories of his spell in charge brought a wry smile to his face when he was doing England proud in Russia.*

"I'll tell you a story about me and superstitions," he told the press conference ahead of the semi-final with Croatia in Moscow.

"When I was managing at Middlesbrough we had a game at Reading and I was under a bit of pressure.

"When I went to get changed at the hotel, I'd forgotten my socks. So I went to the kit man and I borrowed a pair of black goalkeepers socks.

"Anyway, we won and the staff made this big thing about my lucky socks, saying I had to wear them next game.

"So we were at home and I went to get changed and I thought, 'Hmm, shall I wear those socks?' We still needed the win, but I thought, 'No, it's ridiculous.'

"We lost the game and then on the Tuesday we were playing again, so I thought, 'Well, I'd better put the socks on.'

"So I did and we won 2-0. And then I went upstairs and got sacked. From that moment, superstitions have rather gone out the window."

Acknowledgements

This book would not have been possible had it not been for Dave Allan, the former Boro media chief turned who continues to fly the flag for the region through his own PR business and the Teesside Philanthropic Foundation.

It was Dave who entrusted me with the responsibility of tracking down and interviewing former players across the world for the award-winning club programme, *Red Square*.

The success of the programme was very much a team effort and I remain thankful to Dave's behind-the-scenes colleagues, editor Graham Bell and all-round media experts Mike McGeary and Martin, who were a constant source of support for my endeavours.

I am so grateful to all the former Boro players, managers and coaches, right from Rolando Ugolini to Juninho and Jack Charlton to Gareth Southgate, who have generously given up their time to roll back the years.

Former Boro goalkeeper Jim Platt has been a constant source of help with his boyish enthusiasm, generosity and a contacts book that most football reporters would cherish.

I am also indebted to the families of great Boro personalities, like Brian Clough, Peter Taylor and Harold Shepherdson, who have helped me paint a picture of lives and times on Teesside.

I have been overwhelmed by the offers of help from Boro fans as well, including Alf Common's priceless postcards home from Harold Stephenson.

An array of extraordinary images from artist Richard Piers Rayner has been the icing on the cake.

A word of thanks also has to go to Dave Burrill, of publishers Great Northern Books, for having faith in me and backing my vision to turn *Boro Tales* into a reality.

Above all, I have to be grateful to Boro owner Steve Gibson because he enabled football reporters like me who have covered the North East patch, to enjoy an amazing journey.

Those trips across Europe in the UEFA Cup were extraordinary, but what happened in Cardiff on February 29, 2004, still stands out as the highlight of my time as a football journalist. That momentous occasion inspired me to produce *Boro Tales*.

Rob Stewart

Boro Fans

Sean Allen
Claire Ayden
Andrea Bailey
Thom Baker
Shane Bell
Leanne Bingham
Alex Bloomfield
Claire Bloomfield
Mike Bloomfield
Tony Bloomfield
Albert Bowes
Dave Brack
David Buck
Jonathon Bull (Bully)
Ollie Clews
Terry Cowen
Neil Cowen
Samuel George Cumpson
Marc Dale
Chris Dane
Tom Daniels
Stephen Davison
Thomas Dixon
Trevor Dixon
Christopher Downey
John M Duggan
Doug Embleton
Joe Embleton
Brian Exelby
Paul Galloway
Rod Garbutt
David Graham
Colin Gregg
James Donald Hall
Neil Harbisher

Alfie Harrison
Paul Hartshorne
Nick Henegan
Christ Hobson
Mr James Peter Hodgson
Mr Morgan David Hodgson
Paul Michael Hogan
Thomas Brian Hope (Sam)
Mark Joynes
Sue Kane
Sue Kane
Seb Kramer
Jim Lawson
Geoff Lewin
Mark Longstaff
Janet Lynch
Janet Lynch
Stephen Mason
Michael McGowan
Debbie Meek
Geoff Mitchell
Alan Musgrave
Barry Park
John Pearson
Adam Richardson
Nathan Richardson
Stephen Savage
Andrew Shepherd
Lucie Swales
John F Taylor
Jonathan Tweddle
Paul Welford
Stuart Whittingham
Eric L T Williams